THE SOCIOLOGY
OF COMMUNITY

THE SOCIOLOGY OF COMMUNITY

Jessie Bernard
The Pennsylvania State University

**SCOTT, FORESMAN
INTRODUCTION TO MODERN SOCIETY SERIES**

Albert J. Reiss, Jr.
Harold L. Wilensky

Editors

Scott, Foresman and Company
GLENVIEW, ILLINOIS   JAY   LONDON

Acknowledgments

Cover: Dan Ben-Schmuel, Egan Gallery, New York.

P. v, pp. 6–13, and p. 41:   Quotations from Thomas S. Kuhn, *The Structure of Scientific Revolutions* (pp. 4–6). Copyright © 1962 by the University of Chicago. Reprinted by permission.

Pp. 29–30:   Quotation from Kenneth E. Boulding, "The City as an Element in the International System," *Daedalus,* Fall 1968 (pp. 1120–22). Copyright © 1968 by the American Academy of Arts and Sciences. Reprinted by permission of *Daedalus,* Journal of the American Academy of Arts and Sciences, Boston, Mass. Fall 1968, *The Consicence of the City.*

Pp. 65–66:   Quotation from William Kornhauser, "Mass Society," in the *International Encyclopedia of the Social Sciences,* edited by David L. Sills, Vol. 10 (p. 60). Copyright © 1968 by The Macmillan Company and The Free Press. Reprinted by permission.

P. 104:   Table from Joseph W. Eaton and Robert J. Weil, *Culture and Mental Disorders* (p. 75). © by The Free Press, a Corporation, 1955. Reprinted with permission of The Macmillan Company.

4/12/00   SBEN CAM6204

This book is for Michele Linda,
whose world I hope will be one of humane communities.

"When normal science . . . goes astray . . . —when, that is, the profession can no longer evade anomalies that subvert the existing traditions of scientific practice—then begin the extraordinary investigations that lead the profession at last to a new set of commitments, a new basis for the practice of science. The extraordinary episodes in which that shift of professional commitments occurs are the ones known . . . as scientific revolutions. They are the tradition-shattering complements to the tradition-bound activity of normal science" (Thomas S. Kuhn, *The Structure of Scientific Revolutions* [Chicago: The University of Chicago Press, 1962], p. 6).

"What has distinguished periods of great social creativity . . . is not the degree or intensity of activity alone—especially received patterns of activity—but rather the emergence of fundamentally new modes of analysis from which patterns of behavior flow. These are the great dividing points in political and social history: It is at such moments as these that historians record the end of an old era and the beginning of a new one" (Daniel Patrick Moynihan, "One Step We Must Take," *Saturday Review,* May 23, 1970, pp. 21–22).

Foreword

Modern societies are complex territorial organizations whose populations are more-or-less integrated by economic, legal, military, and political institutions and by the media of mass communication and entertainment. Sociology reflects this complexity. It is often packaged in separate sociologies such as those of work, religion, minorities, politics, and the community.

By looking at modernization as a process and urban-industrial ("modern" "affluent") society as a distinctive social system, this series hopes to avoid fragmentation into separate sociologies and at the same time provide intensive treatment of major institutional areas (economy, polity, kinship), units of social organization (society, community, complex organization, family), and of processes that cut across all institutional areas (social differentiation and stratification, social control, demographic and technological change). The series is "relevant" in that all authors address themselves to a single question: "What is modern about modern society?" It is comparative in that all authors know that we cannot answer that question unless we compare the different shapes of modern and premodern societies and of contemporary nations, totalitarian and pluralist, "capitalist" and "socialist." Our abiding concern is the macroscopic, comparative analysis of social structure and change.

Each book in this series can stand alone for specialized courses; each can also be used in combination with others as a flexible substitute for conventional textbooks.

The Sociology of Community begins with two overarching paradigms or models that define problems and their solutions, namely, those of capitalism and functionalism. The author then explains several classic models of the community. She views the community as an ecological organization and structured systems of status and of power, contrasting these with a complex or mass society. The author argues that events of the last fifty years have created anomalies in all the models for understanding communities and community life today. Especially important in creating these anomalies is the substitution of conflict for competition and the resulting change in the nature of power in communities. The older models, the book concludes, can no longer account for the changing nature of life in modern communities. Thus, they are inadequate guides to policy planning for cities, race relations, and social welfare at home or for the problems of new nations abroad.

The book deals also with the drive for power in the black community. The author suggests that functionalist theory originally defended the status quo, only to be used now by both youth and black leaders against it. She analyzes resistance to change in the community and to the role of "change agents." The book also recounts the "clash of paradigms," especially the anthropological and the capitalist, among social scientists in the last two decades as they sought to apply Western social theories to research in the Third World. It concludes that failures were inevitable because so much of Western social science was irrelevant to the problems of very poor countries.

In her final chapter, Bernard tackles the question of the need for the concept of community in a day when technology has all but erased physical community boundaries. She concludes that locale is still important enough for a large number of people to warrant the retention of the settlement conception of community; but clearly new paradigms are needed for understanding them.

Albert J. Reiss, Jr.
Harold L. Wilensky

Preface

The editors of this series refrained from imposing uniformity on the several volumes and encouraged the authors to find the most appropriate way to present their materials. They requested either a synthesizing of disparate views and data or a fresh organization of traditional materials, with thematic development a main consideration. After surveying the field assigned to me, I concluded that the best service a book dealing with community could render at this time was to alert the reader to the disarray which now prevails in the sociology of community.

To state that the sociology of community is in disarray does not mean that there is not a vast reservoir of data dealing with communities. An enormous, sophisticated, and powerful research apparatus pours an endless stream of printouts from the computers. There is therefore no lack of data available for students of the community. It is not data that are lacking so much as a conceptual and paradigmatic apparatus to help interpret them. The very richness of the data may almost be viewed as dysfunctional so far as science-building is concerned. So dense a growth of data may block our view of the forest.

This book is about the sociology of community, that is, about models for explaining and interpreting the facts, rather than about the facts themselves that the researchers provide us with in such great abundance. Facts are extremely perishable; they become of primarily historical value almost overnight. But a good model for interpreting them lasts longer—not forever, as this book shows—but longer than facts. It is such models or guides that concern us here. The theme developed is that the sociology of community is in serious need of what Thomas S. Kuhn has called a scientific revolution, that is, new paradigms to help us understand the processes shaping communities today.

J.B.

Washington, D.C.

CONTENTS

PART ONE
INTRODUCTION 1

1 COMMUNITY PARADIGMS IN CRISIS 3
Definitions: "The Community" and "Community" *3*
The Community of Scientists *5*
The Key Role of Paradigms *6*
Community Paradigms *7*
The Inertia of Paradigms *8*
Normal Science and Scientific Revolutions *10*
Outside Influences on Paradigm Changes *11*
Plan of Presentation *14*

2 TWO OVERARCHING PARADIGMS 15
The Paradigmatic Context of Community Study *15*
The Paradigm of Capitalism *16*
The Paradigm for Functional Analysis *22*
Ideology and Paradigmatic Predilections *26*
Conflicting Policy Implications
    of the Two Overarching Paradigms *27*

PART TWO
THE CLASSIC COMMUNITY PARADIGMS 31

3 THE ECOLOGICAL MODEL 33
The Allocation of Land *34*
Natural Areas *35*
Community Structure *37*
Ecological Processes *38*
Normal-Science Fallout *39*
Paradigm Crisis *41*
Intervention *42*
Structure or Congeries? *43*
Stalled Processes *45*
New Ways to Make Decisions *47*

4 THE COMMUNITY CLASS STRUCTURE   51

Class and the Paradigms   *51*
Class at the Community Level   *52*
The Class Structure of Communities   *53*
Ethnic- into Class-Status: The Melting Pot   *55*
Class in the Black Community   *58*
What Holds Communities Together?   *62*
Mass Society and Community Class Structure   *64*
The Fate of the Community-Integrating Factors
   in the Yankee City Paradigm   *68*

5 THE COMMUNITY POWER STRUCTURE   71

Impersonal Power Paradigms   *71*
The Personalizing of Power:
   Middletown in Transition and The Power Elite   *73*
The Community Power Structure   *75*
The Normal-Science Research
   on Community Power   *78*
The Phantom Power Structure   *79*
The Hollow Power Structure   *80*
What Power Structure?   *82*
Apathy and Participation   *82*
The Power of Direct Action   *84*
Where Is the Locus of Power?   *85*

**6 GEMEINSCHAFT AND GESELLSCHAFT:
   RURAL AND URBAN COMMUNITIES   91**

"The Soil" and the City   *91*
Description Versus Glorification:
   The Gemeinschaft Mystique   *92*
Gemeinschaft and the Folk   *93*
What Do You Mean, Rural?   *96*
Selectivity of Rural-Urban Migration   *98*
Communitarian Communities   *100*
Community and Mental Health   *102*
Children of the Dream   *103*
Off-Beat Communities   *106*
The Great Nostalgia for the Impossible Dream   *106*
The Animus Against Cities   *107*
Urbanism as a Way of Life   *109*
Coping with Urbanism   *111*
The Black Version of Urbanism   *113*
Suburbanism as a Way of Life   *115*

PART THREE
"MODERNIZATION" AT HOME AND IN THE THIRD WORLD
AS A TEST OF COMMUNITY PARADIGMS   121

7   THE COMMUNITY AS TARGET OF CHANGE:
BLACK PEOPLE AND POOR PEOPLE   123
"Modernizing" Race Relations   123
"Modernizing" Welfare   139

8   DEFENSE AND RESISTANCE   149
The Community as Victim   149
"Urban Unease" and Defense
of Beleaguered Neighborhoods   150
On Ne Passe Pas!   153
Defense of Communities
Against Invasion by Outsiders   154
Stability and Change   156
Case in Point: Fluoridation and Other Threats   158
Class Conflict, New Style:
Embattled Populism Versus New Urban Life Styles   160

9   "COMMUNITY DEVELOPMENT":
THE THIRD-WORLD TEST   163
Modernization   163
Community Development   164
Conflicting Paradigms   165
Where Do You Start?
The Village as a Unit of Modernization   167
Disappointment and Disillusion   169
The Costs of Change:
The Cultural Lag Paradigm   173

PART FOUR
REVOLUTION ANYONE?   177

10   THE FUTURE OF THE CONCEPT OF THE COMMUNITY
AND COMMUNITY PARADIGMS   179
Two Questions   179
"Community" sans Locale   180
Is the Concept of the Community Viable?   180
The Mass Media and the Erosion of Community   181
The Disappearance of Space   182

The Persistence of Locale   *185*
Revolution Anyone?   *189*
How Abstract? How General?   *190*
If . . . Then   *191*

SELECTED READINGS   193

INDEX   209

Part One

Introduction

Community Paradigms in Crisis

DEFINITIONS:
"THE COMMUNITY" AND "COMMUNITY"

It is not always easy to see what the diverse entities known as communities have in common. What, if anything, do a nomadic tribe of Bedouins and a megalopolis like New York City, for example, have in common? Among the many different definitions of community that have been offered, three characteristics are usually agreed upon as a minimum, namely, locale, common ties, and social interaction.[1] The apparent simplicity of this formulation is, however, deceptive. It encompasses two quite different, though related, concepts, one referring to "the community" and one to "community."

"The community" as it is currently conceived usually refers to settlements of the kind encompassed in the definition implied above in which *locale* is a basic component. The community in

---

[1] George A. Hillery, Jr., "Definitions of Community: Areas of Agreement," *Rural Sociology* 20 (1955), pp. 194–204.

this sense came with agriculture. Among hunting peoples who had to go where the food was, or grazing peoples who had to follow their herds, locale had a different meaning than it had among agricultural peoples who settled down in fixed locations. The nomadic peoples were no less dependent on their land resources than were the agricultural peoples, but if you have to pull up stakes every season, your emotional attachments to any one locale have to be more brittle.

"Community," as distinguished from "the community," emphasizes the common-ties and social-interaction components of the definition. In this sense community is viewed by some sociologists as "the most fundamental and far-reaching of sociology's unit ideas."[2] It is characterized not so much by locale as by "a high degree of personal intimacy, emotional depth, moral commitment, social cohesion, and continuity in time."[3] A German term, *Gemeinschaft,* has been invoked to refer to community in this sense. It is older than the local community, being characteristic of nomadic tribes as well as of fixed agricultural settlements. It persists even today among gypsies who have no fixed locale at all.

In both the local and the Gemeinschaft conceptualization we are dealing with some kind of unity, of co-unity, whatever the nature of the uniting bond may be. We shall accept at least provisionally as a starting point this twofold conceptualization of community without cavil, and the context in which the term is used will indicate which form of community is referred to in specific instances.

Still we cannot proceed further without anticipating a more detailed discussion in Chapter 10 of some of the critical issues emerging today. Students of the community are catching it at one of the most critical moments in its history. For just as agricultural technology, heralded by some scientists as the greatest revolution of all time, marked the advent of the community, so now modern technology may be marking its demise, heralding a revolution of perhaps equal significance. For modern transportation and communication are changing the significance of locale and space for human relationships as profoundly as agriculture did some ten thousand years ago. As a result, some observers conclude that the settlement or locale concept of the community may soon become

---

[2] Robert A. Nisbet, *The Sociological Tradition* (New York: Basic Books, Inc., Publishers, 1967), p. 47.

[3] Ibid.

archaic or even disappear, or, if retained, be restricted to the backwaters of the postcity era.[4]

Students of community in the Gemeinschaft sense are also concerned with the effects of modern technology. They note that the new locale- and space-independent relationships that modern transportation makes possible are no substitute for Gemeinschaft, and that they leave modern man in a fruitless "quest for community."[5]

The impact, direct and indirect, of these trends has changed communities and community so drastically that old ways of viewing them no longer suffice. The result is a crisis in the study of community well documented by the call for new paradigms by outstanding leaders in the field.[6] They are well aware of the handicaps we labor under without a conceptual apparatus suitable for the study of the community today.

THE COMMUNITY OF SCIENTISTS

There is still another conceptualization of community, as yet not so much researched as those mentioned above, which, although not the focus of study here, is of some relevance. It refers to those "unities" in which the "co" or organizing factor is neither locale nor an emotional tie but a common intellectual or professional bond. In this sense, Thomas S. Kuhn speaks of science as the work of "communities of scientists" and the sociology of such scientific communities as the key to an understanding of science itself—in our case the sociology of community—including the problems it attacks, the solutions it accepts, and the direction in

---

[4] Melvin M. Webber, "The Post-City Age," *Daedalus,* Fall 1968, p. 1099.

[5] Robert A. Nisbet, *The Quest for Community* (New York: Oxford University Press, Inc., 1953), pp. 11–12.

[6] Roland L. Warren, *The Community in America* (Chicago: Rand McNally & Co., 1963), pp. ix, 2, 6, 9; Edmund N. Bacon, "Urban Process," *Daedalus,* Fall 1968, p. 1165; Kenneth E. Boulding, "The City as an Element in the International System," *Daedalus,* Fall 1968, p. 1122; Webber, "The Post-City Age," p. 1093; John R. Seeley, "Remaking the Urban Scene: New Youth in an Old Environment," *Daedalus,* Fall 1968, p. 1126; Daniel Patrick Moynihan, *Maximum Feasible Misunderstanding: Community Action in the War on Poverty* (New York: The Free Press, 1969); Kenneth Keniston, "Student Unrest and the Two Revolutions," *Washington University Alumni News,* March 1969, p. 7; Alfred Dean, Review of *Community Dynamics and Mental Health* by Donald C. Klein in *Social Forces* 47 (September 1969), pp. 141–142. See also Chapter 10 in this book.

which it moves.[7] The current dissatisfaction of community sociologists with the state of the discipline is therefore significant.

THE KEY ROLE OF PARADIGMS

Scientific communities are organized around paradigms. Paradigms "are universally recognized scientific achievements that for a time provide model problems and solutions to a community of practitioners."[8] Such achievements may include almost any aspect of the practice of science such as, for example, "law, theory, applications, and instrumentation [which] together provide models from which spring particular coherent traditions of scientific research."[9] These achievements are acknowledged by a specific scientific community "as supplying the foundations for its further practice."

But a paradigm, though it is, as the dictionary defines it, an example, an exemplar, a model, a mold, or pattern, is also something more. There is also a value component in paradigms, including not only those usually attributed to science, such as accuracy, parsimony, consistency, and plausibility, but also a conviction that science should (or need not) be socially useful. The concept of paradigm also includes a belief component. No scientific group "could practice its trade without some set of received beliefs."[10]

This belief component is especially salient in community paradigms. In general, for example, sociologists "believe" that class explains more variance between individuals and groups than does race. No community of scientists in the field of sociology would be likely to offer or accept a racial explanation for any community phenomenon. Especially compelling in all community research and thinking are the egalitarian beliefs that characterize the American ethos. Class structure, social mobility, and social stratification have been major preoccupations in community study. The study of poverty has been shaped by egalitari-

[7] Thomas S. Kuhn, *The Structure of Scientific Revolutions* (Chicago: University of Chicago Press, 1962), p. x.

[8] Ibid.

[9] Ibid., p. 10.

[10] Ibid., p. 4.

an beliefs; the study of crime, by certain beliefs about the nature of human nature.

A paradigm, then, is a body of beliefs, values, ideas, theories, and data accepted by a community of scientists which then guides their selection of problems, methods of attack, choice of instruments, "hardware," "software," techniques, and forms of explanatory conceptualization. It is, in brief, the "fundamental unit for the study of scientific development."[11]

Kuhn emphasizes the difficulties involved in achieving such paradigms and is not certain how many there are in the social sciences today, if any. The answer depends on the way one defines "scientific achievement." If the criteria are as rigorous as those in the physical sciences, the answer is that there probably are no social-science paradigms—in any case, certainly not many. But if the criteria for what is scientific are relaxed, the answer is yes there are such paradigms. For example, in the area of instrumentation, the Simon-Binet tests of intelligence which served as an exemplar or model for a wide gamut of researchers and inaugurated a great movement toward measurement of all kinds of social-psychological variables such as attitudes, opinions, judgments, institutionalization, and alienation, to mention only a few, seems to qualify as scientific. Among generalizations, the *law of diminishing returns* seems also to be worthy of characterization as scientific.

Whether or not the achievements in the study of community are scientific in the strictest sense, many have served the function of paradigms for communities of scientists. They have attracted such scientists and supplied them with the foundations for a research tradition. They are therefore accorded the status of scientific—or at least quasi-scientific—paradigms here.

COMMUNITY PARADIGMS

Four classical paradigms encompass most of what we know about the sociology of the community. All have served as the focus of a community of scientists, given rise to "coherent traditions of scientific research" and provided "model problems and solutions" to these communities of scientific practitioners. Their rise and current crisis status constitute a major focus of the

---

[11] Ibid., p. 11.

present book. All have taken the locale component of community for granted.

One community of scientists was organized around the so-called ecological paradigm which explained how populations have distributed themselves, how the resulting settlements have become spatially structured, and how the structural components have varied sociologically. The "exemplar" or model here was the city of Chicago. Another community of scientists was organized around the ranked-status or social class paradigm based on research of an "exemplar" named Yankee City. A third, including both sociologists and political scientists, was organized around problems of community power. Two "exemplars" were salient here, Regional City and New Haven. A fourth classic community paradigm that goes under the rubric Gemeinschaft-Gesellschaft has dealt with the meaning of the spatial aspects of settlements for human relationships. The major component of this paradigm was a generalization about the differential impact of rural and urban life styles.

These paradigms might be stated in the "if . . . then" form. If such and such conditions prevail, then such and such results can be expected. If, for example, you have a raw, new land without a feudal tradition, operating under the capitalist laissez-faire policy, with an achievement-oriented labor force, then you can expect cities like Chicago to arise at certain places and to grow this way (Chapter 3). Or if a city is well integrated and not too large, with a certain ethnic composition and a certain industrial structure, then you can expect a class system based on ranked status like that of Yankee City (Chapter 4). Or if you have a community with such and such characteristics then you can expect a power structure like Regional City's or New Haven's (Chapter 5). Or if you have such and such conditions in a community, then you will find such and such effects on the residents (Chapter 6). The catch lies in the fact that we do not always know what the "ifs" are.

THE INERTIA OF PARADIGMS

Inertia tends to be built into scientific paradigms by the very nature of the communities organized around them. Individuals learn paradigms in school from teachers who also learned paradigms in school before them, so there is an unbroken tradition received and passed on. All are therefore "committed to the same rules and standards for scientific practice. That commitment and the apparent consensus it produces are prerequisites . . . for the genesis and continuation of a particular research tradition."[12] All are in the same "club" whose conventions constitute a kind of boundary-maintenance device. Members are loathe to violate its canons and thus invite sanctions. If one does not conform he can be read out of the profession, his work ignored or figuratively denounced. The power of the community thus to determine the fate of paradigms has a conservative effect.

This does not imply that communities of scientists are capricious or irresponsible in their acceptance and transmission of paradigms. It is just that some limits must be imposed: "Observation and experience can and must drastically restrict the range of admissible scientific belief, else there could be no science."[13] But observation and experience do not by themselves determine a specific body of scientific belief. For "an apparently arbitrary element, compounded of personal and historical accident, is always a formative ingredient of the beliefs espoused by a given scientific community at a given time."[14]

In the case of the sociology of community, this "arbitrary element compounded of personal and historical accident" may be illustrated by two quite disparate research traditions that developed in the United States, one concentrating on rural communities and one on urban. For reasons we need not specify here, enormous resources of personnel were invested in research on the rural community, and rural sociology early became a major field of the profession. Not until well into the present century did the sociology of urban communities begin to attract commensurate research attention, and for many years after it became a recognized area of investigation it did not receive the same amount of government support. It seemed "natural" that there should be two separate scientific communities studying communities, one with a rural and one with an urban orientation. Another "arbitrary element" that has influenced the acceptance or rejection of paradigms of any given scientific community has been the prestige of the university or of the scientist presenting it.[15] Still

12 Ibid., pp. 10–11.

13 Ibid., p. 4.

14 Ibid.

15 Ibid., p. 152.

another such arbitrary element has been the sex of the scientist offering the paradigm, those produced by women being less likely than those offered by men to receive a hearing.[16]

Conservatism is also fostered by the fact that it is easier to receive and transmit paradigms than to challenge them. Some members of the scientific community are therefore content to add a little here, subtract a little there. Some are rewarded by having their contribution incorporated into the received tradition. Such replicative, additive, cumulative research is the kind most scientists spend all their time on. It is, in fact, what Kuhn calls normal science.[17]

NORMAL SCIENCE
AND SCIENTIFIC REVOLUTIONS

However, this placid picture is deceptive. The course of science is not serene. Anomalies begin to show up in research findings. Exceptions become numerous. Results that do not fit the accepted paradigm cloud the picture, or positively conflicting results appear.

Many members of the scientific community, especially the older ones, are willing to make the adjustments necessary to maintain the old paradigm. But others, usually the younger, are less acquiescent. Finally, "when the profession can no longer evade anomalies that subvert the existing tradition of scientific practice . . . begin the extraordinary investigations that lead the profession at last to a new set of commitments, a new basis for the practice of [its] science."[18] These shifts of professional commitments constitute scientific revolutions. They are "tradition-shattering complements to the tradition-bound activity of normal science."[19]

Such scientific revolutions are not easy. There may be resistance, for quite human and understandable reasons. Older members especially may find it difficult to change their way of

---

[16] Jessie Bernard, *Academic Women* (University Park, Pa.: The Pennsylvania State University Press, 1964), Chapter 10; also "Sexism and Discrimination," *The American Sociologist* 5 (November 1970), pp. 374–75.

[17] Kuhn, *The Structure of Scientific Revolutions*, p. 5.

[18] Ibid., p. 6.

[19] Ibid.

thinking and jettison a traditional approach; the old way often seems just as good for practical purposes as the new one. At least it works; they are used to it, so they cleave to it. What difference does it make, really, whether the sun goes around the earth or the earth around the sun?

Younger members, however, less identified with the accepted paradigms are more hospitable to innovation. For a while there may be controversy. In time, the older, more resistant members die off, or are read out of the profession, or are isolated; neither their articles are accepted by the journals nor their books by publishers; and the new paradigm takes over. The new one takes over, it should be noted, not necessarily because it is superior (although it usually is), nor because it has been "proved" or validated against "nature," but because it has succeeded in the competition for adherents.[20]

Because new paradigms require reconstruction of accepted commitments and even reevaluation of prior facts, it takes time to establish them. Scientific revolutions therefore are not sudden. The old hangs on at least until the surviving generation takes it with them from the stage. In the meanwhile the processes of normal science—improvement, modification, and adjustment of the new paradigm—take over until once more the "new" paradigm in turn proves less effective than another and the process repeats itself. An example of a scientific revolution in the field of the social sciences is offered in Chapter 2, where the story of the paradigm of preindustrial capitalism is sketched.

Conservative influences have been strong in the case of community paradigms and work in this field has been characterized by normal-science research more than by scientific revolutions. Normal science, then, accepts the paradigms and tries to improve them; it does not seek to be innovative. Revolutionary science, on the other hand, is not merely an accumulation of knowledge. It seeks better ways to look at problems and better ways to explain or interpret findings. It does not fundamentally alter old paradigms; it seeks to create new ones.

OUTSIDE INFLUENCES
ON PARADIGM CHANGES

The discussion so far has focused on the scientific community itself as a determinant of inertia or change. But Kuhn does

---

[20] Ibid., p. 19.

not rule out the influence of outside factors also, especially the effect of technological advances and of external social, economic, and intellectual conditions.[21] These extrinsic forces are especially important in the field of the social sciences. In the last third of the twentieth century they are bringing old community paradigms close to crisis.

With respect to technological innovations, paradigms in the social sciences respond in ways not very different from the ways in which paradigms in the physical and biological sciences respond. Computers, for example, have an impact in the social sciences as great as in the physical and biological sciences. With respect to other kinds of external conditions, however, there is a difference.

It is true that despite the protection of ivory towers all kinds of scientific paradigms are subject to outside influence. The treatment of Galileo at the hands of the Church was only one of many examples. Darwin's theory of evolution had to fight the same kind of battle. Eugene Dubois withdrew his Pithecanthropus Erectus bones to protect himself against calumnious attack. The Freudian paradigm of infant sexuality had hard sledding not only because of the rejection by scientists but also because of popular outcry against it. There are still great lacunae in our knowledge about sex and sexuality, because until recently these subjects were taboo for scientific inquiry.[22] Paradigms in the social sciences are even more vulnerable to such hazards. A study of integration in a community was once denied support by a Congressman until it was explained to him that it was a plant community being studied.

In addition, social science paradigms have peculiar problems of their own. In the physical and biological sciences the new data, or "novelties of fact,"[23] that lead to paradigm shifts tend to result from the research of normal science. But in the social sciences the new data which force modification or supplanting of old paradigms come not only from the researches of normal science but also from historical experience. That is, "current history" as well as controlled or improved observation and research provide the anomalies that have to be incorporated into paradigms. A modern

[21] Ibid., p. xii.

[22] Jessie Bernard, "Technology, Science, and Sex Attitudes," *Impact of Science on Society* 18 (October-December 1968), pp. 213-28.

[23] Kuhn, *The Structure of Scientific Revolutions*, p. 52.

industrialized community generates such "novelties of fact" even faster than a scientist does in his laboratory. Community paradigms are therefore more perishable than those of the physical or biological sciences which deal with a more stable universe.

For the most part, the result of novelties of fact in the form of current history has produced tinkering rather than revolution in community paradigms. As a result, current community paradigms do not tell us how cities function; we are at a loss to interpret the nature and operation of power in the community; old criteria of social class no longer seem to fit the current scene. Events, in brief, have overtaken old paradigms. And research-as-usual will not do what has to be done, for "paradigms are not corrigible by normal science at all."[24] The upheavals of the last third of the century in the United States as well as in the Third World have produced novelties of fact which are so anomalous in relation to old paradigms that merely tinkering with old paradigms does not seem to be enough. Paradigm shifts seem to be called for. We need paradigms which "tell us different things about the population of the universe [of communities] and about that population's behavior."[25]

The lag between new data and paradigm change tends to be greater in the social than in the physical and biological sciences. We have to resign ourselves to the fact that in the social sciences we never know the world as it is right now. It takes an enormous number of specialized personnel to tell us what it was like this morning, yesterday, last year, a generation ago, or a thousand years ago. It takes the efforts of newspaper reporters and columnists, political commentators and analysts, mass media, census enumerators and poll-takers, as well as scientific researchers, to keep us au courant. In time we get a fairly good idea of what it was like, if not what it is like. This process of catching up with events took considerably longer before modern mass media were available, but even today our knowledge always tends to be behind the times. Paradigms show us how to see what was, rather than what is. No matter how much tinkering we do, anomalies persist and grow. The suspicion strengthens that the classic community paradigms are not guiding either policy or research in the most useful way. They are being rejected by planners and revolutionaries because they are not programmatic on the one hand nor, on the other hand, adequate to handle causality.

[24] Ibid., p. 121.

[25] Ibid., p. 102.

PLAN OF PRESENTATION

The general "scenario" of the present book may be sketched as follows. After a brief look at the two overarching paradigms that have served as the intellectual matrix in which all community paradigms have been shaped, Part Two presents the four classic community paradigms—the ecological, the social class, the community power, and the Gemeinschaft-Gesellschaft—which have constituted the major contents of the sociology of community to date, showing in each case how anomalies have resulted from the "novelties of fact" that recent events have introduced. Part Three deals with the failure of the classic paradigms to deal with change; Chapter 7, with change in race relations and in the status of poor people; Chapter 8, with resistance to change; and Chapter 9, with the failure of the paradigms when applied to change or modernization in the Third World. Part Four returns to the questions raised in Chapter 1: Can we dispense with the locale component of the community? Has technology so altered the nature of the community as to render all our thinking on the subject up to now not only useless but even so dysfunctional as to call for a scientific revolution? The answers offered are no to the first question and yes to the second.

2

Two Overarching Paradigms

THE PARADIGMATIC CONTEXT
OF COMMUNITY STUDY

Two general paradigms—capitalism and structure-functional-ism—formed the ambience in which community study has taken place, and the community paradigms that guided such study can be understood only in the context of this ambience. Although not themselves specifically community paradigms, they constituted the encompassing matrix within which community research took place.

At the end of the eighteenth century and the beginning of the nineteenth, when countries in the West were entering the industrial age, modernization was taking place on many fronts—religious, political, and intellectual. All of these changes, especially those taking place in the polity and the economy, were to have dramatic impact on communities. The guide to the understanding of the processes involved came from the paradigms of political economy, especially the paradigm of capitalism.

THE PARADIGM OF CAPITALISM

This "system of beliefs, standards, values, laws, [and] theories" which shaped thought and policy for decades was based to a
large extent on theories presented with systematic elegance by
Adam Smith in 1776. The modernization under way in agriculture—for the agricultural revolution was as fundamental as that in
commerce or manufacture—was releasing workers from rural
occupations and making them available for the mills, factories,
shops, and services in the towns. And the remarkable series of
innovations which began what we now call the first industrial
revolution had already begun when Adam Smith presented the
revolutionary and triumphant paradigm that was to crystallize a
new discipline, political economy, and teach generations of
followers what to see and what to do. It supplanted the mercantilist paradigm that preceded it and won a competitive contest
over the physiocratic—land-based—paradigm that paralleled it.

The capitalist paradigm had repercussions for the study of
community in two directions. First, the market mechanism became the foundation for one of the greatest of the classic community paradigms, the ecological. Second, the psychological and
sociological concomitants of the market essential for its operation
came to be known as Gesellschaft and, as such, were viewed as the
great destroyer of community in the Gemeinschaft sense.[1]

Some Characterizing Concepts
of the Paradigm of Capitalism

The new paradigm saw the production of goods, not gold, as
constituting the wealth of nations. Adam Smith emphasized the
importance of the division of labor in producing those goods,
especially the specialization it fostered, not only at home but also
among nations, thus showing how the principle of comparative
advantage—each person or nation doing not necessarily what he
or it was best at, but what he or it was *relatively* best at—would
increase the total productivity of every nation. Equally important,
Adam Smith showed the importance of laissez-faire, or noninter-
vention by the state, no tariffs, and no attempts to direct the flow
of goods; free trade among nations and reliance on individual

[1] The concept of Gesellschaft is analyzed in Chapter 6.

initiative at home; and, most important, the market, not bureaucrats, making the decisions about the allocation of the factors of production. Adam Smith saw the market mechanism as an alternative far superior to political control as a regulator of the economy. It eliminated the incompetent planners; it produced the "feedback" that alerted businessmen and industrialists in the allocation of resources; it decentralized economic decisions. The market was always a private market and always an alternative to planning.[2] It was to be a long time before the fallacies of the market as a decision-making mechanism became manifest in such forms, for example, as slums and environmental pollution. (The fascination with the market mechanism is still so great that even in the last third of this century arguments are beginning to be heard for turning public services like schools over to the market.)

In addition to the key concept of the market as a decision-making mechanism, the new paradigm was characterized by several psychological and sociological beliefs and assumptions. It presupposed that rational individuals would make the market decisions in ways to maximize gains and minimize losses. It presupposed that they were acquisitive and achievement-oriented individuals who wanted to succeed, who liked competition, and who wanted to be left alone. The paradigm showed how, if given their head, such enterprising persons, each specializing in the work he could do relatively best and exchanging his products in the market for the goods and services of others also doing their best, would indeed maximize the welfare of all. In earlier paradigms it had been assumed that, without controls, the greed of men would destroy the social order. Not so, the new paradigm taught.

To speak of the characterizing concepts or elements of the paradigm of capitalism does not imply that capitalism was viewed as merely a congeries. It was conceived of as a *system.* The components or elements might exist separately or in a different context, but they would then not necessarily function in the same way. For example, the profit motive might appear anywhere in any system. But if it existed in a setting where it was not used as information to guide the allocation of the factors of production but, let us say, merely to finance a borrower's consumption, it might simply be usury or exploitation. Achievement orientation

---

[2] Charles E. Lindblom, "The Rediscovery of the Market," *The Public Interest*, Summer 1966, pp. 90–91.

might be toward nonproductive achievement: counting coups and potlatch burning of goods, for example. Work ethos might be an escape. Laissez-faire might simply mean that there was no state or government at all. It was the peculiar concatenation of functions in a system that characterized the system known as capitalism delineated in the Smith paradigm.

Some Corollaries
of the Paradigm of Capitalism

A paradigm based on rational, achievement-oriented, acquisitive, enterprising human beings full of initiative and out to win, socialized by their religion into an ethos of work, exalting competition, using profit as information for decision making, viewing the new industrial order as a great beneficent natural force, could not help but color thinking about all aspects of human relationships in communities. Not only did Adam Smith extol the merits of his model as it operated in the market but Charles Darwin later showed how it operated in the "struggle for existence" and Herbert Spencer, combining the two ideas, how it led to the "survival of the fittest."

If competition was accorded an exalted function in the great design of nature in the paradigm of capitalism, the same was not true of conflict. The classic paradigm recognized the existence of conflict but deplored and denigrated it. Law and order were its key desiderata. Conflict interfered with social order; it was disruptive. Herbert Spencer taught that industrialism and militarism were antithetical; in time, industrialization would get rid of war, for nations would become too interdependent to be able to afford it. Within the local community, too, the division of labor or specialization fostered interdependence and was therefore integrative; it created what Emile Durkheim called organic solidarity and conflict disturbed it.

The typical or modal modern man under capitalism was thus not only rationalistic and calculating, but also peaceable. He had to be, as communities grew in complexity. "The modern type is the man of mild personality, shunning the appearance of self-assertion, slow to anger, patient of contradiction, mindful of the feelings of those about him, unwilling to 'make trouble.' . . . This . . . has been wrought by the slow but incessant modification of the social environment to which each generation of men has had to conform its action . . . [with] the continuous growth of the community in size and complexity."[3] Modern man was aggressive and competitive, yes, but not in the manner of the "primitive type" who was intense, "easily roused to paroxysms of anger, brooking no contradiction." Conflict was the recourse of incompetents, of those, that is, who could not compete successfully. The victim of conflict might deserve sympathy as an underdog, but the instigator did not, for he upset the applecart. Conflict had a bad name among the successful competitors.[4]

The early response, especially of those who profited from the policies that flowed from the new paradigm, was a loud hurrah! These policies set men free, for they led to the erosion of other controls as well. Men were no longer hemmed in, no longer bound to the soil or to the family or to the place of their birth. They could move. And social as well as geographical mobility became increasingly possible. Obligations, responsibilities, and duties could be discharged by way of money for the "cash nexus" operated in the social as well as in the economic order. One could buy services now formerly only available in the family on the basis of love or duty. If you could get the money you could get the other things too. And if you understood the system you could get the money.

It is quite possible, of course, that the same policies may have been pursued and the same results achieved even if some other paradigm had guided policy. Still, it is also possible that if the physiocratic paradigm, with its emphasis on agriculture and the extractive industries, had won the minds of policy makers industrialization and urbanization could have taken a somewhat different course. The physiocratic paradigm included some of the same components as Adam Smith's, such as, for example, an emphasis on self-interest, economic freedom, and competition. But it also included state control for realizing "individual-transcending purposes."[5] One example, perhaps, is environmental control.

[3] John Fiske, *Outlines of Cosmic Philosophy*, vol. 2 (Boston: Houghton Mifflin Company, 1890), p. 208.

[4] For discussion of conflict and competition in the community see Jessie Bernard, *American Community Behavior*, 2nd ed. (New York: Holt, Rinehart & Winston, Inc., 1962), Parts IV and V.

[5] Joseph J. Spengler, "Physiocratic Thought," in David L. Sills, ed., *International Encyclopedia of the Social Sciences*, vol. 4 (New York: The Macmillan Company and The Free Press, 1968), p. 445.

Be that as it may, the new paradigm was enormously successful. Its conception of the world seemed eminently "natural." It
seemed to describe the only way to allocate the factors of
production and distribute consumer goods and services. The kind
of people it presupposed seemed to represent normal, universal,
"human nature." It set the stage for much that was to happen in
communities in the West in the nineteenth and twentieth centuries.

The Fate of the Classic Paradigm
of Capitalism

After Adam Smith's creative statement of the paradigm of
capitalism, a long normal-science literature ensued. A community
of scientists watched its implementation, scrutinizing in detail
the way each of the factors of production—land, labor, and
capital—operated. The theory of rent was elaborated; an iron law
of wages was propounded. Interest, with which the Church had
wrestled for so long, was rationalized and profit almost apothe-
osized. The nature of exchange value was examined in detail. A
new factor of production, entrepreneurial skill and management,
was added.

After half a century or so, more was known about how the
new system actually operated than had been known originally
when Adam Smith wrote. History was providing "novelties of
fact." Anomalies began to show up in the paradigm. Karl Marx
was merely the greatest, not the only, critic; he forced a reex-
amination of some of its basic assumptions. The so-called institutional school of economics forced recognition of the nonrational,
even in some cases irrational, aspects of market behavior. Thor-
stein Veblen had a field day with the work ethos. Thurman Arnold
pointed out how much of received economic doctrine was merely
folklore. J. K. Galbraith poked fun at the conventional wisdom of
capitalism, noting that profit was no longer sparking its motors.
The nature of competition was scrutinized as it operated on a
scene totally different from that envisaged by Adam Smith and it
was found to have fallen into desuetude.

The model was modified to take account of the new information generated by the record of its operation and by the defects
noted by the critics. It was tinkered with here, trimmed there. But
basically, despite a century and a half of tinkering, the paradigm

remained. It was still addressed to a world of scarcity in which production was the major problem. And although economists had long since been reporting its demise, the community of scientists that was organized around this paradigm successfully warded off all revolutionary competitors.

Not until well into the twentieth century, when the incredible success of science and technology had inaugurated the so-called postindustrial or "technetronic" age, did a paradigmatic revolution occur. A new paradigm built around a "welfare function" and known as welfare economics then arose to challenge the old paradigmatic assumptions and the policies based on them. It jettisoned laissez-faire, recognized the validity of a managed economy, and found income inequalities economically dysfunctional, along with many tenets of the Protestant ethic.

We anticipate later discussion in pointing out here that the erosion of laissez-faire meant that many policy decisions were no longer left to competition in the market but were returned to the polity where they were made by those with power. Conflict came to supplant competition as the great process for decision making.[6]

It was not only the policies of laissez-faire with respect to the market that came under attack, but also the assumptions about economic man on which they rested. The cheerful individuals of the capitalism paradigm, profitably exchanging goods with one another in a market where every transaction left all parties better off than before, were, in the new Gemeinschaft-Gesellschaft paradigm, replaced by sullen, suspicious, power-endowed individuals trying to do one another in. The Gesellschaft paradigm of capitalist society[7] saw in every exchange a zero-sum game in which "the loss of one is the profit of the other."[8] Gesellschaft was viewed as the very antithesis of community; it became the target of virulent protest. When modern young people attack "capitalism" it is not likely to be as a market-oriented economic system and certainly not as a laissez-faire political system primarily, but as the epitome of Gesellschaft.

The period of policy domination by the paradigm of capital-

[6] See Chapters 7–9 in this book.

[7] "Capitalistic society . . . is the most distinct form of the many phenomena represented by the sociological concept of the Gesellschaft." Ferdinand Tönnies, *Community and Society*, edited and translated by Charles P. Loomis (New York: Harper Torchbook, 1957), p. 258.

[8] Ibid., p. 77.

ism may, as Gunnar Myrdal says, have been merely an interlude between a period dominated by policies based on the mercantilist paradigm and the period dominated by policies supplied by the paradigm of the welfare state;[9] but while it lasted, it exerted enormous influence. We can gauge the enormity of its influence by the difficulty we experience in trying to overcome it. Every city in the United States is a monument to its power.

THE PARADIGM FOR FUNCTIONAL ANALYSIS

The second all-encompassing paradigm, not itself specifically a community paradigm but one which has guided thinking and research in the field of community, has variously taken the form of structure-functionalism or of social-systems analysis. Although it is possible to make fine conceptual distinctions between the two forms, they resemble one another more than they differ.[10] The structural emphasis tends to concern itself more with the institutions of a system; the social·systems emphasis concerns itself with the overall system to which the structures belong. Both have been used in community study.[11]

Two classic formulations of the functional paradigm were those presented by Robert K. Merton and Talcott Parsons.[12] The differences between them might be encapsulated by the statement that Merton's would guide one to look for the functions being performed by a given structure, and Parsons' would guide one to look for the way the functions of a system were structured. The heart of the analysis in any event would lie in the central but, as it proved, disconcerting concept of function. One could be equally naive using either form so long as one saw only the civics-textbook functions, such as, for example, education, maintenance

[9] Gunnar Myrdal, Christian Herter lecture, Johns Hopkins University, March 20, 1969.

[10] Alvin W. Gouldner,"Reciprocity and Autonomy in Functional Theory," in Llewellyn Gross, ed., *Symposium on Sociological Theory* (Chicago: Harper & Row, Publishers, 1959), pp. 243, 244.

[11] For example, see Marvin Sussman, ed., *Community Structure and Analysis* (New York: Thomas Y. Crowell Company, 1959); Irwin Sanders, *The Community, an Introduction to a Social System* (New York: The Ronald Press Company, 1958); and Roland E. Warren, *The Community in America* (Chicago: Rand McNally & Co., 1963).

[12] Robert K. Merton, *Social Theory and Social Structure* (New York: The Free Press, 1958), pp. 50–54; Talcott Parsons, "General Theory in Sociology," in Robert K. Merton et al., eds., *Sociology Today: Problems and Prospects* (New York: Basic Books, Inc., Publishers, 1959), pp. 4–8.

of order, production, and the like, or their structural or institutional counterparts, such as schools, government, or factories. A conventional approach to the study of community would analyze the formal institutions—family, school, church, industry, and government—that performed the functions required for its ongoing life and show how they intermeshed with one another in a coherent whole. But the concept of function proved far subtler than it first appeared.

What Do You Mean, Function?

Merton sketched at least five different meanings which have been assigned to the term *function* and even more different terms—*use, utility, purpose, motive, intention, aim, consequences*—which have been given the same meaning as function. The confusion is not a result of carelessness.

What criteria should be used in assessing functionality? Survival, maintenance, adaptation, and adjustment have been proposed, although none is wholly satisfactory. Every community that sociologists study today has, obviously, survived, some of them bearing what, in the eyes of the West at least, would seem like a heavy load of dysfunctional elements. W. G. Sumner once summarized a host of dysfunctional, or what he called harmful, folkways, including the destruction of an individual's wealth at his death; expenditures of labor and capital on graves, temples, pyramids, and the like; food taboos which reduced the food supply; and protective taboos which forbade destruction of harmful animals.[13] Many communities studied by archaeologists—like Troy or Pompeii, for example—have not survived, but for reasons not always altogether clear. We know why some of them vanished. Some biblical communities, for example, were leveled by war; great natural catastrophes have destroyed others. We have no way of knowing how many have been wiped out by plagues of one kind or another or by famine. Some waste away when technology destroys their economic raison d'être. Some have disappeared and are disappearing almost before our eyes. But the part played by structural dysfunction is not always obvious.

More serious still is the fact that often what we are really talking about is survival or maintenance of a particular status quo rather than the community as such. One status quo succeeds

13 W. G. Sumner, *Folkways* (Boston: Ginn and Company, 1906), pp. 26–27.

another, but the community itself—its people, their language, their interests, their culture—remains.

Still, one can go along with the survival criterion of functionality. Prehuman beings were living in communities long before they even became human; they must have been doing something right, for all communities that survive do have to see that certain functions are performed. They do have to replenish themselves or recruit new members somehow or other. This may sound like a verbose statement of the obvious. Of course if a community wishes to survive it has to be able to get new members. So what?

It is not quite as simplistic as it sounds. If it were, then a simple review of the facts of biological reproduction would be all we needed to know in order to understand this function. But knowing all about biological reproduction would tell us little if anything about the replenishment function. We have to know more. We have to know about birth and death rates, for example. So we have to extend our focus to include more demographic data. This is still not enough, because the matings that produce the birth rate do not occur at random among human beings. Universally they are controlled by a vast set of norms specifying who may mate with whom. So we have to learn about marriage and a vast array of sex taboos and proscriptions. Further, if a community is to survive, merely adding members will not be enough. There has to be some way to protect and care for the new members. Most communities give this child-care responsibility to the mother. Still, again, there is more here than meets the eye.

For just keeping babies alive and well is not enough either. In fact, if that were all we did for them we would not even have normal human beings, much less members of a community.[14] In addition to being kept alive and healthy, infants have to be taught how to perform roles in the community. They have to be located somewhere in it and prepared or socialized into some status. To achieve all this as a minimum, in all surviving communities there will have to be at least a modicum of functional differentiation and division of labor on the basis of sex or age or both, if on no other, and, perhaps somewhat later, on the basis of lineage. We know that all of the above will be related, either as antecedent or as consequence, to inequalities in privileges, obligations, rights, duties, and responsibilities, so that some kind of ranking may be

[14] Kingsley Davis, "Extreme Social Isolation of a Child," *American Journal of Sociology* 45 (January 1940), pp. 554–564, and "Final Note on a Case of Extreme Isolation," *American Journal of Sociology* 50 (March 1947), pp. 432–37.

expected. And controls of one kind or another will be present to regulate all this. These functions are required merely for replenishment and survival. One can, of course, go on almost endlessly.

Latent Functions

One of the most useful contributions of the functionalist paradigm was the concept of latent functions. These are functions which are not formally or openly institutionalized by the community but are intrinsic in its operation; their existence may not even be admitted by the community. This concept was especially useful in explaining patterns viewed as bad or wrong; it was not needed for those viewed as good or right, for they could be judged on their merits.

The concept of latent functions was analogous to the psychoanalyst's concept of the unconscious. It made room for anything that had to be openly disavowed; it showed that the observer knew the observed better than the observed did himself. Of course the community does not approve of crime, the analyst of latent functions could soothingly say, and then proceed to show exactly how crime suited the ends of the community and how "deviance can play an important role in keeping the social order intact."[15] Crime served to draw the community together against the criminal. Or, viewed from a somewhat different angle, the Mafia served the community by supplying markets for forbidden goods and services. Of course the community does not approve of racism, the analyst of latent functions could say, and then show exactly how racism served the community's purposes by protecting itself against competition from blacks. Of course the community disapproves of ignorance; then the functional analyst could show exactly what functions ignorance performs.[16] Of course the community does not approve of slums; then the functional analyst could enumerate all the functions performed by slums.[17] In the case of Russia, it could be shown that corruption performed an invaluable function in making the economy operate; without it,

[15] Kai T. Erikson, "Note on the Sociology of Deviance," *Social Problems* 9 (Spring 1962), p. 309.

[16] Wilbert E. Moore and Melvin Tumin, "Some Social Functions of Ignorance," *American Sociological Review* 14 (December 1949), pp, 787–95.

[17] John R. Seeley, "The Slum: Its Nature, Use, and Users," *Journal of American Institutional Planners* 25 (February 1959), pp. 7–14.

the Russian economy would collapse.[18] Latent functions were not, however, intrinsically sinister. The latent function of the Protestant ethic, for example, was to shape a kind of character that would work and save and thus create the capital to finance industrialization. But the chances were that the functions performed latently rather than manifestly were those that could not stand the light of day.

The functionalist paradigm could be reduced to an absurdity. In the hands of some it was used as a moral whip. What they disapproved of could be proved dysfunctional to survival. Conventional morality tends to rely implicitly on some kind of survival criterion of functionality: Immorality leads to the downfall of a society, as the fall of Rome so majestically proves. Or Sodom and Gomorrah are used as examples of what moral deviance can bring about. The military also can use the survival criterion of functionality: Without enormous military power our survival is endangered. Others could just as easily defend the same behavior as performing latent functions; without it, the system would break down.

IDEOLOGY AND PARADIGMATIC PREDILECTIONS

Although Merton concluded that since "functional analysis can be seen by some as inherently conservative and by others as inherently radical . . . it may be inherently neither one nor the other; it . . . may involve no intrinsic ideological commitment although . . . it can be infused with any one of a wide range of ideological values,"[19] still it did, in the middle decades of the twentieth century, attract conservative users. The paradigm itself may not be biased in the direction of justifying the status quo, but many of those who have used it have seemed to be. If the manifest function of any scientific paradigm is merely to serve as a guide for research or to help us understand the world we live in, latent functions may also be served.

In the case of the functional paradigm itself, for example, one latent function it allegedly served was the justification it supplied for the existence of a class system. Thus the most famous use of

---

[18] Edward Crankshaw, *Khrushchev's Russia* (Baltimore: Penguin Books, Inc., 1959), p. 75.

[19] Merton, *Social Theory and Social Structure*, p. 42.

the paradigm to explain stratification saw the unequal rewards attached to social positions as a functional necessity. "Social inequality is . . . an unconsciously evolved device by which societies insure that the most important positions are conscientiously filled by the most qualified persons."[20] All communities have to differentiate their members in terms of prestige and esteem and "must therefore possess a certain amount of institutionalized inequality."[21] This analysis was faulted by those with other predilections on the basis that it did not distinguish between differentiation, which was incontrovertibly a functional necessity, and stratification, which implied a certain degree of fixity. One such critic scored the conservatism that he believed inherent in the functionalist paradigm: "The frequent stress of functionalism on the 'survival of society' easily leads one to look very hard for, or find very easily, some existing structural arrangement which, under the guise of explaining the survival of 'society,' . . . succeeds only in justifying the persistence of some existing structure, e.g., a class system."[22] (In any event, whatever functionalism may have taught with respect to stratification in societies as wholes, it did not tally with what citizens in the local communities could see with their own eyes; here they could see that family background was as important as talent in determining one's position.)

It did seem true that, whatever the intrinsic nature of the functionalist paradigm may have been, those who were attracted to it seemed to use it in ways that were ideologically conservative. And, conversely, among radical young sociologists in the 1960s, *functionalism* had become a dirty word. They snickered when they heard it, but used it, nevertheless, with deadly impact against the status quo.

CONFLICTING POLICY IMPLICATIONS
OF THE TWO OVERARCHING PARADIGMS

The coexistence of inconsistent paradigms is not necessarily anomalous, as illustrated by the two paradigms with respect to

---

[20] Kingsley Davis, *Human Society* (New York: The Macmillan Company, 1948), pp. 366–68.

[21] Ibid., p. 368.

[22] Walter Buckley, "Social Stratification and the Functional Theory of Social Differentiation," *American Sociological Review* 23 (August 1958), p. 375.

light, the wave, and the corpuscular. Research could proceed around both without interfering with one another. It is only when policy turns to the paradigms for guidance that inconsistencies confound.

At the beginning of the last third of the twentieth century paradigmatic inconsistencies were beginning to be felt in policy decisions. A program for developing social indicators was being inaugurated which would show us how the welfare as well as the wealth or gross national product of the nation increased or decreased according to different policies. Could it be assumed that policies designed to increase the gross national product would also increase the general welfare? Were the indicators of economic productivity also indicators of social welfare?

The economist assigned the task of devising such social indicators, Mancur Olson, Jr., concluded that the reply to questions like these was no. He contrasted, with respect to several key concepts, the paradigm of capitalism with the social-system paradigm as delineated by Parsons. The first assumed, as regards rationality, that it was a universal part of human nature; the second, that rationality was only a concomitant of the Protestant or capitalist ethos. As regards stability, or the factors that held a society together, the first emphasized diversity and pluralism, which made it profitable to specialize and thus to increase productivity; the second emphasized similarities of attitudes and values resulting from socialization. With respect to "ideal" societies, the paradigm of capitalism envisioned maximum income which, in turn, depended on the optimal allocation of resources; the Parsons paradigm sought a minimization of alienation. As a corollary, the paradigm of capitalism encouraged innovation, which meant constant change and therefore few stable relationships; it was therefore anticommunity in its emphasis. The Parsons paradigm, with its emphasis on stability, would tend to favor policies discouraging change and thus lead to stagnation. The two paradigms, Olson concluded, led to ideals which were "not only different, but polar opposites; if either one were attained, the society would be a nightmare in terms of the other."[23] Their contradiction with one another expressed "the most fundamental alternatives human societies face."[24]

And, indeed, we shall find these contrasting emphases crop-

[23] Mancur Olson, Jr., "Economics, Sociology, and the Best of All Possible Worlds," *The Public Interest*, No. 12 (Summer 1968), p. 114.

[24] Ibid., p. 144.

ping up in one form or another throughout our discussion here. They may take different forms in different contexts, but they remain ineffable. In planning communities do we want segregated, homogeneous ethnic or class enclaves, or do we want ethnic groups and different classes distributed throughout the community? Do we want pluralism or a melting pot? Do we want business and residential use of land segregated so that certain parts of the city become deserted after working hours? Or do we want all—at least congenial—kinds of land uses to be mixed up together? The conclusion drawn by Olson is, indeed, incontrovertible: We are faced by fundamental alternatives.

Another economist, Kenneth E. Boulding, without referring specifically to the two paradigms, has made a similar point and arrived at a similar conclusion:

> On the one hand, there is the . . . ideal of the individual acting as an individual and independent person in a larger community, exchanging his capacities with other individuals in a social contract and in a market economy, expressing his political activity primarily by voting in elections on the one-man, one-vote basis. In political organization this leads to what we might call "atomistic parliamentarism." In economic organization, it leads to capitalism and the free market. . . . It goes along with the life style of mobility and rootlessness, entrepreneurship, achieved rather than ascribed status, and so on. On the other side, we have the collective ideal stressing the notion that the identity of the individual is so bound up with the community with which he identifies that he can only become an individual as part of a community. His political activity here is exercised by activity influencing the decisions and the bargaining power of a series of concentric communities, rather than as an individual among other individuals. This leads toward a consensus-oriented society, totalitarianism, socialism, catholicism, monasticism, associationism, such things as trade unions and professional associations, collective rather than individual bargaining, and the corporate rather than the parliamentary state. Each of these philosophies has its own virtues and vices, and almost any political system is some sort of uneasy compromise between the two. . . .
>
> The synthesis and reconciliation in both structure and philosophy of the two political "modes," as they might be called, of individualism and collectivism perhaps represent

the greatest single long-run problem of the human race at its present state of development. The city, or at least the urban collectivity, is one of the principal arenas in which this problem is or is not being worked out, as the case may be.[25]

It is, basically, the same conflict as that between Gemeinschaft and Gesellschaft.

Different people place different values on the goals reflected in the two paradigms. Some relish the "rugged individualism" of the paradigm of capitalism; others reject the alienation it leads to, preferring the security of communitarianism. It may well be that the most intractable conflict of our time will prove to be precisely that between (1) those who hate the whole Gesellschaft scheme of life, its rationalism, its impersonality, and its competitiveness, and (2) those who glory in it, who are hard-driving, competitive, out to win, and who enjoy the affluence that goes with it. If we were dealing only with a scientific problem, there would be less basis for concern. But it is more than a scientific problem. It is a value problem demanding scrutiny of goals. The individuals who fit the capitalist paradigm and those who do not are engaged in one of the major conflicts of the nineteenth and twentieth centuries—and even the twenty-first.

So much, then, for the two overarching paradigms that have supplied the matrix in which thinking and research on "the community" and "community" have taken place, and which have also guided policy. We turn now, in Part Two, to an examination of four classic paradigms that have constituted the basic core of the sociology of the community, namely, the ecological, the social class or ranked-status, the power structure, and the Gemeinschaft-Gesellschaft paradigms.

---

[25] Kenneth E. Boulding, "The City as an Element in the International System," *Daedalus,* Fall 1968, pp. 1120–22.

Part Two

The Classic Community Paradigms

3

The Ecological Model

The ecological model, despite its evocative title, could be subsumed under either or both of the overarching paradigms. The paradigm of capitalism had incorporated the factors of production and answered the question of what would be their effect on the wealth of the nation. The ecological model of this paradigm incorporated different land uses and asked what would be their effect on the nature of the community and the relations among its inhabitants. The "hidden hand" in both cases was competition in a market with a minimum amount of regulation in which knowledgeable individuals, with profit as feedback information, made rational decisions. But the ecological model could also be viewed as an offshoot of the structure-functional or social-systems paradigm as applied to one particular aspect of the community—its spatial parameters. For functions were implicit in the concept of land use, and the interconnectedness of subsystems was intrinsic to it.

But sociologists in the nineteenth century had found biological analogies particularly appealing; in the twentieth, many still did. The biological analogy of ecology seemed especially apt for the study of communities. Indeed, R. E. Park stated that "the plant community offers the simplest and least qualified example of the community . . . which is not a society."[1] The term *community* implied diversity but also implied organized uniformity.[2] There were so many analogies between plant and animal communities and human communities that the term *ecological* came to characterize the new paradigm. And it served the functions that any successful revolutionary paradigm must serve: It focused a large but scattered body of knowledge which had been accumulated by muckrakers, social workers, reformers, and surveys of one kind or another by government commissions—on sanitary conditions, pauperism, immigrant groups, housing, and crime and delinquency, to mention only the most salient—for over a century. But as yet there was no paradigm to give these great accumulations of data coherence. Such a paradigm was supplied in the second decade of the twentieth century when Park and Burgess organized a wide gamut of observations and studies into a model that made sense out of the welter of facts, figures, and data of all kinds that had been lying around for a long time and continued to flood the presses. To the "if" supplied by the data (the "givens"), they supplied the "then." It was under their tutelage that the ecological model was launched. It was eagerly seized upon and it harvested a rich crop of normal-science research.

THE ALLOCATION OF LAND

It was one of the "facts . . . accessible to casual observation," easily seen and far from recondite that, by design or not—and equally natural in either case—the uses to which land was put were not randomly distributed over space, inside or outside of community limits. For at least a thousand years, it was obvious, some land was used for agriculture, some for grazing, some for fortresses and castles, and some for highways. Within towns, for at least that long, it was obvious that there was convenience in having a Milk Street or a Bread Street or a Market Street. And whether by edict or by choice, ethnic enclaves in towns and cities found segregation useful. In the case of some, dietary and ritual requirements demanded it; in the case of others, cultural bonds.

These different functional and ethnic allocations of land could be arrived at by different routes; some—like the location of a

---

[1] Robert E. Park and Ernest W. Burgess, *Introduction to the Science of Sociology* (Chicago: University of Chicago Press, 1921), p. 165.

[2] Ibid., p. 177.

fortress—by rational, perhaps even engineering, decisions; some by the tendency formulated in the folk observation that birds of a feather tend to flock together, that like seeks like, or the more sophisticated concept of Franklin Giddings of "consciousness of kind."[3] They could result from either differentiation or accretion.

In any event, these specialized land uses were far older than the paradigm of capitalism. What the ecological model did for modern communities was to begin with these so-called natural areas, describe them and their interrelations with one another, explain them in terms derived from the paradigm of capitalism, and show how they changed over time, again under the specifications set forth in that paradigm.

For our purposes here, scrutiny may be focused on three aspects of the ecological paradigm: the units involved in community structure, that is, the "natural areas"; the spatial arrangement of these units and the resulting overall structure or pattern; and the underlying processes which generated them and the processes that determined their relationship with one another.

NATURAL AREAS - *internally homogeneous*

The broadest categories for studying the uses to which land can be put are: heavy industry; commerce, business, or light industry; and residence. Each of these may, in turn, be subcategorized into increasingly fine units. Thus, for example, residential use may be differentiated by class, ethnic composition, race, type of dwelling, or any other relevant variable. Business use may be broken down into the financial district, the warehouse district, the theater district, the boutique district, and so on in as great detail as one wishes to go.

If such uses were distributed at random, there would be no ecological pattern. Heavy industry might be next door to either a hovel or a mansion; banks might be next door to either junk yards or specialty shops. The ecological model predicts no such chance distribution and resulting heterogeneity. Rather it assumes that the use to which land is put has a fundamental rationale which results in patterns of homogeneous use. We noted earlier that historically the patterned uses of land could result from different processes, including law or edict. The ecological model, while

[3] F. H. Giddings, *Principles of Sociology* (New York: The Macmillan Company, 1896), pp. 17–19.

recognizing this fact, chose to emphasize market processes. The result of similar demands on the environment and similar ability to pay for them was at least a rough kind of homogeneity, never complete, always relative, but always expectable. Although human decisions were recognized as involved in all area specializations, there was no official plan or policy to allocate land use. The areas of the city were natural in the sense that they resulted from the unconcerted decisions of thousands of individuals and families under a given market system. And that they were natural in some sense or other was shown by the fact that whatever index one used—income, education, ethnic origin, or occupation—people did tend to settle in more-or-less homogeneous clusters.

On the other hand, the natural-area concept did not in and of itself require any specific distribution of land use. Rich and poor might live side by side, as in the lower North Side of Chicago in the 1920s.[4] Poor blacks and wealthy white families might live back to back as they did for many years after the Civil War in New Orleans. But the more usual thing would be for rich and poor, black and white, to live in separated areas. The boundaries of these areas might be geographic, such as a hill or a stream. But they might also be human artifacts, such as wide, heavily traveled streets or avenues, railroad tracks, or public parks; for once a city's physical plant was built, social life had to conform to it and might even become strait-jacketed by it. The boundaries might be even subtler, visible only to the residents themselves. In one study of the behavior of public housing residents it was found that the mere color of the bricks in a building could serve as boundaries and affect the relationships among the residents.

There was no complete, clear-cut consensus among members of the community of scientists organized around the ecological paradigm with respect to the precise character or utility of the concept of natural areas. One member, who found the concept useful, felt it was the unplanned character of such areas that was crucial;[5] another, however, discarded the unplanned criterion in favor of a culture criterion.[6] In actual fact, the several criteria eventuated in very similar results, especially with respect to

---

[4] Harvey W. Zorbaugh, *The Gold Coast and the Slum* (Chicago: University of Chicago Press, 1929).

[5] James A. Quinn, *Human Ecology* (Englewood Cliffs, N.J.: Prentice-Hall, Inc., 1950), p. 268.

[6] Amos Hawley, *Human Ecology: A Theory of Community Structure* (New York: The Ronald Press Company, 1950), p. 287.

ethnic groups where it was precisely the cultural homogeneity
that made their areas so "natural."

COMMUNITY STRUCTURE

The spatial relationships among the several kinds of natural
or cultural areas—the way they were distributed in the community—were no more random than the land uses themselves.
Several patterns were discernible, all fundamentally shaped by
market processes. One was the so-called concentric circle pattern,
espoused especially by the students of the city of Chicago.[7]
Another was the so-called sector or axial pattern, propounded by
Homer Hoyt.[8] And another was the so-called multinuclear pattern
of Chauncey D. Harris and E. L. Ullman.[9]

The concentric circle pattern, held by some to be "universally
observable in all types of communities," was one of growth
outward from a center along radii, evolving five circles or zones
around the center "in relation to their ability to bear the time and
cost of transportation to and from the central point."[10] The zones
were: (1) a business center; (2) an area of residential deterioration;
(3) an area of workingmen's homes; (4) an area of better residences, including single-family dwellings and high-class apartment buildings; and (5) the commuters' zone. These zones were
not entirely symmetrical nor wholly homogeneous, for to-
pography, transportation routes, and other physical factors might
distort both the shape and the uses of the zones.

The sector or axial pattern stated that any particular land use
tended to grow out from the center along a given axis forming a
sector or quadrant.[11] The effect would resemble a pie cut into

---

[7] E. W. Burgess, "The Growth of the City: An Introduction to a Research Project," *Publications of American Sociological Society*, vol. 18 (Chicago: University of Chicago Press, 1924), pp. 85–97. See also Robert E. Park, E. W. Burgess, and R. D. McKenzie, *The City* (Chicago: University of Chicago Press, 1925), pp. 47–62.

[8] Homer Hoyt, *The Structure and Growth of Residential Neighborhoods in American Cities* (Washington, D.C.: Federal Housing Administration, 1939), pp. 15–26.

[9] Chauncey D. Harris and Edward L. Ullman, "The Nature of Cities," *Annals of American Academy of Political and Social Science*, 242 (November 1945), p. 14.

[10] Hawley, *Human Ecology*, p. 286.

[11] Hoyt, *The Structure and Growth of Residential Neighborhoods*, pp. 15–26.

several pieces; the same land use would prevail from the center to the periphery.

The multicentered pattern was one in which "every center and subcenter in the metropolitan community tends to be a specialized territorial unit with the largest or major center serving as the integrating point for all functions in the community."[12] There could be nuclei or centers within the nuclei or centers that shared the service functions of the central business district. An interesting example of the way such centers or nuclei function was offered by the strike in Paris in 1968 which brought transportation to a halt. Many of these subcenters then became a series of isolated small villages.[13]

It is not so important to determine which pattern best fit the actual structure of American cities as it is to recognize that in no case were these communities merely hodge-podge congeries. They always reflected an underlying logic. The ecological paradigm was designed to explain that logic.

ECOLOGICAL PROCESSES

The ecological paradigm, while recognizing that the patterned uses of land could result from different processes, chose, as noted earlier, to emphasize market processes. Thus *competition among land uses was the basic ecological process explaining community structure*. Competition, in turn, resulted in the *segregation* of these functions into natural and cultural areas. At any one moment in time, competition and the resulting segregation produced one or another of the characteristic structural patterns just described. But communities were not static entities, frozen forever in a given format. There was constant interaction among the parts. There was *invasion of one use by another* which, over time, resulted in a *succession* of land uses in the same space.

Two focuses of ecological invasion particularly engaged the interest of researchers: one, the invasion by central business of the area immediately surrounding it, and the other, the invasion of one ethnic group by another. The first reflected in blatant nakedness the impact of market processes as landlords in the second zone held property for speculative increase in value without

---

[12] Hawley, *Human Ecology*, . 287.

[13] *Washington Post*, May 27, 1968.

maintaining it in proper condition, thus reducing the area to slums. The second showed how the complexion of a community changed as Irish, let us say, succeeded German and as they, in turn, were succeeded by Jews, Italians, Greeks, and, at length, black people. The "normal" process was one in which one ethnic group merely *re*placed another when the first group left the old area for an "area of second settlement" as its economic position improved. Later on it became a process in which one group *dis*placed another, "forcing" them to leave before they would ordinarily have done so; but that puts us ahead of our story. The whole set of processes—competition, segregation, invasion, and succession—was assumed to be as natural as the processes by which fauna and flora related to one another in nature.

NORMAL-SCIENCE FALLOUT

The normal-science research fallout of the ecological model was prodigious. Sociologists in a wide variety of communities applied it, replicated it, confirmed or challenged it, debated it, argued about it, criticized it, modified it, and refined and polished it. Few paradigms have generated more normal-science research.

One of the first research contributions was to fill in and document the concentric circle pattern of urban structure and growth as exemplified by the city of Chicago. Each of the circles was found to have its peculiar and characteristic sociological qualities. There were intensive studies of specific areas, such as ghetto, gold coast, slums, and vice areas.[14] E. Franklin Frazier applied the paradigm to black settlements in Chicago and in Harlem and, even taking into account the effect of race prejudice, he found that "the general character of these Negro communities has been determined by the same economic and cultural forces that have shaped the organization of the community as a whole," especially "competition for land."[15] He quoted Burgess to the effect that even in black communities "a process of distribution takes place which sifts and sorts and relocates individuals and groups by residence and occupation." He later extended his analyses to other black urban communities, in the South as well as the North, and showed that the ecological paradigm was success-

---

[14] See the Selected Readings at the end of this book.

[15] E. Franklin Frazier, *The Negro Family in the United States* (New York: Dryden Press, 1948), p. 232.

ful in explaining the expulsion of the agricultural worker from the land and in charting his course to the cities.

Some of the normal-science research was based on instrumental subparadigms having to do with improving techniques of measurement that were designed to do better the kinds of things that had already been done: better indexes of segregation, mobility, and the time element—"diatronic" as well as "synchronic" measures—rather than fundamental modifications of the paradigm as a whole.

This, in brief, was the ecological model. It was revolutionary in the sense that it set the pattern for thinking about urban communities for a generation and gave normal science years of work modifying, adjusting, and replicating. Despite its biological terminology, it was actually an application of the paradigm of capitalism to communities in which individual initiative was given a free reign with a minimum of outside intervention to operate competitively in a market situation. It did very well explaining anything that could be related to market values. It could show why, for example, heavy industry got certain choice locations like river fronts; it made clear why slums arose. It could not, in and of itself, tell us why certain things had value. To do this, it had to be modified. One such modification resulted from the criticism of Walter Firey who showed how, in Boston, cultural and sentimental factors interfered with the results anticipated from ecological processes alone.[16] The incorporation of this seeming anomaly by taking account of cultural factors in the paradigm was not too difficult. It simply required that all kinds of characteristics which gave value to an area be considered, including even sentimental ones. Other modifications were added and adjustments made as is expected in the wake of any revolutionary paradigm. And with improved census data, improved research instruments, and better "hardware," smaller and smaller as well as larger and larger ecological units came under scrutiny.

Still, despite the prodigious talent and technical skill invested in normal-science research under the guidance of the ecological model, paradigmatic anomalies piled up alarmingly. It finally became clear that more was needed than sheer technical skill. "Novelties of fact" had appeared in unassimilable amounts. Market processes were no longer producing the same results. Rather, they were producing urban shambles. The paradigm was approaching crisis.

[16] Walter Firey, *Land Use in Central Boston* (Cambridge: Harvard University Press, 1947).

PARADIGM CRISIS

Thomas S. Kuhn said little about the part played by "external social, economic, and intellectual conditions in the development of the sciences."[17] But he recognized that these factors could well transform anomalies into acute crises and influence "the range of alternatives available to the man who seeks to end a crisis by proposing one or another revolutionary reform."[18] In the second half of the twentieth century the ecological model was approaching such a crisis, not because of any intrinsic factors—normal-science research could have taken care of them if the specifications, the "ifs," on which the paradigm rested had remained the same—but because of extrinsic ones. External social, economic, and intellectual forces had so modified urban conditions that they no longer paralleled the paradigm of capitalism; that paradigm could therefore no longer support the ecological model. We have already, in Chapter 2, referred to the fate of the paradigm of capitalism in the twentieth century. No model based on it could be expected to survive when the basic assumptions—laissez-faire or free competition, for example—on which it rested were no longer valid, as they no longer were now.

Sylvia Fava has surveyed the factors involved in the crisis.[19] She notes that all four of the elements of ecological analysis as specified by Duncan and Schnore—population, environment, technology, and organization—have changed. Populations are larger and more heterogeneous; technologies have made both transportation and the transmission of power more rapid; demands made on the space and water facilities of the community have increased; and the organization of business units has become less centralized. But most significant of all is the fact that "the ecological process differs very much today . . . in terms of the conscious control which is exerted at many points."[20]

[17] Thomas S. Kuhn, *The Structure of Scientific Revolutions* (Chicago: University of Chicago Press, 1962), p. xiii.

[18] Ibid., p. xii.

[19] Sylvia Fava, "Ecological Patterns Reviewed," in Sylvia Fava, ed., *Urbanism in World Perspective: Selected Readings* (New York: Thomas Y. Crowell Company, 1968), Introduction to Part II.

[20] Sylvia Fava, "Some Implications of Metropolitan Development for Human Ecology" (Paper read at meetings of Eastern Sociological Society, 1961).

INTERVENTION

Even the most ardent exponents of the tenets of laissez-faire had never viewed them as absolute. They had always granted that there were some things the government had to do. They had always recognized, for example, that defense and certain common services such as the post, dredging rivers, and maintaining harbors were not suitable for market control and that there were some private enterprises that had to be regulated. Thus throughout the nineteenth century the exceptions, adaptations, revampings, and tinkerings went on apace. Gradually more and more functions were withdrawn from market control and turned over to regulated monopolies, to the government itself, or to nonprofit corporations. It was called creeping socialism by some.

Actually, as related to cities, the increasing intervention of government was not based on ideological or even, for that matter, on paradigmatic grounds at all. It was not based on socialist doctrine or even on welfare-state economics. It was pragmatic, practical, and even anti-ideological. It was, in fact, the hit-or-miss, antisystematic, noncoordinated form of intervention that almost assured dysfunctional results, as later sociological critics noted. It ignored, as they pointed out, what little we knew about the structure of neighborhoods, often resulting in the destruction of natural areas.[21]

Still, intervention in some form was necessary, for by midcentury it was becoming increasingly evident that the market was operating perversely. Feedback in the form of profit was directing the allocation of resources in socially dysfunctional ways. What was profitable for individual entrepreneurs rather than what was desirable for the community as a whole was being produced on the basis of these signals. The results were often finally negative for everyone rather than positive, as in the case of the laissez-faire policy that had led to the piling up of populations in such cities as New York, which was originally profitable for some but ultimately costly to all. Reliance on market mechanisms, further, meant that essential goods and services such as housing and public transportation were not being provided in many communities because they were not profitable and no one seemed to know how to get enough housing when it was not profitable for anyone to supply it. Enlightened self-interest was not resulting in the public good. The

---

[21] Herbert Gans, *The Urban Villagers: Group and Class in the Life of Italian-Americans* (New York: The Free Press, 1962), pp. x–xi.

market was not making the right social decisions. According to the market paradigm, that was quite all right. If there was no profit to be gleaned from housing, that was the signal not to produce housing.

Government intervention took a variety of forms. Beginning with zoning ordinances and city plans (usually toothless), intervention took such varied forms as: mortgage policies that made home ownership feasible for millions of middle-income and even low-income families; freeways that encouraged them to move to the suburbs; and legislation such as slum clearance, urban redevelopment, urban conservation, urban renewal, subsidized housing, public housing, and rent control, all of which intervened to distort the old ecological paradigm.

STRUCTURE OR CONGERIES?

As a result of the accumulation of a wide variety of changes, then, the conception of either the concentric zones or axial sectors was becoming anachronistic. Sylvia Fava has shown, zone by zone, how permeated with anomalies the old concentric circle pattern had become.[22] The offices of many commercial, industrial, and related enterprises were no longer concentrated in the central business district but were distributed throughout the metropolitan area; even recreational facilities such as outdoor moving-picture establishments were increasingly being located in outlying areas. The core of the city might still be its "nerve center," for it retained some central offices, sales rooms, and major cultural and entertainment activities, but shopping centers followed families into the outskirts and the new-style space-consuming manufacturing plants—no longer the tall factories of old—settled where land was plentiful, in "industrial parks." There was even some question about the survival of the central zone in the old sense at all. Rather than a natural area, its existence became an issue, a matter of policy, with people lining up pro and con. This is a far cry from classic ecological theory.

The old zone of transition had now become even more heterogeneous than in the original formulation, land values showing a broader range than formerly. The third and fourth zones were now a "gray zone" of gradual deterioration. The fifth,

---

[22] Fava, "Some Implications of Metropolitan Development for Human Ecology"; also Introduction to Part II: Urbanism in World Perspective.

or commuters' zone, had become far more polarized and differentiated. And beyond that zone there was now the urban fringe, including scores of real estate developments or instant communities. In brief, zone by zone, the old concentric circle pattern had ceased to have validity.

Nor did the sector pattern fare any better. It suffered the same fate as that of the concentric circle pattern, as its original formulator conceded:

> [There is] a fundamental conflict between the nature of city growth in the type of society in which the sector theory was formulated and the welfare state. . . . It is conceded that if the new welfare state triumphs completely the sector theory will be only a historical account of city growth in the capitalistic society in the early twentieth century.[23]

The multinuclear pattern was no longer adequate either. As originally envisaged, the subnuclei were part and parcel of the city. Some of the smaller business units were mama-and-papa shops and stores. Increasingly the new nuclei were large shopping centers no longer within urban boundaries. And the prospect was that they would become increasingly dispersed. "The new centers will be located at a central point between a number of large and small cities . . . which can tap a population of 1,500,000 living in numerous towns, cities, and villages by means of . . . belt highways . . . and connecting roads, aptly termed 'women's roads' because they are free from the congestion of through traffic."[24]

None of these structural results in and of themselves need have spelled crisis for the ecological model. If they had reflected the classic ecological processes, they could have been accommodated by it. The model would have been salvageable to the extent that the results were the outgrowth of competition for the use of land. The new patterns need not have constituted anomalies. Something in the way of technology, let us say, could have altered the concentric circle pattern, or the sector pattern, or the mul-

---

[23] Homer Hoyt, "Residential Sectors Revisited," *Appraisal Journal* 18 (October 1950), p. 449. See also, by the same author, "Recent Distortions of the Classical Models of Urban Structure," *Land Economics* 40 (May 1964), pp. 199–212.

[24] Homer Hoyt, "Classification and Significant Characteristics of Shopping Centers," *Appraisal Journal* 26 (April 1958), cited by Sylvia Fava in "Some Implications of Metropolitan Development for Human Ecology."

tinuclear pattern by altering market values. That is, the mere fact that the natural areas and the concomitant distribution of related sociological phenomena had a different spatial pattern would not of itself have invalidated the ecological model so long as the underlying processes which produced these patterns remained the same. But the processes were not the same.

STALLED PROCESSES

Competition was not operating as the model specified. Black families who could afford good housing were not able to buy it. People sold houses at a loss or refused to sell at a profit. The old pattern of succession exploded when it came time for black people to take part in it on a sizeable scale. The influx of black people into cities might be adequately interpreted by means of the classic paradigm. It was part of a well-researched migratory process that had been going on everywhere in the West since the beginning of the industrial revolution. There was no paradigmatic problem there. Nor was the taking over of the slum areas by blacks contrary to the classic paradigm. That, too, was an old story well provided for in the paradigm. Like other in-migrants they came unprepared for the new style of living imposed by cities. As long as there had been a relatively small proportion of black people in cities and space available for them, segregation could be accommodated by the ecological model.

In the past, once members of an ethnic group had learned their way about in an urban environment, and if they had the resources, they moved out of the slums—perhaps into an area of second settlement, perhaps into "integrated" areas or "melting pots." If they did not, almost certainly their children could and would. But as the concentration of black populations in cities grew, the inability of even the affluent to "compete" their way out had a disturbing effect on all aspects of the community. Black areas grew and segregation increased. In addition, to exacerbate the situation, by the time black people had succeeded to an area most of it was almost completely worn out for residential use. When the data about black in-migrants were fed into the ecological model, then, all the lights blinked, gears did not mesh, and the computer sent out an SOS. There was nothing in the memory bank to instruct further processing. Clearly the old processes were not working as programmed by the model. The up-and-out pattern by which one ethnic group had succeeded another was distorted.

The community structure that had been relatively permeable with respect to the Germans, the Irish, the Italians, the Poles, the Jews, and other ethnic groups became tight and rigid when the black man's turn came.

Among whites, occupation, financial standing, and educational attainment were all positively related to vertical housing mobility; this was much less so in the case of nonwhites. Among them, education and occupation helped relatively little. This meant that even when education, occupation, and financial standing would normally have eventuated in upward residential mobility, such upward mobility was not occurring among black people. Those who could compete for good housing were not permitted to. Even if they could pay they were prevented from buying or renting the house or apartment they wanted. The result was a "significant distortion of metropolitan development" in which "little of the existing pattern of Negro residential segregation . . . could be explained by income or other socioeconomic characteristics."[25] Otis Dudley Duncan could state unequivocally that:

> We now know, absolutely for certain, that the Ghetto is *not* the outcome of a market process in which some sectors of the population merely have less money to spend for housing than others, but spend it where they choose. If people were distributed over the urban landscape in proportion to their income levels, the degree of segregation would be no more (conservatively) than one quarter as great as it now is and probably (realistically) no more than one tenth as great.[26]

Nor was succession in other areas following the old pattern. It had posited contiguity of zones so that invasion of one land use by another could proceed by gradual steps, one block at a time, almost imperceptibly, resulting in a more or less orderly succession of land uses. And at any one time, the overall structure showed some coherence. But by mid-century succession no longer seemed orderly. The invasion by business of residential areas was no longer the characteristic pattern. Commercial enterprises no longer inched into old residential areas, producing a transitional zone with characteristic sociological composition. Business was leapfrogging, jumping out over the intervening areas

[25] John F. Kain and Joseph J. Persky, "Alternatives to the Gilded Ghetto," *The Public Interest*, no. 14 (Winter 1969), p. 75.

[26] Otis Dudley Duncan, "After the Riots," *The Public Interest*, no. 7 (Fall 1967), p. 4.

into outlying districts, outside as well as inside of city borders, into open fields and former farmlands. Business use was not stalled, as in the case of black families, but explosively accelerated. The intervention which resulted from the malfunctioning of competition as a process of decision making was like a great geological upheaval that changed ocean currents, air currents, and continental contours so greatly that meteorologists could no longer depend on their old subparadigms for predicting weather. In communities, as elsewhere, the mechanism for decision making changed from one based primarily on competition to one based largely on conflict.[27]

NEW WAYS TO MAKE DECISIONS

One of the great selling points of laissez-faire capitalism had been that it took decision making out of the hands of kings, ministers, bureaucrats, and even parliaments, and distributed it among millions of individuals who could make themselves felt by way of the market. Competition was impersonal; it played no favorites. It minimized occasions for conflict. True, there had never been a time in the twentieth century when conflict in the sense of power plays and pressure was not a fundamental aspect of decision making in all kinds of communities. But not until well into the century did it have an impact equal to, if not greater than, that of market processes.

Sometimes the conflicts were between or among the goals to be sought by intervention. Should the ghetto, for example, be "gilded," that is, be preserved and made more attractive, or should it be dispersed?[28] Should the neighborhood school be preserved or should schools be concentrated in great educational parks? Should the central core of the city be preserved or abandoned as anachronistic? Should the very idea of the city be abandoned as itself anachronistic in this day and age and supplanted by planned new towns?

Some of the issues, like that between diversity and homogeneity as goals, which was sometimes couched in the terms *pluralism* versus *the melting pot,* came to grips with the very

---

[27] Neither of the standard textbooks on human ecology (Hawley, *Human Ecology: A Theory of Community Structure* and Quinn, *Human Ecology)* had indexed conflict.

[28] Kain and Persky, "Alternatives to the Gilded Ghetto," pp. 74–87.

nature of our society. If there was to be intervention, said proponents of one school of thought, let it aim for heterogeneity. No, said the proponents of the other point of view, let the goal be homogeneity. We recognize here an example of the conflict between paradigms sketched by Mancur Olson in Chapter 2.

Diversity rather than homogeneity was advocated by those who saw it as an integrating force.[29] This argument had been adumbrated by Adna Ferrin Weber at the end of the nineteenth century. He had seen the isolation of classes as an evil.[30] Now class diversification, as well as racial or ethnic diversification, was being urged. Both ends of the class ladder were being criticized. The homogeneity of the suburbs was characterized as dysfunctional not only because it exerted a deadening influence on young people by depriving them of contact with the wider world, but also because it insulated adults from life as it was lived outside and detached them from the problems of the city. At the other end of the class structure, public housing was criticized as creating, in effect, prisons for the poor, walls that isolated and insulated them from the outside world and deprived them of opportunities to participate in it. The resulting frustration generated so much fury that vandalism often made such public housing almost uninhabitable. Efforts to distribute poor families among other families rather than concentrate them in class-homogeneous slums were felt to be necessary.

The integrative effect of heterogeneity for the whole community was the emphasis of those who advocated diversity as a goal of intervention; the integrative effect of homogeneity within natural areas was the emphasis of those who emphasized homogeneity. To them the effect of intervention had been catastrophic. Herbert Gans documented the social and psychological losses that had resulted from the destruction of Italian neighborhoods in Boston;[31] and Sylvia Fava, in effect documenting Gans' point, showed how those displaced by intervention came as "intruding 'alien' elements" to other areas, destroying their homogeneity.[32] The proponents of homogeneity in natural areas might have cited

---

[29] Jane Jacobs, *The Death and Life of Great American Cities* (New York: Random House, Inc., 1961), Part II: The Conditions for City Diversity.

[30] Adna Ferrin Weber, *The Growth of Cities in the Nineteenth Century* (New York: Columbia University Press, 1899), p. 434.

[31] Gans, *The Urban Villagers*, p. 320.

[32] Fava, "Some Implications of Metropolitan Development for Human Ecology."

the prescient Charles Booth who had reported of London at the end of the nineteenth century that "only by the greatest care can the living together of rich and poor in one parish be to the advantage of either."[33] Failure was more usual than success. In modern American cities it had been found that where income differences were not too great, such failure was not necessarily inevitable; on the basis of a study of the interaction between residents of housing projects and residents of surrounding areas, it was reported, for example, that "socioeconomic status differences are not a particularly important barrier to social interaction."[34] But neither, of course, does propinquity necessarily facilitate the kind of integration its advocates seek. It has long been known that such physical propinquity does not necessarily mean social closeness.

Kenneth Boulding looked for the best of both worlds in a "mosaic" society for a reconciliation between the point of view emphasizing community-wide integration and the point of view emphasizing integration within natural areas. Such a mosaic society would consist of "many small subcultures, each of which would give its participants a sense of community and identity which is so desperately needed in a mass world, and which could at the same time remain at peace with its neighbors and not threaten to pull the society apart."[35]

When the goal of policy had been to optimize the wealth of nations, there had been a paradigm to show how it could be achieved. When there was not even consensus with respect to the goal of policy, such guidance was not available. Even when there was consensus, powerful interest groups could challenge it, for, when conflict rather than competition was becoming the main process determining the uses of land, decisions became a matter of power. Should the land be preempted for freeways which benefit the suburban commuter or should it be used for low-income housing? Should the land be saved for recreational purposes or should it be used for environment-polluting power plants? Should the land be used for high-rise or garden apartments? While advocates of different criteria debated and interest

---

[33] Charles Booth, *Life and Labour of the People in London: Final Volume* (London: Macmillan & Co., Ltd., 1902), p. 414.

[34] Louis Kriesberg, "Neighborhood Setting and the Isolation of Public Housing Tenants," *American Institute of Planning Journal*, January 1968, p. 49.

[35] Kenneth E. Boulding, *Beyond Economics: Essays on Society, Religion, and Ethics* (Ann Arbor: The University of Michigan Press, 1968), p. 173.

groups fought one another to a standstill, urban communities wilted. Some said they were dying. "Urban decision making in the public sector" had become "a major unsolved problem in today's society."[36] This is true in the uses of land as well as in other decision areas.

In the 1960s and 1970s the term *ecology* had reverted to its original orientation and the emphasis was on the way human beings were violating the natural environment. It may be noted parenthetically here that the ecological community model had not completely ignored environmental pollution. The soot and grime associated with factories were among the factors which led to the separation of residential and industrial land use. Otherwise, however, since it was not then so much as it later became a spatial matter, environmental pollution did not enter the ecological picture, although it might well have. Market decisions were now bringing a host of new environmental ills upon the community, for environmental pollution was an expectable result when profit gave the signals. Nonpolluting ways of disposing of the wastes of industry were costly and ate into profits; reducing the pollutants from automobiles was costly; keeping rivers and lakes clean was costly; withdrawing land from industrial or grazing or other profitable use to devote it to recreational use was costly. Profit was giving signals that led to policies that were dysfunctional for the community. Leaving basic decisions about land use within the community to the vagaries of the market, functioning well or ill, was leading to disastrous results. The first storm signals were not raised by sociologists but by biologists.

The ecological model had been enormously successful in its heyday. None of the technical criticisms, however justified, could detract from the contribution it had made to our understanding of how cities were growing in the first quarter of the century, how the processes at work distributed people, how classes and ethnic groups worked out spatial relations among themselves, and how natural areas took on certain sociological characteristics. Only when the processes which it posited ceased to operate as assumed did a fundamental flaw show through. "Novelties of fact" rendered the old "if" no longer acceptable.

---

[36] Thomas O. Paine, a NASA administrator, quoted in the *Washington Post*, December 2, 1969.

4

The Community Class Structure

CLASS AND THE PARADIGMS

Class in the functional sense was implicit in the paradigm of capitalism, based as it was on the division of labor. It was explicit in the structure-functional paradigm. In terms of function there were ruling classes, governing classes, working classes, entrepreneurial classes, peasants, yeomen, intelligentsia, and even leisure classes who, to use T. B. Veblen's ironic phrase, "performed" the leisure function by conspicuous consumption. Specialized functions were built into any differentiated system, even precapitalist ones. Class in this functional sense was inevitable.

But class in a functional sense was not necessarily the same as class in a ranked-status sense. And it was in a ranked-status aspect that class was incorporated into community paradigms. "All the parts of a complex society are always evaluated and ranked"; in fact, "it is certain that no populous society can [even] exist without one or more systems of rank."[1] In this conception, classes were characterized entirely in terms of rank, namely, upper, middle, and lower.

---

[1] W. Lloyd Warner and Associates, *Democracy in Jonesville: A Study in Quality and Inequality* (New York: Harper & Row, Publishers, 1949), p. 297.

The emphases on function and rank were not incompatible. For even in the functional view, some functions were "higher" than others. Auguste Comte had noted the hierarchical nature of different functions in a social structure: The more general the function, the higher its position. And certainly capitalistic bureaucratic organization was functionally hierarchical. Even children learn this fact; by the age of nine they can already read an organization chart and correctly interpret who is above whom and who below.[2] They also learn very early—by the fourth grade—their own class position in the community and that of other children.[3]

The paradigm of capitalism had never contemplated equality, nor had the ecological model, for inequality was "an inevitable accompaniment of functional differentiation."[4] Competition guaranteed inequality; in fact, demanded it. Without differences there could be no competition; winning would be a matter of chance.[5] There had to be inequality to make the system work. It was the function of competition to locate winners. The structure-functional paradigm implied a similar process: Certain key positions offered more privileges and perquisites precisely in order to encourage qualified people to compete for them.[6] Rank and function, in brief, were related in two ways: Functions were ranked and rank was functional.

CLASS AT THE COMMUNITY LEVEL

Most of the enormous theoretical literature on class deals primarily with societal or national units rather than community units. Class is not the same in both kinds of units. At the societal level a major emphasis is on power; at the community level ranked status is emphasized. Class at the societal level is abstract; what the upper classes do at work or at play is not immediately

---

[2] Herbert C. Wilcox, "Hierarchy and Children," *Transaction* 6 (December 1968), p. 5.

[3] Celia Burns Stendler, *Children of Brasstown* (Urbana: University of Illinois Press, 1949).

[4] Amos H. Hawley, *Human Ecology: A Theory of Community Structure* (New York: John Wiley & Sons, Inc., 1950), p. 221.

[5] Jessie Bernard, *American Community Behavior* (New York: Holt, Rinehart & Winston, Inc., 1962), Chapter 5.

[6] Kingsley Davis, *Human Society* (New York: The Macmillan Company, 1949), pp. 366–69.

visible to people in the local community (or was not before television). What the upper classes in the community do is more conspicuous. The people who live on the hill can actually be seen at the bank or in the mill, driving around town, boating on the river, or playing golf at the club. The people who live in the river flats on relief are far from invisible in the local community. Social class is therefore more meaningful, more personal, and more immediate at the local level. It touches closer to home. The prestige accorded to high status may be great at both the societal and the community levels, but occasions to express deference are more frequent at the local level. The consumption of housing, clothing, and leisure are more important as aspects of social class in the local community than on the national or societal scene.

Consumption criteria of class are far from new. In the Middle Ages the so-called sumptuary laws prescribed the kinds of consumption suitable for the several ranks of society. Conspicuous consumption was long a major function of royalty, the object being to extort deference. And Veblen built an intriguing theory of consumption as a class phenomenon. Characteristic styles of clothes and grooming, he told us, were designed to show that certain people did not have to work. Esthetic taste was expensive; it had to be "cultivated" over a period of years. The gear for most sports was costly so that only those with money could indulge in them. Since consumption is very largely in the hands of women, they may exert more influence at the local class level than men. At the societal level, where power is the major criterion of class, women have relatively little impact.

THE CLASS STRUCTURE OF COMMUNITIES

Social class was implicit in the ecological model. There was ample room in it for slums, Gold Coasts, working class homes, middle class residences, and commuters. But there was no great preoccupation with class per se. The classic statement of the community class structure paradigm in the exemplar sense was that by W. Lloyd Warner, an anthropologist who wished to apply the same techniques as those he had used in Australia to the study of a modern community.

Although the name of Warner became associated primarily with the class paradigm, his own major interest had originally been in community integration and stability. He wanted to know what held communities together. The criteria he used for selecting a community for study, therefore, had to be designed to fit a community suitable for answering this question. To begin with, it had to be well integrated. There should be little confusion or conflict. It had to have a long tradition, "where the social organization had become firmly organized and the relations of the various members . . . exactly placed and known by the individuals who made up the group."[7] It should not have undergone disruptive change that upset the balanced groupings of the members. The ethnic composition should be predominantly old American; there should, however, be varying levels of dominance, for otherwise "total-community integration would tend to be low, subcommunity integration high, and ethnic conflict probable."[8] There should be few industries, several factories only, and the community should be surrounded by a farming area. Finally, it should not be too large.[9] These were the "ifs" which led to his "then."

Applying these criteria, Warner rejected Chicago or any of its industrial subcommunities as exemplars because they were too disorganized; their social organization was dysfunctional, even partially disintegrated. He found what he was looking for in Yankee City, a New England community of about 17,000, and began work in the early 1930s. In a series of volumes [10] he and his associates showed how their "New England subjects live a well-ordered existence according to a status system maintained by . . . several social institutions."[11] The researchers were not so much concerned about how the class system they found had come into being as they were about how its parts—including ethnic groups —related to one another.

By means of detailed interviews, Warner and his staff "discovered"—their term—a clear-cut class structure in Yankee City. Their informants could rank all the people they knew in a status hierarchy on the basis of criteria which all understood quite well and which the researchers generalized as wealth, source of income, education, residence, and "family" or lineage. Six classes

---

[7] W. Lloyd Warner and Paul S. Lunt, *The Social Life of a Modern Community* (New Haven: Yale University Press, 1941), p. 38.

[8] Ibid.

[9] Ibid., p. 39.

[10] See the Selected Readings at the end of this book.

[11] Warner and Lunt, *The Social Life of a Modern Community*, p. xix.

were thus discovered in Yankee City—upper-upper, lower-upper, upper-middle, lower-middle, upper-lower, and lower-lower—each with a characteristic life style or culture. Newer communities might have fewer, as did rural communities.[12] Metropolitan communities might have more. But a normal complement would be six. The several classes differed in biological composition, ethnic composition, ecological distribution, control of property, consumption patterns, church affiliation, schooling, associational patterns, political participation, symbolic behavior, and social characteristics.

ETHNIC- INTO CLASS-STATUS: THE MELTING POT

All studies of communities in the United States have had to wrestle with the part played by ethnic groups. In fact, ethnicity has rivaled class as a major preoccupation of community researchers. Both engaged the attention of Warner and his associates.

In the early years of the century the lower classes in cities were often immigrants whose low status was only temporary. They were poor only until they became acculturated enough to raise themselves out of their poverty, and they fully expected to do so. The emphasis in thinking was therefore on their ethnicity rather than on their class, and on mobility rather than on stratification.

In fact, the old immigrant component in the community did become greatly attenuated. The children might still live in ethnic areas but they looked and acted like everyone else. They became, in research and in theory, blue-collar workers, the working class or the lower-middle class rather than immigrants or ethnics. The fading—though not the disappearance—of ethnicity as such thus left the class rather than the ethnic characteristics of this generation highlighted.

While this process was going on, there was considerable research interest as to the relative weight of class and ethnicity in community life. Herbert Gans tended to see class as more important than ethnicity in Levittown;[13] Glazer and Moynihan

---

[12] Warner and Associates, *Democracy in Jonesville*, p. 263.

[13] Herbert Gans, *The Levittowners, How People Live in Suburbia* (New York: Pantheon Books, Inc., 1967).

documented the persistence of ethnic culture and organization in New York,[14] but Bennett M. Berger documented the salience of class in suburbia.[15] In the case of blacks, the issue of ethnic culture was complicated by race; some observers were arguing that almost all differences between races were class differences, others that they were ethnic or cultural.[16]

The Yankee City studies highlighted the class aspect. Thus, despite the title of one of the books in the series, *The Social Systems of American Ethnic Groups,* which would lead one to expect an analysis of their internal class structures, there is, rather, an analysis of the processes by which the several ethnic groups climbed the class ladder of the total community.

At the time Yankee City was being studied in the 1930s there were no ethnics in the upper-upper class, since membership in that class depended on lineage and most ethnics had not been in the community long enough to acquire that prerequisite. But the upper-upper class was the only one with such ethnic homogeneity; all the others included ethnic as well as "Yankee" members. The class position of the nine ethnic groups—ten if Yankees were included—was directly related to the length of time they had been in the community. It took about twenty years for "a substantial proportion" of the first generation to achieve upper-lower class membership; in about thirty years the more successful, including a small proportion of the first generation, had reached the lower-middle class; after forty years a handful of the first generation, and more of succeeding generations, had reached the upper-middle class. The rate of this upward class mobility varied for different ethnic groups and races, but the processes were the same for all. The processes were "acquisition of material symbols, including residences, increased occupational status, extension of formal and informal relations in the society, and change in behavior modes."[17]

The process by which residential mobility reflected upward

[14] Nathan Glazer and Daniel Patrick Moynihan, *Beyond the Melting Pot* (Cambridge: The M.I.T. Press, 1963).

[15] Bennett M. Berger, "Suburbia and the American Dream," *The Public Interest,* no. 2 (Winter 1966), pp. 80–92.

[16] James Q. Wilson, "The Urban Unease: Community versus City," *The Public Interest,* no. 12 (Summer 1968), p. 34.

[17] W. Lloyd Warner and Leo Srole, *The Social Systems of American Ethnic Groups* (New Haven: Yale University Press, 1945), Chapter 5.

class mobility in Yankee City differed from that in Chicago or New York City in detail, but in general it followed the familiar Chicago-type pattern of segregation by accretion, invasion by *dis*placement rather than by *re*placement, and succession in the up-and-out process. Such spatial mobility was the major factor in the dissolution of an ethnic group's residential base. Once they moved out of the area of first settlement, they dispersed throughout the community.

Ethnic survival as separate groups was viewed by Warner as a negative phenomenon, as the result of failure by some members to make the grade in the outside world. Those who were frustrated in their efforts to gain acceptance by others or who preferred to cling to the ways of their fathers constructed separate social worlds of their own. But that was not approved of by the Warner school. Although by and large "our class system functions . . . to destroy the ethnic subsystems," it does not succeed with all members and so "some of the unsuccessfully mobile turn hostile to the host culture, develop increased feelings of loyalty to their ethnic traditions, become active in maintaining their ethnic subsystems, and prevent others from becoming assimilated."[18] They, in effect, were subverting the model by their anomalous behavior. This curiously unperceptive and bland melting-pot community model of Warner and his school, anticipating, albeit not immediately in the case of blacks, the ultimate homogenization of the community, proved unsuitable and was discarded by later students.

For as it turned out, Warner had caught ethnic groups in a certain—and apparently transitory—phase of their history in this country. Will Herberg later found that the rejection of ethnic background was but a passing phase peculiar to the second generation, that is, to the children of immigrants. The third generation tended to return to their ethnic roots, albeit in a greatly diluted and "Americanized" version. There was a surprising recrudescence of ethnic group consciousness in the early 1970s, in part at least as an aspect of an anti-black movement.

Warner and Srole noted that the melting-pot concept did not apply to black people; they remained separate. The class paradigm was admittedly not enough to interpret their position because, regardless of numbers, not only were they low in ranked status but they were also subordinate in position as measured on five indexes, namely: (1) freedom of residential choice; (2) freedom to marry out of one's group; (3) occupational freedom; (4)

---

[18] Ibid., p. 284.

attitudes in the host community permitting participation in associations and cliques; and (5) level of vertical mobility permitted in the host community.[19] On the basis of this schema, black people of all cultural types showed, not unexpectedly, great degrees of subordination, that is, caste restriction. Warner and Srole knew well the answer to the question the successful ethnic groups were later to hurl at their black successors, "We made it, why can't you?" They may have overemphasized the influence of class vis-à-vis white ethnic groups, but they were well aware of its limitations vis-à-vis blacks.

Warner and Srole may have been justified in their neglect of the internal class structure of ethnic communities because Yankee City was too small to support large, highly differentiated ethnic communities; and it had been selected in the first place precisely because ethnicity as such was minor and assimilation high. Among their criteria of selection, it will be remembered, was avoidance of a community in which total-community integration was low and subcommunity integration high. But as other studies of ethnic groups showed, each did have its own class structure, resembling in general the Yankee City pattern but distorted in characteristic ways, each ethnic group becoming middle or upper class in its own way. In the case of blacks, however, the process was somewhat different.

CLASS IN THE BLACK COMMUNITY

The black population before emancipation had been differentiated as individuals along several axes and there were many ranks in the resulting structure. Some blacks were free; some were slaves. Some were light; some were dark. Some had aristocratic lineage; some did not even know their fathers. Some were house slaves; some were field hands. Some were literate; some were not. Some were skilled; some were not. Although relations among such differentiated individuals might assume a dominance-submission pattern (as inevitably human relations seem to do), this pattern tended not to be a sociological or structural, but rather an interpersonal, phenomenon based on personality characteristics rather than structural imperatives, a personal pecking order rather than an institutionalized pattern, and a matter of dom-

---

[19] Ibid., pp. 288–89.

inance rather than status. For class as such could hardly exist under conditions of slavery.

Even the concept of community as applied to the black population was late in achieving recognition. In the 1950s, E. Franklin Frazier felt called upon to defend the very idea that there was such a thing as a black community, to controvert the "implicit assumption that Negroes are merely atomized individuals."[20] He emphasized the importance of the ecological structure of black communities which he himself had thoroughly researched. There should have been no doubt about the existence of black communities, for Frazier himself had contributed greatly to the description and analysis of the institutional structure of such communities, rural and urban, North and South.

In addition, there was a very old tradition of research on class in black community study. No model for the study of black communities has, in fact, been more widely accepted or produced more research than the class-structure model. From the beginning, all the serious studies of black communities had played up the yawning chasm among social classes.

Frazier reviewed the historical and current research on class and summarized the findings with respect to the existence and/or emergence of social distinctions among slaves and among the free blacks; among blacks after emancipation; among blacks in rural communities; and among blacks in southern and border cities, as well as in northern cities. He showed what had been the criteria for individual and class differentiation and the changes that had taken place over time. Under slavery, for example, type of work, skilled or unskilled, was important for status among individuals, as well as proximity to the owner's family; later the common bases for class differentiation were, in addition to occupation, land ownership, education, income, property, color (analogous to lineage in the Warner paradigm), and, most especially, "respectability" or conventional moral behavior.[21]

Moral criteria had always loomed large. In one of the earliest studies of a black community, W. E. B. Du Bois's study of Philadelphia in 1899, they were basic. Although Du Bois distinguished families on the basis of income, his major emphasis

[20] E. Franklin Frazier, "The Negro Middle Class and Desegregation," *Social Problems* 4 (April 1957), p. 291.

[21] E. Franklin Frazier, *The Negro in the United States* (New York: The Macmillan Company, 1949), Chapter 12, "Social and Economic Stratification."

was on the moral criteria of class. He distinguished four social classes: families of undoubted respectability; the respectable working class; the poor and very poor but honest, if not always industrious, families; and " 'the submerged tenth' of criminals, prostitutes, and loafers."[22] And Frazier comments that such " 'moral considerations' . . . were the criteria which were generally accepted as the basis of social status among Negroes."[23]

Like the authors of all studies of the black community, early and late, Du Bois noted and deplored the chasm that separated the "masses" or lower classes from the middle and upper classes. He rebuked the more successful for refusing to supply leadership to the masses; they were an aristocracy, but, unlike the noblesse-oblige attitude of the upper classes in Yankee City, they refused to accept the responsibilities of one. They should recognize their duty, for the Negro's "social evolution in cities like Philadelphia is approaching a . . . stage when the centrifugal forces of repulsion between social classes are becoming more powerful than those of attraction."[24] (He did not exonerate outsiders who made the situation worse by lack of discrimination in dealing with black people, lumping them all together, and discriminating against all of them equally.)

Du Bois's strictures were far from cold or objective descriptions of a status quo. He was passionately dedicated to the idea that the black community should organize and achieve some sort of unity and cohesion. He placed enormous emphasis on the importance of the skills of organization. Though he deplored the disunity among black people, he did not condemn them, for he knew that it was due primarily to lack of "social education, of group training," and that this "lack can only be supplied by a long, slow process of growth."[25] Even in the face of all kinds of handicaps, some kinds of organization had achieved a great deal; one of its greatest accomplishments was that of "stimulating effort to further more effective organization among a disorganized and headless host."[26] It was precisely to perform this leadership

---

[22] William Edward Burghardt Du Bois, *The Philadelphia Negro* (Philadelphia: University of Pennsylvania Publications in Political Economy and Public Law, 1899), pp. 310–11.

[23] Frazier, *The Negro in the United States*, p. 281.

[24] Du Bois, *The Philadelphia Negro*, p. 392.

[25] Ibid., p. 233.

[26] Ibid., p. 234.

function for a "headless host" that Du Bois emphasized the obligations of the classes toward the masses. "The largest hope for the ultimate rise of the Negro lies in . . . mastery of the art of social organized life."[27] Subsequent events more than half a century later showed how right he was.

Another great classic study dealing with the class structure of a black community was Drake and Cayton's study of Chicago, *Black Metropolis;* it was guided by the work of both the Chicago and the Yankee City models. It presented the ecological, institutional, and cultural patterns that characterized the black community and revealed a far more complex class structure than the one Du Bois had delineated in Philadelphia. For the black population had by now become more differentiated by class in terms of the standard criteria of class. In addition, color itself was now also a class characteristic.[28] Occupation, income, consumption patterns or standards of living, as well as proper public behavior, remained criteria of class and resulted in a tripartite system of upper, middle, and lower class. Within this system there were both respectable and nonrespectable elements.[29] This study, done under the guidance of W. Lloyd Warner, reflected in general perspective the original Yankee City model, modified only to the extent required by the unique situation of black people.

This, then, was the second of the great classic community paradigms. Perhaps because it was so easy to quantify the criteria of class,[30] and perhaps also because of its intrinsic snob appeal, it achieved enormous success. Social class became a major preoccupation of community researchers for a generation and stimulated an incredible amount of normal-science research.[31] In fact, for a while it all but took over the field of community study. In addition, social class became, and remains, an indispensable variable in the study of almost every other kind of sociological or social-psychological phenomenon. And perhaps because of the perennial struggle in the United States to reconcile inequalities

[27] Ibid., p. 233.

[28] St. Clair Drake and Horace R. Cayton, *Black Metropolis: A Study of Negro Life in a Northern City* (New York: Harcourt Brace Jovanovich, 1945; Harper Torchbook, 1962), pp. 495–506.

[29] Ibid., pp. 524–25.

[30] W. Lloyd Warner, Marchia Meeker, and Kenneth Eells, *Social Class in America: A Manual of Procedure for the Measurement of Social Status* (Chicago: Science Research Associates, Inc., 1949).

[31] See the Selected Readings at the end of this book.

with egalitarian ideals, it also achieved astounding popularity with the nonprofessional public. *Upper-middle, lower-lower,* and so on, became standard terms in all kinds of popular discussions. The Yankee City social class paradigm was Apollonian, even soothing, and a welcome relief from the Dionysian, conflict-based conception of class of the Marxists with its emphasis on power. Integration, not conflict, was its major focus.

WHAT HOLDS COMMUNITIES TOGETHER?

Although the social class aspects of the Yankee City studies achieved the greatest success in generating normal-science research, Warner's own interests had been primarily in the integrative aspects of community life. In the paradigm of capitalism, the division of labor and the resulting specialization seemed enough to explain what held communities together. Since this analysis did not loom large in Warner's perspective, he looked elsewhere. Having, by the criteria used in selecting Yankee City as his model, insured in advance a high degree of community integration, Warner now looked for ways to explain it. These he found in certain structures, primarily voluntary associations, and later, in Jonesville, in symbols, especially collective representations.

The importance assigned to voluntary associations in accounting for community integration was based on the fact that their members were most likely to be distributed across at least three classes. Joint participation in associations prevented the alienation of ethnic groups from one another. Associations also facilitated upward social mobility by providing opportunity for those in lower social classes to learn the ways of those in higher social classes and, by such anticipatory socialization, to prepare themselves for ultimately assimilating higher-class cultures. This emphasis on voluntary associations proved to be the least successful aspect of the Yankee City paradigm. It fell on sterile ground and received little recognition from any community of scientists and stimulated little, if any, normal-science research follow-up.

It was not until some years later that Warner felt the need for more than structural factors in explaining community integration. He had recognized the importance of symbolism in the Yankee City studies but it was not until he studied Jonesville, a Midwestern community of 10,000, that he gave great weight to it. He found Jonesville "permeated with two conflicting social princi-

ples," namely, "equality and inequality."[32] The anomalous nature
of ranked status in a democracy now struck him and he found the
reconciliation of the conflicting principles a serious theoretical
problem.

He invoked three nonstructural factors to explain how the
potential divisiveness of class was counteracted. One had to do
with the integrative nature of conflict with an outside enemy, a
factor which had long been recognized; it had, in fact, constituted
a major apologia for war in the nineteenth century. World War II,
Warner reported, had had such an integrating effect in Jonesville.[33]

Another factor serving to mitigate divisiveness was the ideology as well as the actuality of social mobility. Although inequality in work, money, income, and property all violated egalitarian
principles, still the democratic ideology was valid if only because
it permitted achievement-oriented men to realize their ambitions
by upward mobility. Low status was not permanent, fixed, or
unalterable for individuals, however inevitable low status might
be for the structure as a whole. The reality of rank was acceptable
therefore because "the moral code . . . enforces the rules of social
mobility . . . [and provides] that all able men who obey the rules
of the game have 'the right' to climb."[34] Later studies tended to
validate the importance Warner attached to upward mobility as a
method of reducing the resentment of inequalities in rank.[35]

A third powerful integrating factor to which Warner attached
great importance had to do with collective representations including myths, symbols, rites, rituals, and ceremonies which are
accepted by everyone without question. (The concept of collective
representations came from Emile Durkheim, to whom *Democracy
in Jonesville* was dedicated.) Warner found "the integration and
smooth functioning of the social life of a modern community . . .
very difficult because of the heterogeneity of the parts. . . . It is
necessary therefore for the community to provide itself with
symbol systems which function to integrate the people into total
community activities. . . . A considerable degree of unity is

[32] Warner and Associates, *Democracy in Jonesville*, pp. xiii, xv.

[33] Ibid., p. 288.

[34] Ibid., p. 297.

[35] Peter Blau and Otis Dudley Duncan, *The American Occupational Structure* (New York:
John Wiley & Sons, Inc., 1967), pp. 435–36.

necessary if the community is to maintain the ordinary functions of the group."[36]

Warner pointed to patriotic rites such as those of Armistice Day and Memorial Day as dramatically serving such integrative functions. If he seemed to be placing an enormous weight of significance on Memorial Day it was because he felt that extraordinarily powerful common symbols were necessary to counteract the disintegrative effect of the collective representations of conflicting groups.[37]

The effort Warner took to explicate the importance of ways to counteract the conflicts intrinsic in American communities was paralleled by the efforts of another team of researchers studying another small community, Springdale. How does it happen that people accept the discrepancy between the ideals of equality and the existence of inequality? What kept a community together in the face of seemingly flagrant violation of the self-interest of so many of its members? How did people reconcile "symbolic appearances and institutional realities"? Unlike Warner, they found the answer primarily in terms of individual psychological adjustment mechanisms rather than in collective mechanisms in the community itself.[38] But both came to the same conclusion: Either one by one, individually, or collectively as a community, the disparity between ideal and reality, between egalitarian principles and unequal actualities, had to be bridged somehow or other and a modus vivendi arrived at in order to maintain community integration.

The fate of the class component of the Yankee City paradigm was as bleak as the fate of the Chicago paradigm. It broke down under the weight of the anomalies introduced by the "novelties of fact" of the burgeoning of mass society.

MASS SOCIETY
AND COMMUNITY CLASS STRUCTURE

The concept of "the masses" was quite old, as were the concepts of "mass media" and "mass production," but the concept of a "mass society" was relatively new, not becoming a prime

[36] Warner and Associates, *Democracy in Jonesville*, pp. 289–90.

[37] Ibid.

[38] Arthur J. Vidich and Joseph Bensman, *Small Town in Mass Society: Class, Power, and Religion in a Rural Community* (New York: Doubleday-Anchor, 1958), pp. 297–311.

interest among sociologists until the late 1950s.[39] When it did appear, however, it made a strong impact. For a while, in fact, the new paradigm almost eclipsed that of community, giving us a new perspective not only on the nature of the community as a whole but also on the nature of its social class structure.

In 1947, Warner and Low had concluded that "the hierarchical forces operating in our society will increase their power."[40] They conceded that improvement in the conditions of the lower classes and the increased consumption resulting from mass production would modify their relations with higher classes, and that new occupations and positions of power in the world of work would change the relations of economic status and social rank. They agreed that "our class system will continue to change, as will other systems in our society," but they felt such changes were "likely to strengthen rather than to weaken our rank orders."[41] They were, therefore, convinced that "our basic hierarchical social order will remain."[42]

Actually, as it turned out, the effects of mass production and mass consumption have not strengthened our "rank orders." If anything, the effects of mass production and mass consumption have been in the reverse direction. That is, they have had a contra-class or egalitarian effect. For, as William Kornhauser has noted, pervading all relations in a mass society is a "common orientation of equalitarianism. All members of mass society are equally valued as voters, buyers, and spectators. Mass equalitarianism is strengthened by the attenuation of the social bases of inequality, notably membership in ethnic and religious groups and especially in social classes."[43] He summarizes the nature of social classes in mass society this way:

[39] The first title of an article with the word *mass* in it appeared in the *American Sociological Review* in 1945 (D. C. Miller, "A Research Note on Mass Communication," 10 (1945), pp. 691–94. In 1959 William Kornhauser's *The Politics of Mass Society* (New York: The Free Press) appeared; and in 1962 Edward Shils published "The Theory of Mass Society" in *Diogenes*, vol. 39, pp. 45–66. In 1964 Roland Young assembled an anthology on *Individual Participation in Mass Society* (Evanston: Northwestern University Press).

[40] W. Lloyd Warner and J. O. Low, *The Social System of the Modern Factory, the Strike: A Social Analysis* (New Haven: Yale University Press, 1947), p. 188.

[41] Ibid.

[42] Ibid.

[43] William Kornhauser, "Mass Society," in David L. Sills, ed., *International Encyclopedia of the Social Sciences*, vol. 10 (New York: The Macmillan Company and The Free Press, 1968), p. 60.

> Social classes weaken as sources of distinctive values, styles
> of life, and social identity; and they increasingly resemble
> one another in the beliefs, values, and interests of their
> members. Class distinctions are leveled, and class boundaries
> are blurred. Class consciousness and class solidarity dissolve
> into mass consciousness and mass solidarity. . . . Classes
> remain as categories of people who differentially share in
> common ways of life rather than as self-conscious groups
> with distinctive ways of life. Status strivings and anxieties
> abound, but this testifies [merely] to the ambiguity of status
> where fixed social hierarchies no longer exist.[44]

Consumption, work, and the rewards of status all showed the
disruptive effect of the mass society on class structure.

We have already noted that consumption behavior is peculiarly significant at the community level because, in part, it is so
visible. And now a consumption-oriented version of class was
emerging with quite different criteria and different status rank-
ings. The old traditional indexes of social class remained, to be
sure, but as Harold Wilensky noted, they had different significance.[45] Education was assuming different dimensions, with kind
rather than amount making a difference. Residence still made a
difference but, except for the black population, suburbia was
engulfing all income levels. In the field of clothing the direction of
imitation was reversed; the homage of imitation was now be-
stowed not on an upper class élite who patronized haute couture
(itself a casualty of mass society) but on swinging young mods.
The son of the family on the hill might still have all the old
accoutrements of high status, but who was paying attention to
him? The eyes and ears of young people in the community were
now turned to the latest rock singer or moving-picture hero or
Olympic champion.

Perhaps the subtlest contra-class impact of mass society, in
fact, was the effect it had on the allocation of the rewards of high
status in the form of deference, homage, obedience, respect, and
even—as Veblen's wickedly evocative concept of "invidious"
distinctions implied—envy. In the past, for example, the "heroes"
accorded such rewards were "idols of production." Now they

[44] Ibid., p. 59.

[45] Harold Wilensky, "Orderly Careers and Social Participation: The Impact of Work History
on Social Integration in the Middle Mass," *American Sociological Review* 26 (August 1966), p.
529.

were "idols of consumption." No longer were they political figures or industrial tycoons but increasingly entertainers, singers, actors, musicians, and athletes.[46] The mass media exposed the higher classes and, especially on television—the great leveler— they rarely showed up to great advantage. Such familiarity bred, if not contempt, at least a bored ho-hum. The big banker did not come off any better than the union leader; and the families on the hill, no better than the families next door.

And so also in the world of work. Equally subversive of the traditional system of ranked status, if not more so, was the change beginning to take place in the values of some young people in that world. The Yankee City paradigm, like most of the other community paradigms, had taken for granted the striving-orientation of human beings as a given. Thus Warner and Low had confidently predicted that people would "continue to strive for the higher rungs in the ladder of status because prestige, power, and greater rewards are always at the top."[47] But in the 1960s this prediction was not holding up. The so-called rat race was losing its attraction for many young people. "Upper-middle class" was becoming a pejorative, almost a dirty, word to some of them. There was a time when the man who ran the mill or headed the bank or managed the factory was accorded the reward of being looked up to. One might still have such high status in the community, but at what price was it achieved if it no longer garnered the psychic rewards that went with it? At the other end of the occupational ladder, the lowest kinds of jobs were departing the work scene altogether.

Rank did survive, of course; it was still convenient, for example, to short cut descriptions of people by referring to them as middle, upper, or lower class, and Wilensky's use of the term *middle mass* in referring to the lower-middle and upper-working classes illustrated the persistence of rank even in mass society. But mass society did undercut the effect of the old criteria of class. In the old community structure, the upper classes exercised authority in matters of taste and manners, if not necessarily in morals. This is no longer true. The principle propounded by Kornhauser that "decline of authority accompanies the decline of community" might equally well be stated as "the decline of community accompanies the decline of authority."

Like the Chicago model, then, the Yankee City paradigm was

---

[46] Leo Lowenthal, *Literature, Popular Culture, and Society* (Englewood Cliffs, N.J.: Prentice-Hall, Inc., 1961).

[47] Warner and Low, *The Social System of the Modern Factory*, p. 188.

breaking down. "Novelties of fact" were producing unassimilable anomalies. The forms and accoutrements of social class might remain but their significance declined. The mass media broke down the boundaries that had once directed the flow of deference, respect, and homage to the members of the local upper class; attention was now directed toward a new status system, and the rewards of high status now went to those who achieved in that world.

THE FATE OF THE COMMUNITY-INTEGRATING FACTORS IN THE YANKEE CITY PARADIGM

Neither the war- nor the voluntary-association component of the Yankee City paradigm proved any more successful than the social class component in weathering the tests of the last third of the century. So far from serving as an integrating factor, war had become the most divisive force in most communities. We have already noted that the voluntary-association component of community structure which Warner had placed so much emphasis on fell on sterile ground. It was not in this integrating sense that participation in voluntary associations attracted the attention of researchers but in the power-related sense that DeTocqueville had emphasized. The voluntary associations that attracted most research attention tended to be conflict groups such as, for example, trade associations, trade unions, professional organizations, and the like. And the emphasis was on their class exclusivity rather than on their inclusivity. Participation was found not to be pan-class; all the studies showed that participation in voluntary associations tended to be far more common in the higher than in the lower classes.

But unsuccessful as these components of the Yankee City paradigm proved to be, the symbolic component was, in a quite unexpected—and perverse—way, spectacularly successful. In the expectable way, for example, black leaders were creating symbols to integrate the black population and symbols to defy the white population. Spirituals and hymns that had once served an integrative function were rejected by militants; nor were *We Shall Overcome* and *I Have a Dream* any more acceptable to them. But Black Power and Black Is Beautiful were; so was Soul. So were natural hair, African garb, African names, the raised clenched fist, and costumes or uniforms with sacred heraldry. The term *Uncle Tom* was a withering symbol; the term *Negro* an insult; the term *honkie* was meant to be insulting. So far, so good; all this was in line with the Warner paradigm in which symbols served as integrative forces.

Warner had noted that any of the symbolic integrating factors could be used in either a positive or a negative way, to decrease as well as increase solidarity. The beginning of the last third of the century showed how right he was about that. For far from serving a cohesive function, symbols and collective representations were being used by young people for divisive purposes. Like the concept of latent functions, collective representations became weapons. Young people were condemning them as hypocrisy, as techniques for papering over injustice and inequality. To them injustice and inequality were too glaring to be glossed over by collective representations in order to preserve the integrity of the community.

Collective representations and their symbols were thus among the numerous casualties of the last third of the century, and symbolic battles were fought on many fronts. Sacred rites, such as graduation exercises, for example, were disrupted. The Confederate flag, the Viet Cong flag, the black flag of anarchy, and draft-card burning were among the divisive symbols that flourished. The swastika returned and Mao's little red book showed up. Warner had noted how effective symbols could be in political conflict. Now they had become almost schismatic. Police were pigs. Obscenity was stock in trade. Groups competed to outdo one another in divisive symbolic acts. Priests poured blood on purloined draft-board records. Placards vied with one another in symbolic insult. Ku Klux Klan costumes reappeared. *Law-and-order* and *crime-in-the-streets* became symbols for racism. Student rebels relied on such militant symbols as battlefields; they spoke of liberated zones. They rejected the symbolism of Alma Mater, the nourishing mother, and of alumnus, the one who is nourished.

So divisive was the use of symbolism that some observers were asking if it were even possible for a community to function without collective representations, without any "collective emotion and evocative symbolism,"[48] if nothing was sacred, if everything was debunked. Warner had doubted it. "Complex societies," he had said, "must have a common core of basic understanding known and used by everyone or their complex and diverse symbolic superstructures will not stand."[49] They need

---

[48] Warner and Associates, *Democracy in Jonesville*, p. 109.

[49] Ibid., p. 233.

general symbolic systems that everyone not only knows but feels. "The increasing structural diversity and social complexity of contemporary society, the greater development of industrial autonomy, and the proliferation of specialized symbol systems—these and many other factors raise serious difficulties for communication and collaboration."[50]

It was precisely because young radicals did not want the status quo to stand that they were attacking its supporting collective representations. They were fighting the forces that made for community solidarity and stability. In this negative sense, Warner's paradigm passed the test of the 1960s with flying colors. The destruction of collective representations became a weapon of war, a way of destroying a status quo, just as deferring to them had been in Warner's analysis a way of preserving it.

So much, then, for the Warner paradigm of community class structure. Looking back at it now we can see how naive it was to select as a model for understanding the twentieth century a community with the characteristics of Yankee City. The kind of community it represented was already in process of becoming anachronistic. The criteria used for selecting it had already "factored out" the most important challenges in community life today, including conflict and race relations, the impact of mass society, and power.

[50] Ibid

5

The Community Power Structure

IMPERSONAL POWER PARADIGMS

Even plant ecologists had recognized the phenomenon called dominance. "The organism which occupies the niche of key importance in the community is called the dominant."[1] In human communities the ecological model emphasized functions rather than individuals. It noted that "certain functions are by their nature more influential than others; they are strategically placed in the division of labor and thus impinge directly upon a larger number of other functions."[2] Control of the entrance of sustenance into the community (an economic function) is one such strategically placed function; the coordination of other community functions (a governmental function) is another. Other functions are distributed over a scale of dominance or control. Such functional dominance in the community is impersonal; it is not the same as such interorganism, interpersonal relationships as ascendance and submission or "pecking order," studied not only

---

[1] Amos H. Hawley, *Human Ecology: A Theory of Community Structure* (New York: The Ronald Press Company, 1950), p. 45.

[2] Ibid., p. 221.

by biologists but also, among human beings, by social psychologists. Nor is it the same as the institutionalized phenomena of super- and subordination.

The common assumption that "government occupies the dominant position" is not wholly correct, for although "government holds the police power . . . its dominance is not without qualification. The domain of local government is circumscribed by narrowly drawn boundaries,"[3] for it has to compete for dominance with units which "exert a decisive influence on the community's sustenance supply."[4] The ecological model, in brief, interpreted dominance in functional terms, assigning major importance to both the coordinating and the economic functions. The model did not concern itself with the interpersonal relationships among individuals who occupied these positions of dominance, nor with the class implications of dominance.

The functional approach to dominance generated two great research traditions, one concentrating on the economic function and the other on the political function as seats of power. The nature and operation of political power were so basic that a whole scholarly discipline, political science, arose to grapple with it. Even history, for some scholars, was exclusively about political history, that is, the history of such power. And economics as a science began as political economy, an analysis of the relationship between economic productivity and political power. The general idea was that the important coordinating functions could best be performed, as we have pointed out, by way of competition—the less government the better. There should be just enough government, in fact, to permit the "sustenance function" to operate effectively.

The greatest competitor of the Adam Smith paradigm was that of Karl Marx, who saw power in class terms. The owners of the means of production, the bourgeoisie, exercised power over the toiling masses or proletariat. Marx taught millions of people all over the world how to look at an industrial society and what to see. Although his paradigm was not widely applied in research at the local community level, it did, nevertheless, sensitize researchers to the nature of power. The Marxist terms *bourgeois* and *proletariat,* as well as the terms *ruling class* and *governing class,* were not generally used by members of the community of

---

[3] Ibid., p. 229.

[4] Ibid.

researchers in the United States; but such functionally defined terms as *business class* and *working class* were acceptable. And it was likely to be in these terms that the normal-science research on power in the community was first phrased.

THE PERSONALIZING OF POWER: MIDDLETOWN IN TRANSITION AND THE POWER ELITE

Although the ecological paradigm recognized that "a hierarchy of power relations emerges among differentiated units,"[5] for the Chicago model "politics were derivative."[6] The Chicago model made room for both Gold Coast and slum, for working class and middle class areas, but not for class warfare in the Marxist sense nor for the exercise of power. The Yankee City model did not overlook the power that went with high status; it recognized that informal class-based personal associations contributed to the exercise of power in the political structure of the community, but it did not emphasize this power dimension of status. In the first volume of the Yankee City series, the political structure was accorded only 12 out of 450 pages, as contrasted with 24 accorded to the economic life of the community and 55 to associations. The first classic community study to zero in on the power structure was that of Middletown.[7] In the first of two volumes on this community, which appeared in 1924, the authors, Robert S. Lynd and Helen M. Lynd, had emphasized culture change in the first years of the century and paid relatively little attention to power. But in its sequel, *Middletown in Transition,* appearing in 1935, in which the Lynds reported the effect on the community of the depression of the 1930s, they showed greater awareness of the nature of power than had the researchers of either the ecological or the class-structure paradigms. More to the point, they saw the exploitative aspects of power more than had the Yankee City researchers, who emphasized the integrative noblesse oblige norms of the upper-upper class and their expected, taken-

---

[5] Ibid., p. 221.

[6] Morris Janowitz, in a review of Scott Greer's *The Emerging City,* in *Social Problems* 11 (Spring 1964), p. 430.

[7] Robert S. Lynd and Helen Merrill Lynd, *Middletown* (New York: Harcourt Brace Jovanovich, Inc., 1924) and *Middletown in Transition* (New York: Harcourt Brace Jovanovich, Inc., 1937).

for-granted concern for the working class. Even before George Orwell had taught us that some people are more equal than others, the Lynds showed us how those occupying certain positions in the community had at their disposal a wide array of resources, including powerful collective representations, to guarantee their greater equality. Trade unions could be crushed; schools, newspapers, and churches could all be made to toe the line. Loyalty to community, Americanism, and capitalism could be assured by control of the channels of communication. *Middletown in Transition,* in brief, forced "attention to the possibility that systems of social control can operate in the interests of one group and against the interests of others."[8] This study thus linked economic class to the distribution of power, as neither the ecological nor the ranked-status paradigms had done.

Profiting from the Yankee City study, which had pointed out the significance of informal social class contacts in solidifying class structure, C. Wright Mills wedded the power and ranked-status conceptions of class. He rejected the term *ruling class* because it was "badly loaded." "*Class* is an economic term; *rule,* a political one. The phrase *ruling class* thus contains the theory that an economic class rules politically."[9] That was a too simplistic view of the matter. The so-called ruling class was really a coalition of political, economic, and military élites. Mills viewed power as related to community in two senses. He extended the Yankee City model by emphasizing the chasm between the lower-upper and the upper-upper classes, especially in terms of power;[10] and, in addition, he conceived of the power élite—those in charge of the national industrial-military-political complex—as a community itself in terms of the interpersonal associations and relationships Warner had played up. Further, like Warner, he saw a nexus between the two. Local community society was being consolidated and incorporated into a "national system of power and status."[11] Mills' analysis struck a responsive chord. The term *military-industrial complex* became almost synonymous with power.

[8] Maurice Stein, *The Eclipse of Community* (Princeton, N.J.: Princeton University Press, 1960), p. 59.

[9] C. Wright Mills, *The Power Elite* (New York: Oxford University Press, 1956), p. 277.

[10] Ibid., Chapter 2.

[11] Ibid., p. 281.

THE COMMUNITY POWER STRUCTURE

It was not, however, in the Lynds' Marxist-tinged form or in Mills' power-élite form that power was approached by the community of scientists studying the community in the 1950s, but rather in a much blander form that had the advantage of being readily operationalized. The paradigm that generated most normal-science research was based on the work of Floyd Hunter, which was presented in 1953 under the term *community power structure*.[12] In general, two models of the community power-structure paradigm guided research in the 1950s; one élitist in orientation, emphasizing class; and one pluralist in orientation, emphasizing groups.

An Elitist Model

Hunter recognized that he worked in a capitalistic setting, although he made nothing of it. He was deliberately a-historic in orientation. Psychological motivation was only a residual category in his analyses; he did not invoke it to explain or interpret his findings. His paradigm was élitist. He approached community power in terms of the forty men who were in decision-making positions in Regional City, a southern community of about half a million people. Their names were derived from a list of over 175 taken from miscellaneous sources and winnowed down to forty by a set of knowledgeable judges. These men were then intensively studied by means of interviews. This approach became known as the reputational, since it was based on a reputation of power rather than demonstrated exercise of power.

Hunter began with the existence of power, taking it for granted. He was not interested in examining its basis or function. He was not trying to explain why people had power, but only to describe the kinds of people who had it. The actual exercise of political power was only a relatively minor concern in his model. The personal, not the impersonal, aspects of power interested him. He found that, by and large, the decision makers did not constitute a single power pyramid, but several; still the overall chart showed one to be preeminent over the others for several

---

[12] Floyd Hunter, *Community Power Structure: A Study of Decision Makers* (Chapel Hill: University of North Carolina Press, 1953).

kinds of issues. The general ideology of the decision makers he located was, he found, conservative. They were tax conscious, hard-boiled, and fearful of change. At the same time, he reported, many seemed to feel guilt ridden. It might well be said that Hunter's report of the attitudes of his decision makers on most basic issues reads like the bill of particulars against the power structure that young radicals and black militants were to specify a decade later.

Hunter's work was favorably received, and an enormous research effort was invested in replicating it. But as the normal-science research poured from the computers, it came increasingly under fire, especially by those who found Hunter's method superficial. In contrast to the élitist class-based orientation of the Hunter model was the group-based orientation of the so-called pluralist model presented by Robert A. Dahl.

A Pluralist Model

Robert A. Dahl, whose work was based on New Haven, used what became characterized as the decisional method, as contrasted with Hunter's reputational method.[13] It was historical in perspective, using documents as well as statistical data. To Dahl and his students actual participation in decision making, not merely a reputation for such participation, was the true index of membership in a power structure.

Dahl introduced the concept of political resources. And, although the subtitle of his book was "Democracy and Power in an American City," the term *power* is not even in the index. He wrote, instead, of the distribution or concentration of political resources such as jobs; popularity; access to press, radio, and television; social standing; solidarity; and voting practices. He noted that there had been at least three theories to answer the question, Given the existence of actual inequalities in political resources in the community along with the belief in equality, who actually governs in a democracy? One theory answered the question in terms of the competition of political parties, one in terms of conflict among interest groups, and one in terms of an élite who ruled because of their property, income, social status, knowledge, publicity, and focal position. (He recognized, although he did not elaborate, a fourth theory, based on the

[13] Robert A. Dahl, *Who Governs?* (New Haven: Yale University Press, 1961).

so-called revolt-of-the-masses, which posited unscrupulous and exploitative leaders who catered to the rootless masses in return for their support.)

Although all three of these theories seemed superficially applicable to New Haven, Dahl found all of them defective in that they left out the pivotal character, the politician himself. In his model, therefore, the focus of interest is on the "cunning, resourceful, masterful leader" who uses, rather than is used by, majorities, parties, interest groups, and élites. "A leader who knows how to use his resources to the maximum is not so much the agent of others as others are his agents."[14] Such gifted political entrepreneurs do not spring up in every political system; but where they do appear, they make their presence felt. New Haven was one place where they had done so.

Under the general heading of "Equality and Inequality in New Haven," Dahl traced the history of the community, showing the trend away from oligarchy, in which all political resources were concentrated in the hands of patricians, to pluralism, in which many sets of leaders, each with a different combination of political resources, dominated the political scene. (E. Digby Baltzell in a similar analysis of Philadelphia had also argued that an aristocracy could maintain itself only when it was not monopolistic and discriminatory against outside talent.)[15] There was no longer a cohesive élite; but neither was there democratic equality. Dahl showed that leaders, subleaders, and constituents had varying degrees of both direct and indirect influence on decisions. He noted also different structural patterns, namely: (1) spheres of influence, (2) executive-centered coalitions, and (3) rival sovereignties.

Having shown how the system worked, Dahl then asked why it worked that way? His answer lay in the unequal distribution and actual use of the political resources represented by social standing; access to cash, credit, and wealth; access to the legal powers of public office; popularity; and control over information. Some people used whatever resources they had more persistently and skillfully than others. Age, interest in the specific issues involved, and vested interest in politics were among the variables that influenced the extent and skill with which political resources were used. Despite the demonstrable inequality in both the

---

[14] Ibid., p. 6.

[15] E. Digby Baltzell, *The Protestant Establishment: Aristocracy and Caste in America* (New York: Vantage Press, Inc., 1961), pp. 382 ff.

distribution of political resources and skill in their use, belief (collective representations) in democracy and political equality acted as a limit on the power of leaders.

Dahl's model was catholic. It recognized that under some situations, élitism prevailed. But it also recognized that under other conditions, pluralism was more probable. And it did not overlook the part played by specific individual human beings.

THE NORMAL-SCIENCE RESEARCH ON COMMUNITY POWER

An extraordinarily voluminous body of normal-science research was generated by the community power structure paradigms. Two summaries of this extensive corpus of research attacked the problem of explaining the differences in results reported by the two major models.

Since it is contrary to the mores of science to impugn the motives of any certified researchers, if one disagrees, one attacks his method, not his motives or his character. It was not unexpected, therefore, that research method became a major issue in the discussion. An analysis by John Walton of thirty-three studies showed that results were, indeed, dependent on the method used. "The reputational method tends to identify pyramidal hierarchical structures while decision making and combined methods reflect factional, coalitional, and amorphous types."[16] The logical conclusion of those who favored the decisional method was that results obtained by the reputational method should be junked as invalid and the method itself buried;[17] and, of course, vice versa.

But it was further found by Walton that the choice of method in the first place was not itself an independent variable; it was related to the discipline of the researcher: Sociologists tended to favor the reputational, and political scientists, the decisional. This finding then pointed to the discipline of the researcher as the key explanatory factor of the differences in results. But Walton also found that, regardless of discipline, those who used the reputational method tended to find centralized power structures. This finding returned the explanation, then, to method as the determining factor.

[16] John Walton, "Substance and Artifact: The Current Status of Research on Community Power Structure," *American Journal of Sociology* 71 (January 1966), p. 435.

[17] Raymond E. Wolfinger, "A Plea for a Decent Burial," *American Sociological Review* 27 (December 1962), pp. 841–47.

As if the situation were not complicated enough, a second summary of the normal-science research literature offered another interpretation of the differences reported, namely, that "researchers (often sociologists) who chose to use the reputational method also chose (perhaps consciously, perhaps not) to study communities that were characterized by relatively centralized decision-making structures. And, correspondingly, might not other researchers, who chose to use a variety of research methods, also have tended to select for study (again, consciously or unconsciously) communities with more decentralized decision-making structures."[18] In brief, the same factors that led a researcher to select a particular method would also lead him to select a particular kind of community for study.

Following this interpretation, the variable explaining differences in findings reported by different normal-science researchers would be neither political ideology, nor discipline, nor research method, but the actual differences in structures among communities. To test this interpretation, 146 studies of 166 communities were analyzed with respect to the methods used, the nature of the power structure reported, and structural characteristics (mainly demographic and economic) of the communities themselves. While the results showed that the community characteristics studied were by themselves far from completely determinative of the power structure, they were nevertheless "enormously more important than discipline or method in predicting the type of power structure."[19] The power structure, in brief, was related more to the kind of community than it was to the method or the discipline or the ideology of the researcher. This is an eminently reasonable conclusion.

THE PHANTOM POWER STRUCTURE

Some community studies had reported what Walton called amorphousness, an "absence of any persistent pattern of leadership or power exercised on the local level."[20] Such a situation has been conceptualized in terms of a set of institutions, agencies, and

---

[18] Terry N. Clark, William Kornblum, Harold Bloom, and Susan Tobias, "Discipline, Method, Community Structure, and Decision Making: The Role and Limitations of the Sociology of Knowledge," *American Sociologist* 3 (August 1968), p. 215.

[19] Ibid.

[20] Walton, "Substance and Artifact," p. 687.

interest groups (banking, manufacturing, newspaper publishing, contractors, and the like) making use of one another for their own ends, their interaction producing unintended but systematically functional results. The coordination function is seen as being performed not by government but in an unplanned fashion, without personal intervention in the classic ecological tradition.

But one analyst supplies a new twist. "The community vaguely senses that there ought to be a government," so if there is no power élite or community structure one has to be created, if not to perform a coordinating function, then to perform another one which is equally important: the satisfying of "a need for a leadership with the status, capacity, and the role to attend to the general problems of the territory and give substance to a public philosophy."[21] So a collective representation in the form of a "power élite" or a "top leadership" or a "they" is created to supply the need, an illusion dressed in the Emperor's power clothes.

To some people, "they" are benign; to others, malevolent. In either case, belief in "them" imposes order on an otherwise chaotic, hit-or-miss, disorderly, unstructured, chancy world. It supplies a "them" to blame things on. There was a time when human beings, like Job, could finally rest assured that no matter how little sense the world made to them, it made sense to God. That comfortable conviction is no longer possible to many, but a belief in masterminds is a satisfactory, if not a satisfying, substitute. Even a hostile organization is better than mindless chaos.[22] There is a kind of security in knowing that there is an Establishment in charge. Even a conspiracy is more comfortable to some people than a vacuum. It supplies a structure, an enemy to attack. And if the Establishment is viewed as benign, it is comforting to feel that daddy knows best. The new freeway must be all right if "they" say so.

THE HOLLOW POWER STRUCTURE

Another kind of illusory power structure or top leadership is sometimes set up as a front and used as a resource in the Dahl

[21] Norton E. Long, "The Local Community as an Ecology of Games," *American Journal of Sociology* 64 (November 1958), p. 255.

[22] Millions of people all over the world insisted on the existence of a conspiracy to explain the assassination of John F. Kennedy; at least a conspiracy made sense, however malevolent. It supplied "closure."

sense. Newspapers, or individuals interested in the community but lacking any power base of their own, create one to supply them with support. Thus, for example, a "civic technician" or "entrepreneur of ideas," who has ideas he wants to implement, recruits names in order to legitimize his project. He gets a list of prominent people for his letterhead or his committee. "His task may be self-assigned, his perceptions of the problem and its solution may be his own, but he cannot gain acceptance without mobilizing the influentials."[23] They are his resources. He has to create such a hollow structure to achieve his goal. It's all done with mirrors.

Far from being ambitious for power, many such persons recruited to serve as "top leadership" are reluctant to assume even its trappings. They may, in fact, resist the assignment of responsibility. They have to be dragooned, resistant, into even such phony leadership positions because they are newsworthy and are needed as an umbrella by others who really provide the "power." The leadership attributed to them "turns out to be a few telephone calls and, possibly, three luncheons a month."[24] How much leadership these individuals really provide, if any, or if they can be recruited at all, is questionable.

In some large metropolitan areas there may not be enough residents to supply even such a hollow power structure. They are not communities, but mere aggregates of persons and places. We have already met the individuals who live in them in Chapter 1 and will meet them again in Chapter 10. Where they live is of secondary importance to them; their real community identity is elsewhere. In such areas "there is . . . no governing class which is viewed as the source of legitimate leadership. . . . The Mellons of Pittsburgh and the Upjohns of Kalamazoo are still on the scene, but in most communities their ilk has been replaced by the essentially rootless organization man who moves from job to job, but is generally viewed neither as the law-giver . . . [nor] the job-giver. . . . Organization man leads, if he leads the community at all, because he chooses to do so, not because it is an obligation of his class."[25]

---

[23] Long, "The Local Community as an Ecology of Games," p. 250.

[24] Ibid., p. 257.

[25] Charles R. Adrian, *Public Attitudes and Metropolitan Decision Making* (Pittsburgh: University of Pittsburgh Press, 1962), p. 5.

WHAT POWER STRUCTURE?

The élitist or stratification model of the community power structure implied a direct relationship between ranked-status and power, at least power in the form of decision making. In the 1960s, however, people in status positions far below the top, with limited political resources, began to exercise power of a quite different kind. Just as they were denigrating high status symbolically by withholding deference and envy, so were they denigrating institutionalized power by withholding consent and by not acceding to its claims of legitimacy. They were insisting that they did not have to conform to any rule they considered immoral.

Nor was the group-oriented model proving any more helpful. In New York City, for example, civil servants warred with the city government as well as with one another. Although strikes by civil servants were forbidden by law, teachers and sanitary workers closed schools and let the city become buried in garbage. Police and firemen reported in ill and engaged in slowdowns, all with impunity. There was no discernible structure to this kind of power. There was no necessary alignment or coalition apparent among the several groups. They were not engaging in classic pressure politics. Most were not aiming to replace those in the seats of power. Some wanted only to share power; some wanted only to have the power to veto; and some wanted to coerce those in power only on specific issues. Some positively rejected the sharing of power, a situation they labeled co-option, that is, defeat by absorption into the power structure. It was hard to find any discernible structure in the power stasis, this congeries of conflicting forces. It looked in fact quite anarchic, and, in many cases, like communities out of control. If there was such a thing as a community power structure, it seemed to be in hiding.

APATHY AND PARTICIPATION

Power corrupts! was one of the basic tenets of nineteenth-century liberalism and it could corrupt because good men did nothing to prevent it. Citizen apathy was one of the worst defects of government. Participation was the answer. De Tocqueville was the first to state the participation paradigm. Voluntary organizations not only performed functions not taken care of by the deliberately delimited government, but as intermediaries between the individual and the state, they also conferred power and curbed governmental power.[26] Both Hunter and Dahl had placed great emphasis on participation as means for sharing power.[27] And it was certainly true that politicians had shuddered when reformers drummed up a big vote capable of turning the rascals out.

But as the decisions that had to be made in the community became increasingly complex and increasingly dependent on technical and scientific information, it was harder and harder for anyone to make correct ones. Even experts were sometimes baffled. The story of community reaction to fluoridation is a case in point. It is one of the most extensively researched areas in the whole field. The results of an analysis of scores of such studies showed that the locus of the decision strongly affected its nature: The more concentrated power was, the more likely there was to be acceptance of fluoridation; the more the citizens participated in the decision, the less likely. One commentator concluded that participation may not always be such a good thing.

> The experience with fluoridation seems to confirm the inappropriateness of direct citizen involvement in policy making. The technical intricacies of the problem are too great for the average voter to resolve. Administrative agencies and legislatures, with their greater capacity to distinguish among experts, are more able to rationally consider questions of safety and efficacy. Nor would the value aspects of fluoridation be ignored if the decision were to be restricted to administrative agencies or legislatures. On the contrary, they would be clarified by a careful treatment of the technical questions. ... Finally, it must be noted that for the citizen to perform adequately even a restricted role in a scientifically advanced society, he must have at least a slight understanding of science in order to judge wisely the abilities of competing leaders to deal with complex issues.[28]

[26] Alexis De Tocqueville, *Democracy in America* (New York: J. & H. G. Langley, 1840), pp. 115–16.

[27] Hunter, *Community Power Structure*, Chapter 9; Dahl, *Who Governs?*, pp. 276ff.

[28] Harvey M. Sapolsky, "Science, Voters, and the Fluoridation Controversy," *Science*, October 25, 1968, p. 432. See also R. Crain and D. Rosenthal, *The Fluoridation Decision*, Report 2: The Community Confronts an Innovation (Philadelphia: National Analysts, Inc., 1963). See further comment on citizens' reaction to fluoridation and other health programs in Chapter 8 in this book.

Is there a race, perhaps, between the increasing complexity of decisions and the popular education required for making them? This is certainly an élitist formulation of the issue.

Most discussion and research on the participation paradigm had focused on peaceful participation by way of voting, pressure-group lobbying, and taking part in the whole political process. Such participation was envisaged as "within the system." But there was also another kind of participation, one that was especially relevant for the community because it took the form of direct action. And direct action always takes place in a local community.

THE POWER OF DIRECT ACTION

The natural history of the several community power paradigms suggests that the term *power* and even the term *decision making* may have been misnomers. The question might well be raised whether decision makers truly wielded power in the classic sense as contrasted with the civic do-good projects sense. (Hunter had recognized that force was an element of power and noted the use of police force, but the decision when and where and on whom to use it was not in the hands of his decision makers.) In the 1960s, "history"—in the form of the civil rights movement, the war on poverty, the drive for black power, and the "revolt of the classes," that is, of university students—performed a set of "experiments" that yielded "novelties of fact" about the nature of the structure of power in communities which did not always corroborate the findings of normal-science research.

For not yet integrated into the research on community power was the "plebiscitory democracy" which in the form of direct action began to burgeon in the 1960s. Georges Sorel, a French sociologist, had in the early years of the century been one of the first analysts of direct action, so called, against both economic and political power, especially in the form of sabotage and the "general strike."[29] And there had been successful political use of it in the form of civil disobedience in India under Gandhi in the 1940s. But not until after the middle of the century did it come to be used in a wide variety of communities in the United States. Sit-ins, demonstrations, marches, walks, vigils, and disruptions became expectable ways of exerting power, the power of numbers

[29] Georges Sorel, *Reflections on Violence* (New York: The Free Press, 1950).

and of access to the public by way of the media, especially television. Indeed, television—an example of one of Dahl's political resources, control over information—gave direct action an enormous boost. "The whole world's watching" was literally true; political action became high drama.

The management of such exercises of power was becoming a profession itself, quite aside from leadership. Those who used it learned by their own experience how best to make it effective. It was not primarily a way to exert positive power; it was, rather, a means of expressing veto or countervailing power.

Most communities did not have the physical layout or professional staff to accommodate such assemblages; no provision had been made for them. Little by little, however, decision makers were having to take such assemblages into account. New buildings were designed with an eye to their vulnerability to vandalism or take-over; barriers to control the line of marches were contrived; police had to be trained. In brief, a quite new political antiparliamentary form of power was in process of institutionalization in many communities.

Faced with these expressions of power, Hunter's genteel decision makers and those of other community researchers did not seem all that powerful after all. Nor did Dahl's political leaders. True, they might gain victories in police battles, but they usually turned out to be Pyrrhic victories. When the smoke of battle cleared, there still were the enemies, thumbing their noses at them.

For in the gut-fighting of those wars, it was coercive power that counted. The bland "power" of Hunter's decision makers seemed almost irrelevant, as did that of Dahl's politicians. In any event, none of the prodigious normal-science research of the 1950s and even of the 1960s prepared us for the explosion of black power, student power, poor-people's power, flower power, youth power, and female power that challenged the "powers-that-be" as we entered the last third of the twentieth century. The name of the new game was not Dahl's political competition, nor his struggle among interest groups, nor Hunter's decisions; the name of the game was coercion.

WHERE IS THE LOCUS OF POWER?

All the research discussed so far had concentrated on the local community. Floyd Hunter believed that the local com-

munity was a primary power center and the implication of most of
the work on community power structures was consonant with this
view. But all the classic community paradigms had recognized
that local communities had long been faced with an almost
inexorable trend toward increasing control by extracommunity
systems.

Even in the nineteenth century, for example, large corporations had had resources greater than some states'; they could in
effect push communities around. And as the national economy
became increasingly integrated, more and more power over local
communities shifted to outside agencies, economic as well as
political. As we noted in Chapter 1, decisions made in far-off
places affected local communities more and more, prejudicing
their decisions in advance. A Supreme Court decision might be
aimed at a specific community, but it affected thousands of others.
Decisions to open or shut government facilities, impose or not
impose a tariff, or subsidize or tax some industry all reverberated
in local communities as did also decisions of industrial corporations.

The ecological model had long since recognized the phenomena of urban and regional dominance. It had found that the
ecological region was characterized by centers of such dominance: "Unrestrained by the bounds of local government, business and industrial units may exercise control over the sustenance
process long before it reaches the particular community."[30] Hawley had seen a continuum between independent communities at
one end and dependent communities at the other; the first being
self-sufficient, isolated, small, and stable; the last intimately tied
in to a complex system which exposed them "to the effects of
events that occur anywhere within the scope of intercommunity
relations."[31]

A study of five towns in the 1960s illustrated a quasi gradient
between communities at one extreme in which local leadership
was entirely in the hands of residents and, at the other, communities in which ownership, and hence power, was completely out of
the hands of local residents. River City was the most independent.
Ownership and control of most business and industry were in the
hands of local people. Leadership was completely oriented
toward the local community. In three of the others—Minerville,
Factoryville, and Newton—the leadership remained local but it

[30] Hawley, *Human Ecology,* p. 46.

[31] Ibid., p. 47.

was beginning to branch out laterally. Minerville was a declining town with two or three large coal companies which were detached from local affairs; local leaders saw them "as an outside presence, which manipulates the town for self-interested purposes. . . . It . . . assumed that the 'outside' is by definition exploitative."[32] Factoryville, which was middle-sized and midwestern, had a rural past but had become industrialized; it tended to be fairly liberal. At the dependent end of the continuum was Hometown, an upper-middle class metropolitan suburb just in process of industrialization. Although its leaders retained local residence, they were more involved in the national system than were leaders in the other towns; it tended to be conservative.[33]

The process by which power in Yankee City passed from the local leadership to outsiders in the depression of the 1930s was described as it looked to the local residents by Warner and Low. At that time workers in all the shoe factories went out on strike. This, in many ways strange, episode challenged the attention of Warner and Low whose interests, it will be remembered, were in stability and integration. Why had such a conflict broken out in Yankee City? They found their answer in the effect of absentee ownership on old relationships between owners and workers.

Originally the owners and managers of the factories had been local leaders, cultivated gentlemen who were members of the best clubs, full of feelings of responsibility and noblesse oblige toward the community, and "dominated by local sentiments which motivated them 'to take care of their own people'; . . . under the power influence of the numerous organizations to which they belonged. . . . Their personal contacts with the local citizens directly related them to influences from every part of the city."[34] They were anachronistic archetypes of Dahl's patricians. The new owners, by way of contrast, did not even live in Yankee City. They represented "Big City capitalism" rather than the old "small town capitalism." The local men were now only plant managers and were "not in a position to take leadership . . . [or] in a position of great power . . . to make the decisions."[35]

The old financiers of Yankee City, too, like the old factory

---

[32] Lois R. Dean, *Five Towns: A Comparative Community Study* (New York: Random House, Inc., 1967), p. 100.

[33] Ibid.

[34] W. Lloyd Warner and J. O. Low, *The Social System of the Modern Factory, the Strike: A Social Analysis* (New Haven: Yale University Press, 1947), p. 96.

[35] Ibid., p. 97.

owners, had been local leaders, responsible and dominated by local pride. Their philanthropies in the form of parks, libraries, hospitals, foundations, and endowments had enriched it. "Perhaps the price was high, but the product bought by the rest of the community was substantial and of high quality."[36] But to the financial interests that succeeded the local bankers, Yankee City's factories were merely one in a large number of enterprises in which they were interested. "The flow of wealth from Yankee City's banks and factories, once a great local arterial system giving life and strength to the town, now has shrunk to an infinitesimal part of Big City, world-wide capitalism, where it has no vital significance."[37] The effect on Yankee City of such reduction to "colonial" status was embittering. Local men were reduced to inferior positions; their status fell; they could not exert strong leadership. Decisions of great importance in the lives of the residents were made by men at the level of international financial houses which had no interest in Yankee City as such. The takeover of Hollywood by bankers a generation later was a classic example of the same processes.

Although a strike was not an effective way to resist such a take-over by outside forces, it did serve as a form of information, communicating to the threatening absentee owners some of the dangers involved. Little by little the "colonial powers" learned their lessons. Public relations departments of great national corporations learned to devote a considerable amount of time and energy teaching management in local communities how to win friends and influence people at the grass roots. At least the illusion was to be fostered that the "small town in mass society" had a modicum of autonomy. But did it have real power? That was another question.

The old Parsons social systems paradigm had provided for both the internal and the external relations of a community. Now Roland Warren, noting the "increasing orientation of local community units toward extracommunity systems . . . with a corresponding decline in community cohesion and autonomy,"[38] proposed substituting "horizontal" and "vertical" for Parsons' "internal" and "external."

In the 1960s and early 1970s a centrifugal trend was begin-

---

[36] Ibid., p. 98.

[37] Ibid., p. 48.

[38] Roland L. Warren, *The Community in America* (Chicago: Rand McNally & Co., 1963), p. 48.

ning to emerge. <u>There was a movement to return power to local communities if at all possible.</u> National voluntary organizations made a good deal of "grass roots" support. In the government there were fewer guidelines from Washington and more decisions at City Hall. There was talk of a "New Federalism" by which taxes would be shared by states and local communities.

Years of prodigious normal-science research had left us, then, with the conclusion that there was no such thing as *a* "community power structure." The structure of power, where any existed, varied from a monolithic pyramidal structure to an amorphous congeries of separate power structures, depending on the nature of the community itself. It might even be a cleverly managed illusion. Even if it had once had demonstrable reality, it seemed increasingly vulnerable to outside take-over.

The view of the community itself as an independent rather than a dependent variable, shaped by far-flung impersonal forces —urbanization, bureaucratization, and industrialization—and at the mercy perhaps of outside forces and power complexes, leads also to a quite different paradigm, one that deals with the effects that different kinds of communities have not only on the nature of the power structure but also on the inhabitants themselves. Community as the independent rather than as the dependent variable engages the attention of this paradigm, as noted in Chapter 6.

6

Gemeinschaft and Gesellschaft: Rural and Urban Communities

"THE SOIL" AND THE CITY

The fourth great classic community paradigm went under the rubric Gemeinschaft and Gesellschaft proposed by Ferdinand Tönnies. Neither term referred to community in the settlement sense, nor did agrarianism and urbanism, their transmogrified form. But in actual practice, the rural community came to represent one and the city the other; one good and the other bad; one having a benign effect on its members, the other a sinister one.

The terms *Gemeinschaft* and *Gesellschaft,* as Durkheim had regretfully noted, are really not translatable. Gemeinschaft does not imply community in the sense of mere locale—Gemeinde— but in a very special "Blut-und-Boden" sense, and the "Boden" more salient than the "Blut." "A common relation to the soil tends to associate people who may be kinsfolk or believe themselves to be such. Neighborhood . . . is the basis of their union."[1] And Gesellschaft, when all the modifications, circumscriptions, exceptions, and qualifications are duly noted, turns out to be

---

[1] Ferdinand Tönnies, *Community and Society,* edited and translated by Charles P. Loomis (New York: Harper Torchbook, 1957), pp. 160–61.

urban capitalism. "Capitalist society . . . is the most distinct form
of the many phenomena represented by the sociological concept
of the Gesellschaft."[2]

In one form or another the Gemeinschaft-Gesellschaft paradigm has been a major preoccupation of sociology from its
beginning. It has been stated in different forms by different
observers, but essentially they have all referred to the changes that
took place in the nature of human relationships when preindustrial, isolated, "closed," "folk" communities became urbanized or
"open" by becoming integrated into a wider industrial system.
However stated, it was central; one sociologist, in fact, labeled this
paradigm as *the* sociological tradition. When it became operationalized for research purposes, it took the form of the study of rural
and urban communities.

DESCRIPTION VERSUS GLORIFICATION:
THE GEMEINSCHAFT MYSTIQUE

If Tönnies had limited himself to a straightforward description of the nature of Gemeinschaft relationships wherever they
were found, historically or geographically, there would be little to
fault in his concepts. There *are* genuine differences among different kinds of relationships. A tribal community *is* vastly different
from a megalopolis. The difficulty arises when Gemeinschaft
develops a mystique of its own. Tönnies recognized that his
concepts referred to artificial, even forced, abstractions and that
both Gesellschaft and Gemeinschaft could be present in all kinds
of associations. The fatal flaw was in identifying Gemeinschaft
with the rural village—"the outstanding example of an association of this [the Gemeinschaft] type is the rural village community"[3]—and a specific kind of rural village at that, the European, and
with a preindustrial past.

Despite Tönnies' disclaimers, his own values showed. The
Gemeinschaft community was invested with a warm and loving
aura. "The expression 'bad Gemeinschaft' violates the meaning of
the word";[4] "the theory of Gemeinschaft starts from the assump-

[2] Ibid., p. 258.

[3] Ibid.

[4] Ibid., p. 34.

tion of perfect unity of human wills";[5] there is in Gemeinschaft "mutual affirmation"[6] and "an instinctive and naive tenderness of the strong for the weak, a desire to aid and to protect";[7] "mutual furtherance and affirmation predominate."[8] The overriding impression was of Gemeinschaft as a warm, loving, harmonious, emotionally rich, organic wholeness suffused with a tender glow. It had prevailed in a nostalgic past; it was in process of dissolution in the harsh present.

GEMEINSCHAFT AND THE FOLK

The Gemeinschaft paradigm could not stand the test of research examination. The presence or absence of Gemeinschaft in the past cannot be unequivocally determined. But folk communities today can be studied and there is a considerable amount of evidence that they are not always characterized by Gemeinschaft as Tönnies envisaged it. Thus, for example, when we examine preliterate villages today we do not always find the loving warmth implicitly attributed to them by the Gemeinschaft paradigm. Ruth Benedict noted that some preliterates are dour, treacherous, morbidly suspicious of one another, and even schizophrenic; some show paranoid traits and as much competitiveness as do capitalistic or Gesellschaft societies.[9] In Java, village officials have been known to sell their villages to plantation owners.[10] In one Vietnam village, an anthropologist reported that there was not enough trust or sense of social solidarity to run a successful cooperative; the villagers did not have strong social bonds.[11] Another anthropologist, on the basis of studies of peasant

---

[5] Ibid., p. 37.

[6] Ibid.

[7] Ibid., p. 41.

[8] Ibid., p. 44.

[9] Ruth Benedict, *Patterns of Culture* (Baltimore: Penguin Books, Inc., 1946).

[10] Erich H. Jacoby, *Agrarian Unrest in Southeast Asia* (New York: Columbia University Press, 1949), p. 52.

[11] Gerald Cannon Hickey, *Village in Vietnam* (New Haven: Yale University Press, 1964), p. 276.

communities in such countries as Mexico, India, Peru, Italy, Slovenia, Egypt, and China, reported that, far from being irradiated with loving-kindness, these communities were rife with feelings of personal insecurity, suspicion, distrust, tension, hostility, and malice; friendship was viewed as a luxury and endless quarrels were inherited by one generation from another.[12] Feuds, for that matter, have been notorious in certain mountain communities in the United States as well. It is a fallacy that close or deep ties are always loving; they may be the most hostile. When the ties between people are enforced by blood or duty they may be resented; they may generate hate rather than love. The folk recognizes that some people "hate like brothers." Dependency may be galling on both sides. On the other hand, voluntary contractual (in the sense of self-selected) ties may be superficial, but they may also be loving and warm.

Research findings in the Third World did not permit identifying Gemeinschaft with rural life any more than research of the anthropologists permitted identification with folk communities. Gesellschaft could characterize rural as well as urban communities. "A plantation system," Philip Hauser reminded us, "is essentially an industrial organization out in the field, and the work experience on a plantation . . . is essentially within a whole industrial setup, with a managerial hierarchy and operations in the money market."[13] And bureaucracy, one of the characterizing aspects of Gesellschaft, can be as infuriating in the countryside as in the city, exploitation as harsh. Wherever you have "money, exchange, money markets, [and] cash crops" you cease to have Gemeinschaft, whether in the country or in the city.

Conversely, just as anthropologists documented the absence of Gemeinschaft in folk societies, so have a number of sociologists reported its presence in urban communities. Within the seeming turmoil and chaos of cities, for example—even Gesellschaft-type or capitalistic cities—people manage to live in "urban villages." Ethnic groups, for example, insulated from the outside world, show strong kinship and locality bonds. Such "urban villagers"

---

[12] George M. Foster, "Interpersonal Relations in Peasant Society," *Human Organization* 19 (Winter 1960–1961), pp. 174–78.

[13] Philip M. Hauser, "Observations on the Urban-Folk and Urban-Rural Dichotomies as Forms of Western Ethnocentrism," in P. M. Hauser and L. F. Schnore, eds., *The Study of Urbanization* (New York: John Wiley & Sons, Inc., 1965), pp. 503–17.

have been described in Boston,[14] Detroit,[15] and San Antonio.[16]

The Tönnies paradigm was especially inappropriate for American experience, for Tönnies, as noted earlier, had identified Gemeinschaft not only with the rural village, but with the European rural village, in which there was proximity of dwellings, communal fields, intimate knowledge of one another, and the need for cooperation in labor.[17] But "rural" in the United States meant something quite different.

The pattern of settlement that had characterized American experience with the land was one of dispersion, not proximity. Isolated homesteads were the rule rather than villages from which tillers of the soil went out to farm their fields. There was so little natural or intrinsic identification with any village, in fact, that it took a special research procedure to determine the boundaries of "natural communities." (The ecological model, for example, was originally used by Charles J. Galpin to delineate the boundaries of rural communities.) Rural villages were more service- than residential-oriented settlements. Any one family might even belong to several communities—one in which they traded, one in which they worshipped, and one in which they sent their children to school. The farmer's contacts might even be segmented rather than holistic. He was certainly individuated—more so, perhaps, than any other part of the population—and not at all submerged in a common will, as specified in the Gemeinschaft model. There was, to be sure, a great deal of cooperation; it was not only of the informal, neighborly kind illustrated by a barn raising, but also of the formal, highly organized, even corporate, kind among producers and among consumers.

"Rural community" in the United States could mean, finally, anything from a feudal plantation in the South worked by blacks, to a "factory farm" in the West worked by migratory workers, to a stranded Appalachian town, to a small family-size farm in Iowa. In none of them did the Tönnies paradigm fit. When sociologists

[14] Herbert Gans, *The Urban Villagers* (New York: The Free Press, 1962). See also Harold L. Wilensky and Charles N. Lebeaux, *Industrial Society and Social Welfare* (New York: Russell Sage Foundation, 1958), pp. 115 ff.

[15] Erwin H. Johnson, in Arthur J. Field, ed., *Urbanization and Work in Modernizing Societies* (Detroit: Glengary Press, 1967), p. 69.

[16] Ibid., p. 67.

[17] Tönnies, *Community and Society*, p. 48.

put the rural community under their research lenses, they had no need to invoke that paradigm. They found the classic community paradigms quite relevant and suitable—the ecological,[18] the ranked-status,[19] and the power structure.[20] Only rarely was it the seat of Gemeinschaft.

Roy Buck was one of the few rural sociologists who rebuked his colleagues for looking at the rural community through inappropriate paradigms: "Traditional scholarship," he charged, "has tended to look at the American community through stereotypes growing out of European thought." He wanted to dispel "the traditional image of rural life as being wholly rooted in a European peasantry and 'Elysian bliss' or an erosion of this once-upon-a-time mentality." He tried to counteract the romantic idealization of the countryside. He decried the family-farm ideology that pervaded so much thinking about rural communities. However nonscientific farmers elsewhere may have been, science had been incorporated into the rural value system in American rural communities; American farmers were not lacking in experience with large-scale organization; and agriculture was one of the more highly organized industries. As a scientific construct, the Gemeinschaft paradigm was not only useless, it was dysfunctional. It had hindered rather than helped the study of rural communities.[21]

WHAT DO YOU MEAN, RURAL?

It was noted in Chapter 4 that class, like ethnicity, became a standard variable in research on personality and behavior. Com-

[18] Charles J. Galpin, *The Social Anatomy of an Agricultural Community* (Madison: Agricultural Experiment Station, University of Wisconsin, Bulletin No. 1, 1915).

[19] E. A. Schuler, *Social Status and Farm Tenure* (Washington, D.C.: United States Department of Agriculture, 1938); H. C. Hoffsomer, *Social and Economic Significance of Land Tenure in the Southwest States* (Chapel Hill: University of North Carolina Press, 1950); E. A. Schuler, "Social and Economic Status in a Louisiana Hills Community," *Rural Sociology* 5 (1940), pp. 69–87; Harold F. Kaufman, *Prestige Classes in a Rural Community* (Ithaca, N.Y.: Cornell University Press, 1944). Warner found a rural class structure similar to that of Jonesville in the surrounding rural communities, namely, squire farmers, old landowners, dirt farmers, and lower-lower rural residents corresponding to upper-middle, lower-middle, upper-lower, and lower-lower classes in Jonesville (*Democracy in Jonesville*, p. 263).

[20] Seymour Martin Lipset, *Agrarian Socialism: A Study in Political Sociology* (Berkeley: University of California Press, 1950).

[21] Roy Buck, "An Interpretation of Rural Values," in *A Place to Live* (Washington, D.C.: United States Department of Agriculture, 1963), p. 4.

munity background also became a routine variable in such studies. How, actually, did the behavior of human beings and their relations to one another differ in different kinds of communities? How did behavior differ in rural as compared to urban communities? How did the community one lived in affect personality? We were rather cavalier in Chapter 1 about definitions. Still, when one gets down to the drawing board to design a research project at least he has to specify the criteria he uses to operationalize his variables. It did not prove easy to find such criteria for the concept of rurality. "Occupational, demographic, ecological, social-organizational, and cultural characteristics have all been used as defining attributes,"[22] different as such criteria are among themselves in "the ease with which they can be used in research, the degree to which they provide meaningful theoretical and empirical differentiation, their constancy in time and space, their cultural relativity, and their causal connection or interrelationship."[23] In the end, mainly because of the form in which census data came, demographic criteria—size and density—became the major ones applied, and community structure became the major focus of attention.

Numerous studies reported on such variables as community size, location, type of functional specialization, growth and stability, and regional context as related to age, sex, race-nativity, family composition, socioeconomic level, and economic activities. It was found that, in general, rural people married at a younger age, remained married longer, and had more children. Overall, they were less well schooled. The definitive analysis of urban and rural communities, based on 1950 census data, concluded that "the steady progress of urbanization is the cardinal fact about the evolution of community structure in the United States."[24] Whatever the rural-urban differences that had been reported were, they were, in effect, transitory.

Sorokin and Zimmerman had been of the opinion that the magnitude of rural-urban differences followed a parabolic course,

---

[22] Olaf F. Larson, "Rural Society," in David L. Sills, ed., *International Encyclopedia of the Social Sciences,* vol. 13 (New York: The Macmillan Company and The Free Press, 1968), p. 582.

[23] Paul K. Hatt and Albert J. Reiss, Jr., eds., *Cities and Society: The Revised Reader in Urban Sociology,* rev. ed. (New York: The Free Press, 1957), pp. 19–21.

[24] Otis Dudley Duncan and Albert J. Reiss, Jr., *Social Characteristics of Urban and Rural Communities, 1950* (New York: John Wiley & Sons, Inc., 1956), p. xii.

being relatively small in the earliest stages of city growth and increasing as the pace of development accelerated in urban centers more rapidly than in rural areas. But when urbanization spread out over rural areas also, the magnitude of the differences would tend to decline. When rural-urban differences were first reported, they were greater than they are today; rural areas were more isolated and more out of touch with the great world. As modern transportation and communication have urbanized outlying areas, however, rural-urban differences have indeed become attenuated. Today in a state like Pennsylvania, for example, they have all but disappeared. At the historical moment when the rural sociologists "caught" the rural communities, the parabola was already in its descending phase.

The implications for community life in cities were not insignificant. The first great wave of rural-urban migration was truly one between different cultures, from small, rural communities in Europe in the case of immigrants, or from farms in the United States, to great urban centers. The cultural breach between these newcomers and the older city residents could be unbridgeable in many cases. Such "first-wave" types of rural-urban migration still persist in the case of city-directed moves by southern plantation workers or people from the hill country. But "last-wave" types of rural-urban migration are altogether different; the rural in-migrant has already been exposed to the urban culture so thoroughly that there is practically no cultural difference left at all.

SELECTIVITY OF RURAL-URBAN MIGRATION

Before attempting any serious assessment of the effect of community on personality, the perennial chicken-and-egg problem of selectivity has to be faced. It cannot be ignored, for "population characteristics reflect the selective influence of different types of communities"[25] even in such biological aspects of behavior as sexuality. Some observers tend to emphasize the community-determines-behavior point of view; some, the people-determine-the-community point of view. Some straddle.

Both rural and urban sociologists have shared research interest in rural-urban migration. Both wanted to know whether the

---

[25] A. C. Kinsey and Associates, *Sexual Behavior in the Human Male* (Philadelphia: W. B. Saunders Co., 1948), Chapter 12.

city was getting the best or the worst or a cross section of the rural population. A considerable corpus of research arose to answer this question. The results were by no means unequivocal.

The earliest rural-bred recruits to the factory towns included workhouse inmates, children who were parish charges, and society's dregs. The experiment of Robert Owen at New Lanark, Scotland, was posited on the assumption that successful farmers would not be drawn to the harsh factory towns; why should they come? Those who did come or could be recruited would necessarily be the unsuccessful; to be useful as workers they would need to be upgraded, that is, processed for the discipline demanded by the mill. Owen showed how this could be done, firmly but not harshly. Charles Booth, on the other hand, comparing "countrymen" with native Londoners at the end of the nineteenth century, found the countrymen, in general, to be superior.[26] In the United States, research on European immigrants to this country was so clouded by biases that polemic rather than reliable data usually resulted: Immigrants from southern and eastern Europe were inferior, those from western Europe were not, and so on.

With respect to simple rural-urban migration within the country, Adna Ferrin Weber concluded at the end of the nineteenth century that the most enterprising rural people went to cities.[27] E. A. Ross even spoke of "folk depletion" as a consequence. But the conclusion derivable from an extensive twentieth-century body of research seemed to be that rural-urban migration selected top and bottom—the brightest, the most ambitious, and the most talented, but also the least bright, the least ambitious, the least talented, and the least competent. By the beginning of the last third of the century, when only six percent or less of the population lived on farms and seventy percent or more in cities, the selectivity, if any, in rural-urban migration did not seem very relevant.

In any event, in all that has been written about rural-urban differences it is hard to tease out how much is truly rural and how much the result of ecological distribution based on migratory movements, or the result of frontier conditions, or sheer cultural newness and rawness, or the selectivity of migration itself.

Not all of the migration had been from rural to urban

---

[26] Charles Booth, *Life and Labour of the People of London* (New York: The Macmillan Company, 1902), p. 241.

[27] Adna Ferrin Weber, *The Growth of Cities in the 19th Century* (New York: The Macmillan Company, 1899; Ithaca, N.Y.: Cornell University Press, 1963), p. 437.

communities. In the nineteenth century some of it had been from one rural community to another and sometimes from an urban to a rural one, as in the "winning of the West." This movement has been glamorized and romanticized out of all proportion; but the glamorous and romantic myth did contain a grain of factual underpinning. It did take a considerable amount of courage and enterprise to pull up stakes in the East—wherever the East was—and move out to the frontier. But it took unremitting hard work to succeed. The demands on human resources for survival were often brutalizing. Success required character that kept one on the beam, that had, to use David Riesman's picturesque figure of speech, an inner gyroscope to keep one from straying off course. In politics, it has been found, rural voters have been liberal where their interests were concerned, and conservative where those of the city and of labor were concerned. In fact, an overrepresentation of the rural population in legislatures was once justified in terms of guaranteeing greater stability to the nation as a whole, as a counterfoil to the alleged susceptibility to mass psychology of city dwellers. Some investigators uncovered other differences as well. Kinsey and his associates reported slight differences in sexual behavior by community background, though when they occurred the differences were in the unexpected direction of less frequency of sexual behavior among the rural than among the urban males. One study comparing small children in kindergartens in the Cumberland Mountains and in New York City found the latter more rebellious and the mountain children more placid.[28] A later study of rural youth found that they conformed to parental standards to a high degree.[29]

COMMUNITARIAN COMMUNITIES

A considerable number of rural so-called communitarian—that is, communist in the non-Marxist sense—communities arose in the United States in the nineteenth century. Some of them were genuine folk communities; conversely, some were planned, "intentional," utopistic, and nontraditional, but totally opposed

[28] Claudia Lewis, *Children of the Cumberland* (New York: Columbia University Press, 1946).

[29] Robert C. Bealer and Fern K. Willits, "Rural Youth: A Case Study in the Rebelliousness of Adolescents," *Annals of the American Academy of Political and Social Science* 338 (November 1961), pp. 63–69.

to Gesellschaft as it was then revealing itself, designed to be revolutionary. Some reflected authentic Gemeinschaft, others reflected a contrived kind. By and large the genuine Gemeinschaft communities were religious or sectarian in origin, usually transplants originally of peasant communities from Europe, especially, it seems, from Germany. Examples of this kind were: the Rappites (1804); the Separatists (1817); the Inspirationists (1843); and, from Russia, the Hutterites (1874) and the Doukhobors, who went to Canada (1899).

Of quite a different stripe were the intellectually designed communities, some based on "social science" principles, which hoped to counteract the evils of Gesellschaft by a deliberately contrived form of Gemeinschaft.[30] By and large such intellectualistic or utopistic communities did not survive, although new ventures continue to appear even up until today. There was an anarchist phase in the years 1880 to 1915; also, then and later, there were cooperative communities; cooperatives for land settlement, including the Mexican Ejido collectives; urban "communities of work" organized around the place of work; anarcho-syndicalist communes; and, finally, the communes of disaffected young people in the 1960s and 1970s.

One analysis of nine successful and twenty-one unsuccessful historic communities found the key mechanisms that distinguished between them in the nature of the commitment mechanisms that prevailed. The commitment to continued participation in the community required sacrifice—in the forms, for example, of austerity and oral, sexual, or other gratifications—and investment in the forms of time and energy. Commitment in the area of control took such forms as obedience to authority, mortification, and surrender. Most relevant for Gemeinschaft was the commitment to cohesion, creating bonds among the members that could hold up against inner or outer threats to the group's existence. Attachments other than those to the group had to be given up; family or other dyadic relations had to be relinquished. Insulation of the community by spatial isolation, uniforms, language barriers, conceptualization of the outside world as evil, and the like was fostered. The author concludes that "systems which employ the kinds of [commitment] mechanisms enumerated here, whether in the specific forms described or in others which serve

[30] Such as, for example, Brook Farm, New Harmony, and the Icarians, as well as Modern Times and the Fourieristic phalanxes.

the same functions, should find their participants dedicated, obedient, loyal, and involved."[31]

Religious communities seemed to be more successful in achieving these commitments. Are such sacred sanctions, in the technical sense, essential to achieve such commitments, or could ideologies serve as well? Can Gemeinschaft be created artificially by other than religious systems? Can communities that begin without collective representations achieve them by willing them into existence? Can individuals reared to maturity in a Gesellschaft-type society remold their basic personality and character structure to merge into a Gemeinschaft-type community based on the mechanisms of sacrifice, renunciation, and de-individuation? Whatever the answer to these questions may prove to be, the significance for personality and character of such communities continues to challenge research attention. Two examples are offered here, one having to do with mental health and one with general personality.

COMMUNITY AND MENTAL HEALTH

Psychologists and anthropologists interested in the theoretical culture-personality problem, as well as psychiatrists interested in mental health, have found the community a basic variable in their research. One study is singled out for presentation, namely the sectarian and pristinely Gemeinschaftlich Hutterite Community. The more than 162 Hutterite settlements in the United States and Canada, averaging about ninety-four persons each, are descendants of 440 immigrants who came to this country from Russia in the 1870s.[32] These communities are antipodal to the outside world in almost every basic respect: They are anti-capitalistic, anti-industrial, anti-urban, and anti-individualistic. In these communities there is a high level of conformity; great security; and a minimum of stress and strain. They are, in fact, almost archetypically Gemeinschaft communities, and when size threatens their character they divide and establish new communities. They provide protection against poverty and threats against

---

[31] Rosabeth Moss Kanter, "Commitment and Social Organization: A Study of Commitment Mechanisms in Utopian Communities," *American Sociological Review* 33(August 1968), pp. 499–517.

[32] Victor Peters, *All Things in Common* (Minneapolis: University of Minnesota Press, 1965).

health. They also provide guidance against moral uncertainty or anomie as well.

Using the incidence of psychosis in these archetypically Gemeinschaft-type communities as a benchmark, the authors of one study reported extraordinary and, in some cases, unexpected differences among ten quite diverse communities—rural, urban, and peasant—as summarized in the accompanying table.[33] Although the Hutterite community did not protect its members against feelings of guilt, it was supportive and sympathetic rather than punitive and rejecting when mental illness—which took the forms of depression and introjection rather than aggression—did occur. The major traumatic consequences of such illness were therefore minimized.

As the table shows, the incidence of psychosis was far less among the Hutterites than it would have been if New York rates had prevailed; but, conversely, there were some communities that showed even lower incidence than the Hutterites did. Thuringian villages, for example, showed only about a third as many cases as could have been expected if Hutterite rates had prevailed. But an Arctic Norwegian village showed almost twice as many. It is not always clear exactly what the differentiating factors were—latitude, climate, and nationality could be ruled out—but apparently Gemeinschaft in and of itself was not uniquely and unequivocally definitive. Difficult as it may be to specify exactly what it was that differentiated the communities from one another and explained the widely differing incidence of psychoses, it did seem clear that the kind of Gemeinschaft that characterized the Hutterite company protected the community from psychoses, although it did not wholly eliminate them.

CHILDREN OF THE DREAM

We asked earlier, in connection with the communitarian communities in the United States, whether ideologies as well as religious beliefs could achieve the kinds of commitment that research had found essential for their success. The Israeli kibbutz seemed to answer that question affirmatively. For although the founders were Jews, it was ideology rather than religion that fired

---

[33] Joseph W. Eaton and Robert J. Weil, *Culture and Mental Disorders* (New York: The Free Press, 1955), p. 75.

TABLE 6-1 COMPARISON OF TEN LIFETIME MORBIDITY SURVEYS OF PSYCHOSES BY THE STANDARD EXPECTANCY METHOD

Survey	Total Population	Actual Number of Cases Found	Expected Number of Cases		Expectancy Ratios actual cases / expected cases	
			Hutterite Norms	New York State Norms	Hutterite Norms	New York State Norms
Arctic Norwegian Village	1,325	38	19	26	1.97	1.43
North Swedish Area	8,651	107	94	141	1.14	.76
Ethnic Hutterites	8,542	53	53	85	1.00	.62
Rornholm Island	45,694	481	773	1,049	.62	.46
Baltimore Eastern Health District	55,129	507	822	1,144	.62	.44
Williamson County, Tennessee	24,804	156	271	502	.58	.31
West Swedish Island	8,735	94	186	260	.51	.36
Bavarian Villages, Rosenheim Area	3,203	21	49	84	.43	.25
Formosa Area	19,913	76	194	273	.39	.28
Thuringia Villages	37,546	200	617	841	.32	.24

them. The first of these settlements were established in the early years of the century by idealistic young Jews from East European ghettos to reclaim the land of their forefathers. They were Marxist in orientation and antitraditional, overreacting against everything associated with Jewish life in the *shtetl*.[34] Unlike the nineteenth-century communitarian communities in the United States, they were almost doctrinaire in their insistence on equality. Life was hard and demanding. The individual care of children by the full-time attention of their mothers was a luxury that could not be afforded. The children were therefore reared in their own quarters by personnel specialized for this function and had only limited contacts with their parents.

A recent study of the results of such communities on the personalities and characters of the children reared in them concludes that "a radically new personality" had been created in a single generation.[35] Its members lacked the defensiveness with respect to Jewishness which had characterized their parents. They showed a "literalness, a matter-of-fact objectivity which has no place for emotions." They were embarrassed or even disgusted by the emotions their parents exhibited. Although these young people retained many of the original ideals of the settlements, they were otherwise materialistic, Kibbutz-centered, offhand, and often discourteous. They were characterized by "emotional flatness." Their love of the land was no less than that of their parents, but it was less romantic. The parents viewed them as less humanistic and less involved than they were.

To the extent that the West has seen private property and family ties as intrinsic to human nature, the Kibbutz had changed human nature. Kibbutzim-reared young people saw communal property as "the only normal way to live." They viewed the emotional distance between parents and children of the Kibbutz with equanimity. The women were casual about their femininity. A kind of human nature had been created, in brief, that was "not only different from, but more suited to Kibbutz life than that of the parents who devised it."[36]

Despite the conservatism of the Kibbutz-reared generation,

[34] Stanley Diamond, "Kibbutz and Shtetl: The History of an Idea," *Social Problems* 5 (Fall 1957), pp. 71–99.

[35] Bruno Bettelheim, *Children of the Dream* (New York: The Macmillan Company, 1969), p. 276.

[36] Ibid., p. 282.

change does occur; affluence does exact a toll; concessions are made to expedience (workers are hired, for example, a practice contrary to the original Marxist ideals), and to individual whims. The Kibbutzim shed light, clear and almost unequivocal, if not on the nature of Gemeinschaft, at least on the effect of community on personality and character.

OFF-BEAT COMMUNITIES

Not in the mainstream of community research per se, but of considerable tangential interest have been studies of institutional communities such as asylums, hospitals, and prisons; "therapeutic" communities, Synanon communities, and half-way houses; concentration camps; prisoner-of-war camps; refugee camps; hippie communities; gypsy communities; the factory as a community; logging camps and nudist camps; migratory workers' camps; homosexual communities; mobile home "parks"; and so on. In such off-beat communities it is usually the interpersonal, interactional, primary-group nature of the relationships rather than Gemeinschaft as originally conceptualized that is the focus of interest, and the emphasis of the research tends to be that of social psychology rather than that of community per se.

What happens to people when the normal functioning of a community breaks down has also been of research concern, beginning with the so-called Halifax disaster of 1919, continuing through the great depression of the 1930s. World War II, with its accelerated mobility, its boom towns, and its population uprooting, produced more newspaper copy than careful research. The exigencies of the Cold War, especially civil defense, stimulated more technically competent research and a new genre of interdisciplinary community research known as disaster research. As a result a great deal of insight has accumulated on what happens to people when their communities are subjected to unusual stress.

THE GREAT NOSTALGIA
FOR THE IMPOSSIBLE DREAM

We have given so much attention to the Gemeinschaft paradigm not because it proved useful for empirical research but because it has exerted enormous influence on people's imagination. We cannot understand the uneasiness evident at the onset of the last third of the century unless we recognize the pull of the Gemeinschaft mystique. Gemeinschaft is still the dream for millions of people, reflecting a deep longing. That Gemeinschaft in the loving sense is only a fantasy in no way detracts from its appeal. Untold thousands dream of living in a small, congenial, cooperative community of loving, understanding, noncompetitive relationships; they long for togetherness and bemoan the lack of community spirit. The last third of the twentieth century saw a new wave in the long quest for community, new refugees from Gesellschaft, undismayed by the fact that there probably never has existed the kind of community of which they dream.

THE ANIMUS AGAINST CITIES

Along with the nostalgia for the Gemeinschaft past, there had existed through the nineteenth century a strong animus against the modern city. The agrarian concept of the community that guided thinking and policy in the United States from its beginning was not the same as Gemeinschaft but rather one of small, independent farmers cultivating their own land as the basic foundation on which democracy rested. In the towns there were skilled craftsmen who provided mechanical services, using their own tools. But most people were, properly, on the land where, engaged in the most honorable of all occupations, the cultivation of the soil, they could be self-reliant, independent, and solid citizens. Urban communities were, at best, but secondary; at worst, destructive.

Capitalistic and industrial cities were destructive in a variety of ways. Demographically they were vampires, consuming populations. Without constant replenishment from rural areas they would die out.[37] They were destructive aesthetically in that they destroyed beauty; they lacked order and dignity;[38] they were great ugly wens on the beautiful countryside. They were destructive structurally in that they fostered inequality, class distinctions, and social disorganization that led to tyranny.[39] They were, finally, morally destructive also, turning upright people into

---

[37] Tönnies, *Community and Society*, p. 234.

[38] Henry James, quoted by Morton White and Lucia White, *The Intellectual Versus the City* (New York: Mentor Press, 1962), p. 237.

[39] Ibid., p. 47.

sharpers and slickers. As contrasted with agrarian virtue, cities were wicked. (Of course, replied R. E. Park, and properly so.)[40] As late as the middle of the twentieth century this was how cities looked to small-town people: "Cities breed corruption. . . . Cities are an unwholesome environment for children and families, and have had an unhealthy effect on family morals; urban politicians and labor leaders are corrupt and represent antidemocratic forces in American life. . . . Cities are hotbeds of un-American sentiment, harbor the reds, and are incapable of educating their youth to Christian values. . . . Most of the problems of country life have their origin in the effects which urban life has on rural ways."[41] These townspeople were, like their nineteenth-century forebears, viewing cities as "pestilential to the morals, the health, and the liberties of man."[42] And not in a figurative sense either; cities were literally sick.[43] This rural bias dominated thinking even among researchers; long after the urban population had exceeded the rural, it could still be said that "compared to the attention that has been devoted to agriculture and the rural phase of American life, that part of America which is symbolized by the city has been almost completely neglected and has never fully emerged into our national consciousness."[44] Not passively or heedlessly neglected, but positively, even hatefully, rejected.

Understandably, then, the first serious study of urban communities had its roots in city problems. Social reformers, settlement house workers, revolutionaries, disaffected poets, and romantics, as well as intellectuals, set the pattern for viewing cities in a hostile and adverse perspective. And even today most people, when asked, have agreed with these critics; most people say they prefer not to live in cities. Even in the short period between 1966 and 1968, Gallup polls showed the proportion of people who said they liked living in cities dropping from twenty-two to eighteen

[40] R. E. Park, "The City: Suggestions for the Investigation of Human Behavior in the City Environment," *American Journal of Sociology* 20 (March 1916), pp. 577–612.

[41] Arthur J. Vidich and Joseph Bensman, *Small Town in Mass Society: Class, Power, and Religion in a Rural Community*, rev. ed. (Princeton, N.J.: Princeton University Press, 1968), pp. 33–34.

[42] White and White, *The Intellectual Versus the City*, back cover.

[43] Ibid., p. 235. As late as 1946 a book called *Cities Are Abnormal* (Westport, Conn.: Greenwood Press, Inc., 1946) edited by Elmer T. Peterson appeared.

[44] National Resources Committee, *Our Cities* (Washington, D.C.: U.S. Government Printing Office, 1937), p. 4.

percent.[45] Urbanism was decidedly not the preferred way of life for most people.

URBANISM AS A WAY OF LIFE

Many of the most hated aspects of cities, such as crowding, inadequate transportation, and blocked traffic, are ecological or spatial, structural problems. But the community of scientists interested in the city have also been interested in urbanism, a psychosociological phenomenon referring to the ways in which the city affects how people think and feel and interact with one another. The two are not independent of one another but rather complementary. Park had included both the ecological and the social or organizational aspects of the city in his suggestions for studying human behavior in the urban environment, emphasizing communication, culture, and consensus, as well as ecological structure. He agreed with Simmel who had referred to the city as a state of mind.[46]

But the formulation that became the classic and most influential statement on urbanism was that of Louis Wirth in 1938. The problem was not so much to explain why cities had the structure the ecological studies had revealed but rather what the city did to people who lived in it. Urbanism was the human side of urbanization.

Wirth rejected the traditional rural-urban dichotomy and definitions. He wanted a definition that would be independent of locale and apply not only to industrial cities, but also to preindustrial cities as well, and one that did not confuse urbanism with modern capitalism either.[47] He wanted to abstract, out of all the various forms that cities have taken, the essential core traits that characterize them as cities. He finally settled on size, density, permanence, and heterogeneity. He defined a city as "a relatively large, dense, and permanent settlement of socially heterogeneous individuals" and the central problem of the sociology of the city to be "to discover the forms of social action and organization that

[45] Daniel J. Elazar, "Are We a Nation of Cities?"*The Public Interest,* no. 4 (Summer 1966), p. 49.

[46] Georg Simmel, *Die Grosstädte und das Geistesleben* (Dresden, Germany: Zahn und Jaensch, 1903).

[47] Louis Wirth, "Urbanism as a Way of Life," in Albert J. Reiss, ed., *On Cities and City Life* (Chicago: University of Chicago Press, 1964), pp. 60–83.

typically emerge in [such] relatively permanent, compact settlements of large numbers of heterogeneous individuals."

A major effect of the first criterion, large numbers, was the segmentalization of human relations. Relative to the number of contacts one had with others, urbanites knew a smaller proportion and knew even this smaller proportion less intensively than in nonurban settlements. Contacts in cities tended to be secondary rather than primary, impersonal, superficial, and transitory, even when face to face. Superficiality and anonymity fostered sophistication and rationality. Such emancipation from intimate controls constituted *anomie,* a social void. Communication tended to become indirect. Individuals as such counted for little; they could make themselves heard only through representatives.

Density, the second criterion of urbanism, reinforced the effect of numbers and tended to increase reserve. But the propinquity resulting from density increased close physical contacts. Propinquity exposed all kinds of contrasts in wealth, intelligence, ignorance, order, and chaos. "The close living together and working together of individuals who have no sentimental and emotional ties foster a spirit of competition, aggrandizement, and mutual exploitation."[48] Formal controls have to be set up, therefore, to maintain order and counteract irresponsibility. Nervous tensions result from the personal frustrations and the rapid tempo that accompany density.

Heterogeneity, the third characteristic of urbanism, tended to break down caste lines and complicate the class structure. It fostered status heterogeneity in that the same individual might have higher or lower status in different groups. Depersonalization accompanied heterogeneity. Since we cannot behave toward people on the basis of their individuality because the diversity is so great, we deal with categories rather than with individuals. And also as an accompaniment of heterogeneity, there was leveling, as well as what we have called massification.

Wirth's influential paradigm was an interesting attempt to specify what was intrinsically and uniquely urban about a community as distinguished from what was the result of industrialism or capitalism per se. It stimulated a considerable amount of discussion and normal-science research, mostly critical. Philip Hauser, for example, found that oriental cities did not show the characteristics expected from Wirth's formulation of urban-

[48] Ibid., p. 74.

ism.[49] Herbert Gans did not believe that the consequences attributed to size, density, and heterogeneity had been proved. He conceded that, although few areas of a city approached the kind of community implied in the democratic ideology, few approached the anonymity and fragmentation implied in the paradigm either.[50] Don Martindale criticized Wirth's paradigm as an overreaction to the oversimplification of the ecological paradigm,[51] and Scott Greer criticized it as a product of the general *Weltschmerz* engendered by the great depression of the 1930s.[52]

Still, a paradigm that stimulated so much rebuttal must have had something going for it. As a matter of fact, a fairly good case could be made for the point of view that the history of cities in the United States in the twentieth century had been a history of attempts, one way or another, to counteract the effects of size, density, and heterogeneity, or to escape them. With almost tropistic directness Americans sought small, uncrowded, homogeneous settlements in which Wirth's urbanism could be avoided. Those who could escaped to suburbs. Those who were left behind had to find other ways to cope with the consequences of urbanism.

COPING WITH URBANISM

One criticism of Wirth had been that his conception of urbanism really fit only in the inner city. But Gans found that even here people were protected by the social structures and cultural patterns they brought with them from rural backgrounds or developed themselves. Studying the Italians in the west end of Boston, he had found that life there resembled that of villages or small towns. Unlike the earlier Gemeinschaft theoreticians he did not glamorize the small community. His urban villagers were not noble peasants "resisting the mass-produced homogeneity of

[49] Hauser, "Observations on the Urban-Folk and Urban-Rural Dichotomies as Forms of Western Ethnocentrism," pp. 503–17.

[50] Herbert J. Gans, "Urbanism and Suburbanism," in Arnold Rose, ed., *Human Behavior and Social Process* (Boston: Houghton Mifflin Company, 1962), pp. 628 ff.

[51] Don Martindale, in the introduction to Max Weber, *The City* (New York: The Free Press, 1958), p. 42.

[52] Scott Greer, *The Emerging City* (New York: The Free Press, 1962), p. 17.

American culture and overflowing with a cohesive sense of community."[53] But neither were they the alienated, atomized, lonely products of Wirth's urbanism. They were people with low incomes and little education struggling with the day-by-day problems of survival, as villagers in any ambience have to do. Their village was poor, but still a good place to live. By restricting their social world to their own ethnic community they softened the impact of the sheer size of the larger world. Crowding was coped with by means of cultural taboos. Heterogeneity was eliminated by the ethnic character of the village.

Less optimistic was Gerald D. Suttles' report on the way residents of the Adams area in the near west side of Chicago coped with urbanism. His report did not at all resemble the Gans model of villagers in the midst of a large city doggedly, if not spectacularly, coping with urbanism; but neither did it resemble Wirth's shapeless mass of socially heterogeneous individuals. Rather, it resembled reports by anthropologists on hostile villages sharing a restricted area—hostile, but ordered, if not always orderly. One of Suttles' most intriguing contributions, in fact, was his concept of ordered segmentation. Units—they were not always groups— based on age, sex, ethnicity, and territory lined up with and against one another along clear-cut, but not always consistent, lines. When there was a confrontation it was between equivalent units. At the first level, for example, one age-grade unit (a boys' gang, let us say) lined up against another unit of the same age-grade and ethnic background in another territory. At the next level, the ethnic age-grades combined in each area, and those in one area confronted those in another; one ethnic group against its ethnic counterpart in another area. But, surprisingly, at the third level all age and ethnic groups in one area combined against their opposite numbers in another area. In brief, territoriality took precedence over other characteristics in ordering at the third level. Suttles explained this fact in terms of the importance of sheer propinquity; it was safer to have one's enemies, whatever their ethnicity, at a distance rather than in one's own front yard. This ordered segmentation was interpreted as a method for coping with Wirth's density and heterogeneity in a very complex and subtle way. It was not, however, impersonal, superficial, or transitory.[54] There was mutual distrust between and among the

[53] Gans, *The Urban Villagers,* p. 16.

[54] Gerald D. Suttles, *The Social Order of the Slum* (Chicago: University of Chicago Press, 1968), Chapters 1 and 2.

units of this segmentation, to be sure; but there was not the kind of amorphous atomization posited by the Wirth urbanism paradigm. Nor was there the impersonality. There was a personalistic morality, and personal reputation counted.

THE BLACK VERSION OF URBANISM

Whatever might be said about urbanism as related to ethnic groups, the situation of blacks conformed in almost archetypical fashion to the scenario of the Gemeinschaft-Gesellschaft paradigm. In fact, the history of blacks in the United States in the twentieth century was such a precise, almost exact, demonstration of this paradigm as to look almost like a caricature. In less than a century blacks had been catapulted literally from a feudal to an urban society, from a folk community to Gesellschaft. Frazier had called the great trek to the city a flight from feudal America.[55] These migrants had had little experience with Gesellschaft—especially with money—or with its emphasis on achievement and the Protestant ethic. Work for many was an unpleasant necessity which one did under duress; work was not a taken-for-granted obligation with moral underpinnings. Many had been nurtured in dependency. They did not think in terms of individual initiative and enterprise, or in market terms. Frazier, like the nineteenth-century critics, spoke of "the city of destruction."[56] It was not, actually, the city in and of itself that was destructive. In his own work on black communities, Frazier had presented evidence of integrity and achievement among urban blacks; free blacks in the urban North were among the most stable of their race.

Still, as in the case of folk of whatever color, the effects of urban migration were to uproot old ways of life, destroy folkways and mores, and create confusion in thought and contradictions in behavior.[57] As Booth and his predecessors had reported of London and other cities in the nineteenth century,[58] as Chicago

[55] E. Franklin Frazier, *The Negro Family in the United States* (New York: Dryden Press, Inc., 1948), p. 225.

[56] Ibid., Part 4.

[57] Ibid., p. 92.

[58] Booth, *Life and Labour of the People in London*, pp. 353, 41, 335; Sir Edwin Chadwick, in a report on a survey of Reading, England, quoted in Benjamin Ward Richardson, *The Health of Nations* (New York: Longmans, Green, 1887), pp. 407, 328.

researchers had reported of Chicago in the 1920s, and as all the later studies here and in the Third World had shown with such monotonous consistency, so also among black people in city slums researchers found juvenile delinquency, family breakdown, and unconventional sexual behavior. It was a painfully familiar scenario, independent of time, place, ethnicity, or race. The consistency with which the same conditions produce the same results may be reassuring in validating the legitimacy of the social sciences; at the same time it is disheartening to learn how little we profit from this knowledge.

If the Gemeinschaft-Gesellschaft paradigm fit in the case of blacks, the same could not be said of Wirth's paradigm of urbanism. In a microsociological study in the 1960s, for example, it was not heterogeneity that was found to pose problems for blacks, but just the opposite. It was the enforced homogeneity of the housing projects in which they were, for all intents and purposes, incarcerated. It was this enforced homogeneity, according to Suttles, more than anonymity or impersonality, that robbed them of individuality and led them to extremes in "styles of life."

Wirth, following Simmel, had noted that "the urban world puts a premium on visual recognition."[59] The artificially massified black inhabitants of the housing project were thus driven to invest a great deal in the visual presentation of the self. Density means crowding; it means the strains of propinquity. It means that there have to be defenses against mistakes that can easily lead to confrontations and attack. Black people learned how to create such defenses. Orderly relations demanded that the misgivings, suspicions, fears, and doubts of others be assuaged or else that one assume such an awesome appearance of power that one is guaranteed "free passage." "In either case, [people] must exaggerate the available signs that let others know what they 'really are.' The most direct means of doing this is simply to extend, emphasize, and elaborate existing styles of clothing, manners of speech, walk, stance, and demeanor. Colors become extremely loud or entirely lacking, styles advance to the very forefront of the period, and mannerisms become 'way out.' "[60] The analogy with diplomatic ploys in the international community is almost irresistible. And, as in the international community, when signs failed, force or bluffing contests were resorted to. There was never

[59] Wirth, *Urbanism as a Way of Life*, p. 73.

[60] Suttles, *The Social Order of the Slum*, pp. 24–25.

ending fear of deception. "No one is willing to accept another at face value, and extreme proofs of one's identity are required."[61] Neither the "law" that the people in the near west side of Chicago worked out for themselves, nor the order that it produced, might be the kind implied by proponents of "law and order," but, in its own way, the area did achieve a social order.[62]

SUBURBANISM AS A WAY OF LIFE

The other way of coping with the size, density, and heterogeneity of cities, as noted earlier, was an almost tropistic beeline for the suburbs and beyond. For, just as there have been waves of rural-urban migration, so also has there been a continuing undertow pulling people out again.

"Are we really, in fact, a nation of cities, as we believe on the basis of census counts?" asks one student. And he answers with a resounding "No!" We are still agrarians at heart, with deeply rural roots. We have tried to make our cities resemble rural areas as much as possible, with a town-and-country look. Unfenced private lawns, large public parks, tree-lined streets, low density, and free-standing private homes—all neo-agrarian features—are or have been characteristic of American cities.[63] And as long as cities provided opportunities for this kind of neo-ruralness, people remained within city limits, only moving farther out. The push beyond city limits to the suburbs was merely an extension of a very old process. As early as 1820, in fact, such large cities as New York, Boston, Philadelphia, Baltimore, and New Orleans were beginning to show out-migration to suburban areas.[64]

Sociologists had long since reported on these suburbs. They had been watching the outward movement of population for decades. The Chicago school had included a commuter zone as part of the concentric circle model; Charles Booth had noted the suburban trend in London at the end of the nineteenth century.

[61] Ibid., p. 126.

[62] Ibid., passim. The work of Lee Rainwater and his students on the Igoe-Pruitt housing project in St. Louis tallied with that of Suttles. See *Behind Ghetto Walls* (Chicago: Aldine Publishing Company, 1970). Elliot Liebow's study in Washington did not. See his *Tolly's Corner* (Boston: Little, Brown and Company, 1967).

[63] Elazar, "Are We a Nation of Cities?" pp. 42–58.

[64] Ibid., p. 51.

Sociologists had also discovered the urban fringe; they proposed the term "rurban" to refer to communities that fit into neither the urban nor the rural, nor even suburban, categories. They were not, therefore, as surprised as the general public seemed to be in the 1950s by the relative decline of central cities and the growth of suburbs.

Sociologists had distinguished satellite suburbs and dormitory suburbs. They had noted industrial suburbs. They had studied communities that lay along railway lines which, for the most part, had been the remotest concentric circle, inhabited largely by the affluent. But in the 1940s, and especially in the 1950s, the automobile and the highway began to supplement and even supplant the commuter railroad; huge real estate "developments" created new suburbs almost overnight; instant communities sprang up almost everywhere. And in the 1960s scores of so-called new towns "mutated" from the old pattern, deliberately designed to be complete nonurbanized communities and thus to begin the de-urbanization of the population or, at least, to break up the megalopolis.

The new communities differed from the older suburbs. In the old-fashioned suburbs families had entered one by one, as they did in other towns or in other urban areas. They found an established social order into which, in varying degrees, they became assimilated. They came in as strangers or knowing only one or two other families. But in the newest suburbs or suburban places all the families moved in within a short period of time. There was no established order other than the one laid down by the builders. All were newcomers. Whatever order there was tended to be of their own making. A sorting process took place, filtering out natural leaders. Families "tried one another on for size" until they found some that fit their own age, education, income, and other such characteristics.

Only three of the numerous suburban studies can be noted here. One of the first and most influential was made in the early 1950s of Park Forest just outside of Chicago. The organizing paradigm, interestingly enough, was not one in the great classic tradition of community study but rather of bureaucracy, namely "the organization man." The author therefore saw the new suburb primarily as the domestic side of the corporation. The characterizing aspects of the suburban way of life were, therefore, the rootlessness demanded by the corporation compensated for— sometimes overcompensated for—by neighborliness, sharing of property, and participation; determined classlessness as part of the interchangeability demanded by organization; *in*conspicuous consumption (for about the same reasons as Suttles' black housing-project inhabitants engaged in conspicuous consumption, to demonstrate solidarity); child-centeredness or filiarchy; lack of privacy and an almost exaggerated outgoingness or responsiveness to the group; church membership; and strong emphasis on social adjustment as a goal of education.[65] The author did not claim that Park Forest was typical of all suburbs; he did think, though, that it was characteristic of the "twenty-five-to-thirty-five-year-old white collar organization man with a wife, a salary between $6,000 and $7,000 [as of 1953], one child, and another on the way."[66]

A second study of workers in a large corporation disputed the conclusions of Whyte. Bennett M. Berger in 1957 studied a quite different kind of suburb than Park Forest, one peopled by automobile workers who followed a relocated plant from Richmond to Milpitas, California. The men were not, like those in Park Forest, on the make or upwardly mobile, but like Warner's lower-middle class. But, like the Park Forest men, they were family oriented. There was frequent neighboring, but little formal visiting, again as in Park Forest. Unlike Park Forest, however, there was relatively little participation in voluntary organizations. Berger's paradigm was "counter-vanguarding," that is, based on a conviction that the then-current "myth of suburbia" fostered by men like Whyte was wrong. He concluded that suburbanites bring with them their old way of life—based on age, income, occupation, education, and rural-urban background—merely living it in a new environment.[67] The suburb was not merely the domestic aspect of the corporation or "organization"; the upward mobility it reflected was not the mobility of individuals, but rather the mobility of a stratum. These semi-skilled persons moved up the status ladder not individually by their own efforts but as a cohort by the skill of their union bargainers.

One of the researchers involved in the study of Park Forest was Herbert J. Gans who, in the mid-1950s, became interested in the way working class families became acculturated to middle class life styles. Like Berger, he rejected the growing myth of

[65] William H. Whyte, Jr., *The Organization Man* (New York: Simon & Schuster, Inc., 1956).

[66] Ibid., p. 281.

[67] Bennett M. Berger, *Working Class Suburb: A Study of Auto Workers in Suburbia* (Berkeley: University of California Press, 1960).

suburbia and when he saw that it was becoming accepted and actually influencing architects and planners, he felt it was essential that research take the place of irresponsible journalism. Since Berger had already studied a working class suburb, Gans chose a Levittown as the site of his study. He lived in such a community as a participant observer during its first two years, beginning in 1958. It turned out to include components characteristic of both the Berger and the Whyte communities, resulting in a "multinucleated" status structure, one for the working class, one for the lower-middle class, and one for the upper-middle class, each vulnerable to subnucleation by religion. He found that the lives of people were changed by moving to the suburb but, as Berger had also reported, "their basic ways remain the same; they do not develop new styles or ambitions for themselves and their children."[68] Rather than the class-homogeneous suburb described by Whyte and by Berger, Gans advocated more diversified ones. "The ideal solution is more, better, and more variegated new towns and suburbs, but the first priority in the years to come is more . . . communities for the less affluent."[69] Such communities were the answer to the negative concomitants of the size, density, and heterogeneity of urbanism and should be available for all rather than only for the affluent.

Still even Gans had found that the upper-middle class segment of Levittown did show the results reported for Park Forest. He found a difference between residents he labeled Mobiles or Transients, who were, in effect, merely sojourning in Levittown on their way up the class ladder, and those he called Settlers for whom Levittown was the terminal point. The involvements of the Mobiles were likely to be more in the form of participation in organizations; the involvements of the Settlers, in informal visiting. More relevant was the fact that the professional Transients "often develop [deeper] roots in their profession and its social groups [than in community groups; thus] occupational or functional roots . . . [replace] spatial roots."[70] In general, the Transients tended to be what Merton called "cosmopolitans," and the Settlers, "locals" so far as orientation was concerned.[71] R. E. Park

[68] Herbert J. Gans, *The Levittowners* (New York: Pantheon Books, Inc., 1967), pp. 408–9.

[69] Ibid., p. 432.

[70] Ibid., p. 198.

[71] Robert K. Merton, *Social Theory and Social Structure* (New York: The Free Press, 1957), pp. 393–99.

had also commented on the limited involvement of many people with locale. Professional people, he had noted, were not interested in the local community as such, but rather in their professions.[72] If the housekeeping details of the area where they lived were properly taken care of and if security were adequate, they could scarcely care less about neighboring or social contacts with others in the area. And with the further improvement in transportation and burgeoning communication media, there was arising what Marshall McLuhan was calling the global village. The individuals on the jet flying to Switzerland introduce themselves to one another as IBM or AID rather than as Tarrytowners or Bethesdans. Xerox is nearer—and dearer—to them than Westchester. The segment of their personalities that belongs to it is larger than the segment belonging anywhere else. Whyte's organization is, indeed, their community. We shall meet these individuals again in Chapter 10.

Sociologists knew a considerable amount about communities by the middle of the century. They knew how cities grew, how groups distributed themselves in space, and what the concomitants for human relationships were; they knew what the social class structure of communities was like and also about decision makers and power structures. They knew something about rural communities and what living in cities did to people. Then, as we have shown, their paradigms blew up in their faces. They could no longer accommodate the anomalies that the "novelties of fact" were imposing on them.

This debacle of the classic community paradigms came at a peculiarly critical moment of time, a time in which there was enormous preoccupation with change, not in the abstract sense in which it had been studied in the past, but in the very concrete and specific form it was taking at mid-century, the form, that is, known as "modernization." All the classic paradigms had provided for "changes." The growth of cities and the ecological processes themselves all implied changes: the social mobility of the Yankee City model implied changes that would result in the assimilation of ethnic groups; the power paradigms had implied, if they had not explicitly stated, changes in the wielders of power if not in the structure of power itself, although Dahl's model had also shown changes over time even here; the Gemeinschaft-

---

[72] R. E. Park, "Community Organization and the Romantic Temper," in E. C. Hughes et al., eds., *Robert Ezra Park, Human Communities, the City, and Human Ecology* (New York: The Free Press, 1952), pp. 64–72.

Gesellschaft paradigm was, in effect, itself a paradigm of change in the form of urbanization and industrialization.

But none had anticipated the changes of the 1960s when new revolutions were being proclaimed daily. The decade of the 1960s was to be a great testing period during which communities grappled with problems without much help from community paradigms. Not all the revolutions that were proclaimed reverberated through the community, but at least two of them did, one dealing with blacks and one with poor people. Together they constituted profound upheavals. The classic paradigms were either of little help in meeting these tests or they were actually used against communities themselves.

Part Three

"Modernization" at Home and in the Third World
as a Test of Community Paradigms

The Community as Target of Change: Black People and Poor People

"MODERNIZING" RACE RELATIONS

Until the middle of the twentieth century,"modernizing" race relations had meant revamping the old Jim Crow pattern, a hangover from the plantation system where it may have been viable but was now completely anachronistic in an urban industrial society. It had meant bringing the legal, political, economic, and social systems into line with modern industrialism.[1] It had meant making the Bill of Rights apply to black as well as to white citizens. For the inherited community structures were totally unsuited for dealing with race relations in modern, industrial, technological, urban communities. By the last third of the century those forms of modernization, merely bringing to blacks the modernization of the late eighteenth and nineteenth centuries, were no longer enough. By that time modernization was beginning to mean the generation of power in the black community, "decolonization."

---

[1] Joseph S. Himes, "Changing Social Roles in the New South," *Southwestern Social Science Quarterly* 37 (December 1956), pp. 236 ff.

Who Asks What Questions?

The major trends in research on race relations had always been guided by white scientists and answered the questions they asked, questions about white people for the most part. This research had emphasized the nature of race differences with strong emphasis on their cultural origins, the nature of white race prejudice, the nature of white discrimination against black people, the effects of segregation, and similar questions. So far as blacks were concerned, the methods and results might as well have referred to some other species. They implied "white people as actors, feelers, thinkers vis-à-vis a more or less faceless, anonymous, almost inert nonwhite population."[2] Even when white researchers dealt with black people, they still tended to answer questions that interested white people: crime, family disorganization, sexual irregularities, out-of-wedlock births, the female-headed family, the class structure. Even the great giants —E. Franklin Frazier and Charles S. Johnson—had operated in this basically white-oriented research framework, looking at black communities with the aid of white paradigms. Thus, most of what we have known about black communities has been what white social scientists have been interested in studying. The classic paradigms they designed were models of the world and how it functioned from a white perspective; they were not necessarily at all functional for answering the questions that black people were asking.[3]

Blacks in the Classic Paradigms

Black people had both confirmed and confounded the classic—white-oriented—community paradigms. The ecological model had been found suitable only up to a point: Frazier had found it adequate when the number of blacks was not too large; Duncan had proved it demonstrably inadequate a generation later. Warner had found that the upward mobility pattern of ethnic groups did not operate among blacks; for them it was complicated

[2] Jessie Bernard, in a review of H. M. Blalock, Jr., *Toward a Theory of Minority-Group Relations,* in *International Migration Review* 3 (Spring 1969), p. 100.

[3] See, for example, H. M. Blalock, Jr., *Toward a Theory of Minority-Group Relations* (New York: John Wiley & Sons, Inc., 1967), pp. 153–54.

by the subordination factor. The community power paradigms had not even had to take account of blacks; if blacks had any power it was entirely derivative and therefore not worth including. The folk-urban form of the Gemeinschaft-Gesellschaft paradigm had fit moderately well, to be sure, but such a situation was no longer tolerable to blacks.

By the last third of the century a new black élite had grown up who had been exposed to a myriad of modern currents of thought and they were no longer willing to see themselves or their world through the paradigms of white people. They were articulate, educated, and militant. They wanted to define their own problems, derive their own paradigms to interpret their own experience, or apply white-supplied paradigms for their own ends. Instead of the statement, "If whites are to maintain a constant power advantage over Negroes, then the degree of their mobilization relative to that of Negroes must not only increase with percent Negro, but it must also rise at an increasing rate,"[4] they gave their own version, "If we are to achieve a power advantage over whites, then the degree of our mobilization relative to that of whites must not only increase with the percent black, but it must also rise at an increasing rate." They were no longer willing to allow white people alone to define black identity or to allow the paradigms established by white scientists to guide thinking about the black community. They wanted paradigms that led to data that would be useful for interpreting the black community from their own point of view. Or they wanted to use white-originated paradigms in their own way. They wanted to analyze class in the black community according to new criteria, not those that had been evolved for the white community; they wanted more appropriate conceptualizations of upward social mobility, new collective representations, and new approaches to power. They saw black people as no longer a folk but urban men and women who had to be whipped into self-acceptance, remolded, and rescued from the brainwashing they had been subjected to for centuries, which caused them to view themselves always as deviant or imperfect or deficient white people. They had to be taught to respect themselves. A cultural tradition had to be supplied. The blacks envisaged in the paradigms of white scientists had to be replaced by a new black man. The paradigms of white scientists alone could not achieve this goal. If they could be

---

[4] Ibid., p. 153.

used at all, they had to be used for black ends, even against whites if that should prove necessary. In the great upheavals of the 1960s it may have been the violence that garnered most of our attention, but it was the "war of the paradigms" that had the profoundest effects. It was not so much the invention of new paradigms that was involved as the new uses made of old ones.

Class in the Black Community: New Criteria

In the past, Caucasoid features had been incorporated into the black standards of beauty, and by and large a light skin and "good" hair helped raise status. The new élite attacked these standards, which were spurious to them. Knowing the mechanisms through which class structures maintain themselves, they knew how to attack them. They withdrew the rewards of envy from those who accepted white-based class—in this case, Caucasoid—characteristics. They ridiculed rather than envied the pretentious social life that modeled itself on the white world. They upstaged the older élites, withholding deference or positively denigrating them by refusing either respect for their white-accredited achievements or admission to their membership and by expressing contempt, sometimes denouncing them as Uncle Toms. Theirs was not the old sour-grapes resentment of the "masses" but rather a coldly analytic derision based on documentable data drawn from sophisticated paradigms, primarily Fanonist. The upper classes had been co-opted, or bought out. They were whitey's stooges. They were phony or ersatz white people. They may have assumed the role of "spokesmen" for the black community, but they certainly were not its leaders, nor did they wield any real power.

The reaction of the older élites to the challenges of the new was at first one of uncertainty and ambivalence. They were initially fearful that the intransigence of the new élite might endanger their own relations with the outside world. When they learned that at least some of those in the outside world were willing to accept—even encourage—the collectivist approach, if not black militancy, they themselves came to accept and encourage it also. Many caught the excitement. It *was* reassuring to see the upsurge of creativity released by the new self-definition. They found it reassuring to be able to be unashamedly themselves, authentic black men and women.

Social Mobility in the Black Community:
The Dysfunctionality of the Classic Paradigm

The classic community paradigms of upward social mobility had implied a one-by-one, individualistic rise, family by family. And according to this model there was nothing anomalous about the experience of black people in the second half of the century. There was an increase in the size of the black middle class in the 1960s as measured in terms of three of the standard criteria of class—income, occupation, and education.[5] All these indexes gave evidence of upward social mobility as provided for in the class-structure model and were therefore expectable. Black people were merely following the same pattern as that of the ethnic groups described in Chicago and Yankee City. To be sure, the fourth standard class criterion, residence, was equivocal. Unlike the residential dispersion that occurred in Yankee City as ethnic groups left Zone I, segregation in the case of blacks increased.[6] But with this—admittedly crucial—exception, the upward mobility of blacks confirmed the classic paradigms. Why, then, did the new black élite find them inadequate?

There were at least three cogent reasons why accepting them was dysfunctional for black people: (1) the costs of individual upward mobility in terms of mental and emotional health were excessive; (2) the costs to the black community in terms of class schism were excessive; and (3) the vulnerability to exploitation by the white world was enhanced.

When upward social mobility among blacks was viewed as an individual process by which people entered the outside world one by one, single file so to speak, each entrant was extremely vulnerable psychologically; he was, in effect, stripped of emotional support. He entered the outside world presumably as "one of the boys," but knowing full well that he was not. His blackness was treated as a stigma which had to be ignored or overlooked. Humiliating statuses like Tomism and tokenism were inevitable if, hopefully, only transitional. Upward mobility under these circumstances violated almost everything we know about the importance, even indispensability, of a nurturing social matrix for

---

[5] Herman P. Miller and Dorothy K. Newman, *Recent Trends in Social and Economic Conditions of Negroes in the United States* (Bureau of Labor Statistics Report No. 347, July 1968), pp. 8, 16, 18.

[6] Karl Taeuber and Alma Taeuber, *Negroes in Cities* (Chicago: Aldine Publishing Company, 1965).

the normal functioning of human nature. It took an overwhelming, even exhausting, tolerance of stress to be able to undergo this grueling ordeal. No wonder studies of the mental illness of black people in cities showed that they paid an inordinate price for upward mobility in the form of high mental-illness rates.[7]

The costs to the black community were also excessive. Individual upward mobility led to co-optation of successful individuals by the white community, thus alienating them from the black community and depriving it of their leadership. The upwardly mobile had had to keep a distance between themselves and the black masses in order to protect their own status. The fracturing of the black community thus rendered it practically powerless for all intents and purposes.

Cayton and Drake, finally, believed that this atomistic way of dealing with black people according to the specifications of the white paradigm was a deliberate Rightist ploy, used by the Left as well, for controlling them. Such exploiters tried to "smother the Negro problem as a whole" by dealing with blacks as individuals, by making individual deals with them, thus rendering the situation one they could control.[8]

For at least these reasons, and doubtless for many more, the lesson to be learned from the data generated by the classic paradigms of upward mobility and class was, patently, that policies based on the classic paradigms were destructive to black people. Clearly other constructs were needed to guide thinking and policy with respect to black communities. One such was supplied by Nathan Hare and took the form of a collective approach to upward mobility.

A Collectivist Paradigm for Upward Mobility

The old policy of dealing with, let us say, workers one by one had long since been replaced in industry by the more modern idea of collective bargaining. We have already referred to Bennett Berger's contrast between the upward mobility, individual by

---

[7] Seymour Parker and Robert J. Kleiner, *Mental Illness in the Urban Negro Community; A Pointed Inquiry into Goal-Striving and Stress in a Climate of Limited Opportunity* (New York: The Free Press, 1966), Chapter 10.

[8] Horace Cayton and St. Clair Drake, *Black Metropolis* (New York: Harper Torchbook, 1961), p. xxix.

individual, in Park Forest with the stratum-mobility of the workers in his suburb. The two patterns were polar opposites with reverberations not only in the work lives but also in the community lives of those involved. Berger's semiskilled workers were not upper-lower but lower-middle class, a status achieved not one by one, but collectively by way of their representatives' bargaining skill.

Now Hare wanted to have the advantage of a collective approach for blacks too. He wanted them to move forward in a solid phalanx rather than, like the Persians at Thermopylae, single file, to be picked off one by one. He wanted a collective entity for whom leaders spoke rather than a fractionated congeries for whom no one could speak. Black students were to learn to stop thinking individualistically and begin to think collectively. They were to "inspire and sustain a sense of collective destiny as a people and a consciousness of the value of education in a technological society."[9] Even though traditional black education did attempt to rehabilitate students by inculcating pride, dignity, and self-respect in them, still it was in the individualistic white pattern, facilitating upward mobility according to its specifications but not tying it up with the fate of others less privileged. The students did not see the relevance of their own privileges for "an animated communalism." Hare rejected Du Bois's Talented-Tenth schema, the educated élite who were to go forth from the colleges to share their own achievement with their fellows. Even that strategy was too individualistic, super-tokenism even at best; it left out "motivation growing out of collective community involvement."

Hare was clearly not calling for a Gemeinschaft kind of communitarianism. There was nothing of the folk mystique about it. This was to be a fighting phalanx advancing as a unit to take the place of the old ladder image of individuals climbing up rungs one by one or the old serpentine image of an avant-garde pulling a column behind it.

The Mystique of Soul

There had been a fairly lively controversial literature in the 1960s about the validity of the concept of a "black" or "Negro"

---

[9] Quoted by John H. Bunzel, "Black Studies at San Francisco State," *The Public Interest,* no. 13 (Fall 1968), p. 36.

culture. Several communities of scientists had contributed to it. Those interested in marriage and the family had struggled with the question, Should the black family, especially as it appeared in urban ghettos and in the Caribbean, be viewed as the expression of a separate black or Negro culture or should it be viewed as a deviation from the prevailing outside culture? Students of race relations had also pondered the question of the reality of a separate black culture.

For the most part, black students of the subject in the past had resisted the idea of a separate and different black culture. The result of accepting it, however sympathetic in intent, was negative. Black culture was denigrated and assumed somehow or other to be inferior. When the new élite reviewed the matter, however, they saw here, as in the case of other situations, that white paradigms could be used constructively as well as destructively; they could be invoked to explain or interpret positive aspects of black community life as well as negative aspects.

The black version of the culture paradigm came in the form of the concept of Soul. It was analogous to the better articulated concept of *Volkgeist* or folk mentality or "spirit" which had enchanted the romantics of the nineteenth century, especially in Germany, where it had even achieved the status of a scientific paradigm and a community of scientists who devoted themselves to research on folk psychology. Blacks even used the same term as that used by the German theorists, for Soul is an acceptable translation of Geist. Viewing black people by way of this paradigm, they were no longer empty individuals bereft by slavery of a culture of their own or, at best, only marginal or fringe participants in a degraded form of white culture. They had a spiritual bond that they understood and that white people could not. Soul was an indefinable, ineffable, but desirable something; black people had it but white people could hardly even aspire to it. It was the animating spirit behind their music, their dance, and their style. It even expressed itself in their taste in food, their language, and their speech. Not even all black people shared it. Those who rejected their blackness did not. Some rare, exceptional white people might achieve it. This paradigm served the same function as the original romantic prototype: It defined community of spirit. In addition, it served also to help overcome alienation. It took the stigma away from blackness. It demanded recognition of blackness on its own terms, not on white terms. During the riots of the 1960s blacks protected their property by inscribing Soul Brother on its walls. Black shops advertised that they sold soul food. Soul was invoked to counteract the devastation of urbanism.

Another prototype of the paradigm of Soul was more theoretical; it was the Franco-African concept of negritude. Fanon accepted it, but with reservations.[10] He recognized it as useful in a transitional stage, but only then. He did not believe in opposing white racial narcissism with black narcissism, except that such a myth was temporarily necessary in the process of achieving raceless humanism. It had relatively little impact on blacks in the United States. They were beginning to wonder about raceless humanism.

Melting Pot: "Getting Ready"

We noted in Chapter 3 that when intervention in community processes undermined the natural ecological processes there was considerable controversy about the goals of intervention. Should it seek heterogeneity or homogeneity? In Chapter 4 we noted also the goal of assimilation which is expressed in the melting-pot construct as contrasted with the pluralism construct, illustrated by the persistence of ethnicity. American communities have been struggling with the complexities of ethnic and class differences for a very long time. Such differences were exacerbated when race differences were also involved. What, precisely, was the most suitable kind of relationship between black and white?

There had once been an ideal for race relations, as with ethnic groups, that would render race, like ethnicity, irrelevant in all human contacts. There is, for example, Fanon's raceless humanism. People would interact as human beings rather than as members of a race or ethnic groups. There would not be, perhaps, in the case of blacks as in the case of white ethnic groups, a melting pot—although there were some who did look for that among the races also—but at least there would be integration.

But the new black élite did not find that enough. A black man, unsupported, single-handed, could achieve integration only by sacrificing part of his identity. Integration implied inferiority in differences. The black man felt he had to become an ersatz middle class white man in order to achieve acceptance in an integrated community. The new black élite now wanted a different, racist, basis for interaction—interaction based on a recognition rather than a denial of differences. They wanted blacks to be accepted and respected as black people, entitled to their own style.

---

[10] Frantz Fanon, *Black Skin, White Masks* (New York: Grove Press, Inc., 1968), pp. 32 ff. Fanon seems to have gotten the term from Jean-Paul Sartre and was not very happy with it.

Resistant white people fighting desegregation had often put forth the argument that most blacks were not "ready" yet. And the standard answer had been, "We've been waiting over three hundred years and if we continue to wait we will never be 'ready.' " But, as with so many clichés, black leaders were now finding a kernel of truth in this former anathema. It was true that without some kind of preparation the black community was vulnerable to sociological "bends" as the pressure of outside repressive forces relaxed. The preparation needed for them to be able to hold their own was not, however, the kind implied in the old white defense against desegregation—imitation of white patterns and standards—but a cultural and sociological, as well as occupational, one. Black people needed time and privacy to find themselves as a group. Once they had acquired the cultural matrix to give them collective support and backing they would be able to enter the outside world freely, as members of closed ranks rather than as isolated individuals. They could then order chitlings and watermelon in public, as secure Jews could order bagels and lox. The new élite therefore called for a form of separatism that would give them an opportunity to forge this black identity so that when they met with the outside world it would be with at least a modicum of power, without self-consciousness, shame, humiliation, or self-denigration; as bona fide black people, not make-believe white people.

For some, this separatism was not a transitional phase but an ultimate goal. In the 1920s there had been an abortive movement among black people to "return" to Africa. In the 1930s a modified form of spatial separatism was proposed in the form of a Negro Soviet in the confidently expected Soviet America.[11] In the 1960s there was talk of a separate state to be turned over to black people. A variety of arguments ranging from the mystical to the strategic were invoked. The white man was evil and blacks should have nothing to do with him. The separatism was there, not originally of the blacks' making but of the whites'; so be it. The attitude was, Let's make the best of it by accepting the ghetto but controlling it ourselves. Some appealed to localism as a power base. Desegregation would disperse the black population and, in effect, disenfranchise it. Segregated in the largest cities it could exert a swing vote and thus be a major influence in state and national elections.

In any event, the decision with respect to what form separat-

[11] James S. Allen, *The Negro Question in the United States* (New York: International Publishers Co., Inc., 1936).

ism would take was to be a black decision, not one imposed from the outside. "Whether the [Black] Nation is to be a collection of enclaves or a geographical location, existing within or without the United States, is a question we must ultimately answer as a people. Black People . . . [must] be prepared to face and decide that question in the foreseeable future."[12]

This call for separatism was dismaying to many in the outside world who genuinely believed in "one nation, indivisible" or who, in any event, were attempting to prevent the two-society future the Kerner Report had warned against. Separatism seemed to them retrograde, a step backward, a return to segregation. Blacks did not see it that way—not all of them, at any rate. They did not look upon separatism as a final goal but rather as a transitional phase toward ultimate full participation, perhaps even Fanon's raceless humanism. They had in mind the ethnic pluralism that had become the actual substitute for the melting pot.

Black Power: Filling a Paradigmatic Void

The study of power in black communities had been one of the most neglected in all of the social sciences. There was, therefore, little in the normal-science research literature that dealt with it. When black power received attention, it was incidental, mainly in connection with the study of other aspects of community, such as violence, for example. This neglect was understandable since there was so little power in the black community and most of what there was, was derived from the outside world.[13]

Within the black folk communities there had been little occasion for the exercise of power. There were few policy decisions to be made. Order tended to rest on the authority of folkways and those who knew from experience how to interpret them. Where coercion was essential, physical power, even violence, could be invoked, and it often was.

Even in urban communities that had lost their isolated folk character there were few, if any, power resources in the form of jobs, patronage, votes, or other prerogatives. What power there

---

[12] Position paper for the black studies program at the Federal City College, *Washington Post*, March 6, 1969.

[13] For a formal paradigmatic statement of the power relationships between the races, see Blalock, *Toward a Theory of Minority-Group Relations*, Chapter 4.

was, therefore, tended to be derivative, derived, as noted earlier, from the outside world. And the black men who achieved it often did so by manipulating their white sponsors even, sometimes, at the expense of their black constituencies. Thus even in northern urban communities when a modicum of at least token participation in the political system was achieved, there was notably little payoff within the black community.[14]

Black powerlessness had received considerably more attention than black power. Du Bois had analyzed it in terms of undeveloped organizational skills; others had seen the lack of solidarity, especially as revealed in the class schism characteristic of black communities, as an obstacle to the accumulation and exercise of power. In this view, powerlessness implied structural bases; if the structure of the community were changed, power could be achieved. But others saw that sometimes the system was only an intervening variable. For some kinds of powerlessness were subjective, psychological, and socialized into people, so that changes in the system did not immediately and automatically make power available. C. S. Johnson had noted how black urban in-migrants discovered public agencies as means for getting something for nothing, thus fostering dependency and endangering working habits and self-respect.[15] The idea of generating power by their own efforts within their own ranks was therefore slow in maturing. Not, in fact, until the 1960s did the importance of independence as a basis for power become incorporated into the programs and policies of the black community.

So strong was the concept of black powerlessness that when the term "black power" was first used by Stokely Carmichael in 1966 it was immediately interpreted in terms of the only kind of power generally conceded to blacks, namely, physical violence. And it took several years before exegesis, participated in by almost everyone, finally winnowed the frightening chaff and revealed the legitimate grain. Black power came to mean not only self-defense against white aggression and violence (Carmichael's original emphasis), but also the acquisition of such power resources as ownership of property, control of ghetto schools,

---

[14] See Cayton and Drake, *Black Metropolis,* Chapter 13, "Democracy and Political Expediency" for the history of black political power in Chicago in the twentieth century, and Harold M. Baron and Associates, "Black Powerlessness in Chicago," *Transaction* 5 (November 1968), pp. 27–33, for an updating of the Cayton-Drake account.

[15] Charles S. Johnson, *Shadow of the Plantation* (Chicago: University of Chicago Press, 1934), p. 86.

review of local police, and representation in local governments and agencies determining policies that affected black people.

But how is such power achieved? How is powerlessness overcome? With so much to be done by and for the black community, almost any channel toward power that promised anything at all seemed worth a try. To gain economic power, ownership of businesses and industries, accumulation of capital, and positions which enable the offering of jobs and employment are necessary. To gain political power, candidates must be made to compete for the black vote; blacks had to win office themselves. To some blacks, black power meant not primarily such economic and political power—which, in any event, seemed to them unattainable—but physical power, even violence. At least it seemed to work.

There is no more dramatic contrast between "white" and "black" sociology than the research and theorizing with respect to violence in the 1960s. To the communities of white social scientists the major concerns were the urban riots, guerrilla tactics, bombs, and property destruction, and the major question they saw was, What can we do to stop such violence? To the black militants the question was, rather, What is the function of violence in rebellions, in "decolonization," in the achievement of racial identity, or even of violence as therapy? With such different questions in mind the two sets of thinkers selected different paradigms through which to look at the community and sought different kinds of data.

Perhaps no area of concern had elicited a more extensive literature—from aggression of individuals to war among nations—than that on violence. All the behavioral and social sciences had contributed paradigms on the subject. Several were selected as useful by the new leaders. Maoism taught that power came out of the barrel of a gun and the whole concept of guerrilla warfare received elaboration and support from Maoist thinking. Some black leaders applied Fanon's psychiatric paradigm of violence (which even justified murder as therapy) as a method for achieving self-respect. And others, following Fanon, saw it as a necessary reserve weapon in decolonization. Fanon had analyzed the processes by which colonial empires had degraded natives. He taught that the African was no longer to submit or show deference to the white settlers and thus legitimate the status quo; he must cease to accept the white man's brainwashing. In addition, he must be ready for violence at all times. Fanon's thesis had great appeal to militant leaders in the United States, for if it did, indeed, apply to the American scene, there became available the whole armory of intellectual weapons that had been generated by the dismantling of empires. Much that would be judged criminal by white paradigms could be exalted to the level of a necessary aspect of a political war of liberation. Some black leaders did apply the Fanon model literally to the United States; they spoke of the black people as "the colony." They were to be liberated by a revolutionary movement, as other colonial peoples had been in other parts of the world—by violence, if necessary.

In addition to therapeutic violence, cold strategic violence, and "decolonization" violence, violence as communication also became an issue. Violence was justified as producing results faster than other methods. More to the point was the strategic use of violence as threats, for it seemed that both violence and the threat of violence paid off. Violence communicated in a way that got through, as more restrained forms of communication did not. It forced the outside world to pay attention.

White Guilt as a Power Resource

Gunnar Myrdal in his monumental study of race relations in the United States had pointed out that the American creed made white people feel guilty about their treatment of blacks, because it so flagrantly violated the ideals imbedded in that creed. Black leaders learned quite early that this guilt could be used for bringing about change. Martin Luther King had made effective use of such white guilt feelings as a power resource. Some black strategists were less idealistic than King had been; they assessed white guilt more cynically. They could discount the ever predicted white backlash because they knew, or felt, that in a crisis white guilt would triumph. They could use the moral scruples of the conscientious as weapons against them. This guilt, they knew, went beyond its historical roots. Not many people, especially the very large proportion with ethnic backgrounds, could sincerely assume guilt for the slave trade or for slavery itself. But everyone of goodwill could be made to feel guilt as benefactor in a basically unfair "game." There was an intrinsic pathos in the black's position in today's world.

But some black leaders rejected the use of, or dependence on, white guilt. It was too easy to be of any value. Whites with "a hunger for humiliation," who became "so bogged down in guilt" that they lost "their concept of what are decent procedures in dealing with human beings," were of no help.[16] Too-easy victories were worthless. In order to be meaningful, victory had to be wrested from opponents worthy of their steel, not people disarmed by guilt. Sentimental liberals need not apply.

Others raised the question of the value of white goodwill, guilt-motivated or not. Was it really a power resource? Was it an asset? The generation that had fought for civil rights had believed it was. Martin Luther King had relied on it heavily. Now some were asking whether blacks should even try to enter coalitions with whites. That "conventional white aid to blacks is exploitative" was their assessment.[17] They leaned rather toward the Machiavellian point of view: It was better to have people fear than to love you. The threat of violence—at least the rhetoric of violence, if nothing more—was more powerful than the often slothful goodwill of white people.

Fanon had even argued that white ill will was a power resource. Warner, it will be recalled, had noted the importance of an outside enemy as a unifying force in the community. James Q. Wilson noted that "the cultural value of Black Power or race pride depends in part on its being resisted by whites. The existence of a 'white enemy' may be . . . necessary for the growth of Negro self-respect."[18] It was for this reason that too-easy victories were judged of little value, why the capitulation of appeasing liberals without a fight was assessed as just no good. Blacks needed and wanted strong enough opposition to sharpen their claws; they needed earned victories, not concessions.

Internal Power Struggles

The derivative nature of power in the black community had meant that in order to exercise power one had to be able to deal effectively with those who controlled political resources in the outside world. The older upper class had exerted what leadership

[16] Kenneth Guscott, head of the Boston NAACP, quoted in Bernard D. Nossiter, "Ghetto Experiment: Massive Aid Without Strings," *Washington Post,* January 12, 1969.

[17] Ibid.

[18] James Q. Wilson, "The Urban Unease: Community vs. City," *The Public Interest,* no. 12 (Summer 1968), p. 39.

it did exert "by affiliating only with the 'proper' race causes."[19] Being "a race man" was a standard role in the black community.[20] This meant that often the power was in the hands of black persons who were more at home in the outside world than in the black community; they were not "really" black at all. And sometimes, although allegedly speaking in behalf of the black community, they were rejected by the black community itself as in no sense representative of them. They were rejected, perhaps, even as exploitative of them. Often these intermediaries felt no identity with the black community and rejected it as much as it rejected them.

In the last third of the century this situation was no longer tenable. Upheavals were taking place, including power struggles that dramatically modified the traditional class-power structure and forced "the old upper class . . . to identify with *all* Negroes instead of solely with an exclusive class."[21]

The infusion of vast amounts of money into ghetto communities in the 1960s for reform or "modernization" programs of one kind or another provided incentive for struggles to control these funds. Sometimes they took ideological form and were fought with the paradigms of nationhood, solidarity, and unity; their leaders quoted Kwame Nkrumah, Fanon, and Mao. Sometimes they took very practical and nonideological, even violent, form not too different from Mafia-like struggles or old-fashioned gang warfare.[22]

Most modern peoples have gone through the throes of development in "privacy," and their power struggles are revealed—equivocally and indeterminately, if at all—only through history. Blacks of the United States, and colonial peoples everywhere today, do not have such protective covering. Their struggles take place in full view of television, the daily press, and researching social scientists. The Lancasters and the Yorks could fight and murder and maneuver in comparative secrecy; the Urban League, the NAACP, the Black Panthers, SNCC, CORE, RAM, and all the

[19] Seymour Leventman, "Class and Ethnic Tensions: Minority Group Leadership in Transition," *Sociology and Social Research* 50 (April 1966), p. 373.

[20] Cayton and Drake, *Black Metropolis,* pp. 392–95.

[21] Leventman, "Class and Ethnic Tensions," p. 375.

[22] For an example of community power struggle in Philadelphia, see Leventman, "Class and Ethnic Tensions," pp. 371–76; for an example from Boston, see Nossiter, "Ghetto Experiment."

United Black Brothers were accorded no such privilege. Theirs were open and widely heralded "power struggles."

"MODERNIZING" WELFARE

Welfare was another aspect of community life that needed modernizing. Love—medieval Christian charity—had long since proved inadequate for modern communities. So, too, had philanthropy, that is, nineteenth-century humanitarianism, as well as social work or twentieth-century professionalism. The much-tinkered-with legacy of the distant and not-so-distant past, the so-called relief or public welfare system had to be revamped and incorporated into the economic and social systems. Modernization meant, instead of a maze of ad hoc welfare programs, a welfare state. An extremely complex set of economic and political paradigms underlay the thinking invested in the new approach.[23] But, strangely enough, there was relatively little theoretical input from sociology.

The Poor in the Class Paradigms

The great, majestic paradigms had supplied guidance to communities only indirectly, if at all, and then in such an abstract form as to be of little concrete help at the community level. For what the community had to contend with was a very complex phenomenon. At least two categories of poor people had long since been distinguished by those who had to deal with them, the "worthy" and the "unworthy" poor. Some paradigms dealt with one, some with the other.

The "unworthy poor" antedated industrialism and continued through "postindustrialism." From at least the seventeenth century they had been the bane of poor-law administrators. They were "sturdy beggars," people who were not work oriented, who, though apparently able-bodied, were not, as the canons of the Protestant ethic prescribed, working as they should have been. They were the lazy and the shiftless; they were the ne'er-do-wells. They persisted through industrialization in the eighteenth and

---

[23] Harold L. Wilensky and Charles N. Lebeaux, *Industrial Society and Social Welfare* (New York: Russell Sage Foundation, 1958), Part One and pp. 337–51.

nineteenth centuries. They did not share the achievement drive called for by the paradigm of capitalism. Some were incompetents, who could not make the grade; they simply gave up. Some, for whatever reason, were dependent people, unsuited for a competitive economy. Urbanization only highlighted their existence. They were among the homeless persons in boweries, skid rows, and slum rooming houses. In the twentieth century they were still with us, still showing the characteristics Charles Booth had reported at the end of the nineteenth century in London, "ill-regulated" behavior and loose sexual morality, one of the "clearest lines of demarcation between upper- and lower-working class."[24]

By that time the terms *worthy* and *unworthy* had long since been discarded, but the distinction remained. There was *lower-lower* versus *upper-lower, clinical* or *pathological* versus *working class, upper strata,* who responded to encouragement and opportunity for self-help,[25] versus *hard-core.* Whatever the terminology used, some such distinction had always been necessary for dealing with poor people. *Unreachables, multiple-problem families, chiselers,* and *unemployables* were among other terms used to refer to those formerly lumped together as the unworthy poor. One could be unworthy in many ways. Whatever they were called, they were people who found it "increasingly difficult to survive in modern society."[26]

The great paradigms addressed themselves differentially in explaining the existence of the unworthy poor, some in terms of their own defects and others in terms of defects in the economic system.

In the great preindustrial paradigm of capitalism, for example, the unworthy poor were, obviously, the lazy people who did not work and who therefore had to remain poor. In the later Social Darwinian paradigm, they were the incompetents, the unfit, those who were weeded out in the great struggle for existence which resulted benignly in the survival of the fittest: Their existence proved that the system was working. In the Malthusian addendum to the preindustrial paradigm they were the result of excessively

[24] Charles Booth, *Life and Labour of the People in London* (London: Macmillan & Co., Ltd., 1902), p. 335.

[25] Bertram M. Black et al., "Neighborhood Service Centers: A Study and Recommendation," in *Examination of the War on Poverty* (Washington, D.C.: U.S. Government Printing Office, 1967), p. 780.

[26] Herbert J. Gans, *The Urban Villagers* (New York: The Free Press, 1962), p. 268.

high birth rates that held them down in an iron law of wages. In one of the most recent paradigms, known as the "culture of poverty," they were victims of a socialization process that, while it helped them endure their depressed and deprived status, at the same time made it impossible for them to escape it.

On the other hand, in the Marxist paradigm the poor were the exploited proletarians whose sweat and toil produced the surplus value appropriated by the ruling classes. In the Keynesian paradigm they were, by implication, the victims of erroneous fiscal policy that resulted in unemployment. The two sets of paradigms were, clearly, addressing themselves to quite different kinds of phenomena.

There had been only incidental room for the poor in the classic community paradigms. The transitional zone of the ecological model had included inhabitants of slums; areas of disorganization made up of skid rows and boweries that harbored societal discards of all kinds, including failures and deviants; areas of broken and hence poor families; and areas that were the first home of in-migrating ethnic and rural groups as well as of just plain poor people. In the Yankee City model, residence and income were major indexes of class as ranked status and this had to include the lower-lower class. Researchers on the operation of power in the community had studied participation, voting behavior, and, in general, underdogs; they had had to include the poor if for no other reason than to see what coalitions their ward leaders were allying them with. In the wake of these classic paradigms, normal science had accumulated a respectable corpus of research on poor people, but tangentially, as an almost incidental part of other paradigms.

But there had never been much professional mileage for sociologists in the study of poor people as such; there was not much high-level sociological theory that applied to them. True, because of its eclectic heritage, academic sociology had always made room somewhere or other for courses on the "defective and dependent" or the "depressed" classes in departmental offerings.[27] But, as compared to other courses they were without prestige. In later years the study of some of the categories of people who might be encompassed by the term *unworthy poor* was taken over by the community of scientists organized around paradigms of "deviancy."

---

[27] Jessie Bernard and Luther Lee Bernard, *Origins of American Sociology* (New York: Thomas Y. Crowell Company, 1942), Chapters 44–49.

The War on Poverty

The war on poverty, declared in 1964, was designed for the "worthy poor." It presupposed people willing and able to take advantage of any opportunities offered them. It presupposed structural, not deviant, causes for poverty.

Poverty, as distinguished from "the poor," referred to a status rather than to people. As recognized in the classic community paradigms, the status of poverty was a temporary one, and, when combined with hard work and honest behavior, it was considered even an honorable status. It was, in fact, the expected but transitory status of immigrants and rural-urban in-migrants who occupied this low position temporarily until they became acculturated to the ways of the city and worked their way up and out. They might need help from time to time but "with a little-bit-of-luck" and hard work they would in time make the grade. Upward mobility was expectable, if not always for the first generation, at least for succeeding ones. Or poverty might be the result of injustice and exploitation, a condition modifiable by fair wages or steady employment.

Poverty defined as low status is, by definition, ineradicable, since short of complete equality there will always be a lower status. In this sense all that could be hoped for was a social structure so adequate that even those at the bottom were well housed, fed, and educated. And in a free society the ideal was to make the stay at the low status level a transitory, not a permanent, one. Hopefully everyone would sooner or later climb up out of poverty. Not everyone did, to be sure, and, as an almost inevitable corollary, some fell into poverty from a higher status. The war on poverty declared in 1964 implied not the total elimination of inequality but primarily the upgrading of those on the bottom. It posited the kind of normal or remediable poverty accommodated in the community paradigms. There were basically three strategies for prosecuting such a war. One was based on jobs, one on services, and one on income.

The Job Strategy

When the war on poverty was first declared in 1964, the name of the agency charged with prosecuting it, Office of Economic Opportunity, reflected the assumed economic and job-oriented nature of poverty and therefore indicated the strategy contemplated for prosecuting the war against it. Its generals took for granted the creation of jobs as a first priority in any war on poverty. Unfortunately a test of this employment strategy proved not to be feasible; it became a casualty of war itself. To create all the jobs needed to win with this strategy would have called for a public works program of no less than two billion dollars to begin with and perhaps up to ten billion dollars within a few years. By the time the need for such funding was recognized in 1965, the war in Southeast Asia had already begun its heavy drain on the national budget and the poor did not have enough political clout to force their will on the decision makers. A cheaper substitute for jobs had to be found.

The Service Strategy

The substitute took the form of the so-called service strategy implemented by community action programs. In the nineteenth century services to the poor had been performed by "friendly visitors" or by settlement-house workers who went to live among the poor and supplied much-needed services on the basis of humanitarian ideals. But such "charity" and "philanthropy" had become a casualty of Gesellschaft. (Some viewed it as merely a shield of the rich against chiselers, revolutionaries, and the unworthy poor.) Services to or for the poor had become highly bureaucratized. They were delivered family by family by father-knows-best, middle class bureaucrats, who were remote from the grass roots or, rather, from the asphalt streets. Allegedly these workers even developed vested interests in maintaining the demand for their services, thus fostering rather than curing dependency. The services contemplated by the war on poverty were to be different.

Normal-science research on participation had documented the defects of programs that were centrally or bureaucratically concocted and then imposed on passive or apathetic recipients. To be successful, programs had to engage the participants. And that was what the so-called community action programs were originally designed to do. This was a war to be planned and fought by the people themselves. It was to be their war, a do-it-yourself war, and the community was to be its major battleground. The poor were to participate in the planning, advising, and administrative stages, as well as in the actual delivery of services. This could not, obviously, be a return to Gemeinschaft or even to loving "friendly visiting"; but it could be an attack on the bureaucratic rigidities of Gesellschaft, or, one might almost say, on urbanism. There was no lack of imagination in the conception of the services this strategy sought to supply. Among the many kinds of community action programs that developed were Head Start, legal services, health programs, Upward Bound, family planning programs, remedial education and tutorial programs, adult basic education, programs for the older poor, foster grandparents, consumer action programs, Project Enable, rural problems, programs for Indians and for migrants, small business development centers, and VISTA.

The community action program aspect of the war on poverty "tested" two paradigms: participation and power resources. It also shed light on the question, Where is the locus of power?

"Maximum Feasible Participation"

When the expression "maximum feasible participation" by poor people was incorporated into the legislation declaring the war on poverty, no need was felt for extensive discussion of what it meant. Warner, it will be recalled, had placed a great deal of emphasis on participation in associations; Du Bois had done the same for blacks. The De Tocqueville paradigm on participation—"If men are to remain civilized, or to become so, the art of association together must grow and improve, in the same ratio in which the equality of conditions is increased"[28]—was accepted without question. Participation was virtuous. To challenge this belief would have been to violate a cherished collective representation. It is, however, one thing to call for participation; it is quite another to implement it.

Normal-science research had long since documented the class limitation on participation. Large segments of the community did not have access to this powerful tool. They were therefore helpless, vulnerable, and exploitable. In the past, ethnic groups had had indigenous leaders in the form of ward healers or settlement workers to lead them. In recent years, such groups, especially black people, Indians, and Mexican-Americans, had not. What was needed, some poverty warriors argued, was the

---

[28] Alexis De Tocqueville, *Democracy in America*, Part Second (New York: J. & H. G. Langley, 1840), p. 115.

development of indigenous leaders as modern surrogates for the old ward healers and encouragement through such leaders to make their demands known to city hall or any other representative of the bureaucratic establishment. Even if the monetary gains of such action were not monumental, the very process of protest would itself be educational, not to say therapeutic. It would teach participants how power was generated and applied, overcome apathy, and train people to diagnose their own problems and help them figure out means for dealing with them. It would arm them with skills. No one dreamed that action programs might sometimes take the form of civil war.

But, in effect, in some communities they did. The channeling of funds directly into community action programs instead of through city hall or the state house meant that the indigenous leadership for the first time could go to city hall demanding rather than begging. Like participants in the prototype Mobilization for Youth, set up in 1961 to attack problems of juvenile delinquency in New York City, participants in community action programs organized strikes and boycotts; they practiced the tactics of confrontation.

The Establishment was astounded. The idea of poor parents making demands on school principals, or of relief recipients making demands on welfare officials, was more than most bureaucrats could stomach. Nor could the public or Congress. Poor people should be humble and grateful, not arrogantly insisting on their rights. To officials in city hall it looked as though the federal government had entered into a coalition with the slums against them. And they were not men to take this sort of thing lying down. When it dawned on city governments that the Office of Economic Opportunity really was supporting civil wars against school boards, welfare offices, and chiefs of police, to name only a few targets, signals lit up in Congress, and pressure was exerted to cease and desist. Stop subsidizing revolution!

Congress got the message. Increasingly city hall was dealt in. After several years of confusion this campaign of the war on poverty was, in effect, liquidated, one way or another. Despite numerous efforts at the evaluation of its results, it was conceded that adequate evaluation was impossible. Most professional critics, after giving the community action programs A for effort, finally qualified their appreciative comments with a long list of defects and failures.

In the end, the Office of Economic Opportunity proved to have little power. Even if it had had power, it is doubtful if it

could have conferred that power on the local indigenous community leaders. It was not the real thing in the sense of Dahl's
power resources. Such derived or conferred power lacked cred-
ibility. To those reared in traditional power patterns there was
something very odd about relief recipients, for example, making
demands. It didn't quite come off.

There was once more the question of the locus of power. Was
the local community the real battleground in a war on poverty?
With the best will in the world on the part of the establishment
could the community make much of a dent on poverty? Actually,
how much power was there in the community? How much overall
leverage did it have? Decisions in Washington on monetary or
fiscal policy, budgetary priorities, and the allocation of contracts
could have more to do with the success of programs in the local
community than even the maximum participants. However valuable a community action program might be in putting pressure on
landlords by way of rent strikes, on school or welfare bureaucracies, on exploiting shops and markets, or on other local sources of
exploitation or disaffection, the question of how much direct
impact it had on poverty itself still had to be raised.

The Income Maintenance Strategy

However successful the community action strategy may have
been, by the 1970s local communities were buckling under the
weight of their welfare burdens. Some were on the verge of
bankruptcy. It was becoming clear that welfare was no longer
merely a local community matter. The national government
would have to step in to share the load. The new approach was
called an income strategy and was heralded by one of its major
proponents as marking the end of one era and the beginning of
another.[29]

If lack of income is all that poverty is, then the simplest, most
straightforward way to deal with it is to supply income. Simple
and straightforward it might be, but it ran up against one of the
fundamental tenets of the paradigm of capitalism, the Protestant
ethic of work. It also ran up against the hostility of the lower-
middle classes, especially ethnic groups. "We made it the hard
way, why can't they?" became almost a battle cry. Social workers

[29] Daniel Patrick Moynihan, "One Step We Must Take," *Saturday Review*, May 23, 1970,
p. 21.

had been running up against this opposition for decades, walking a fine line between supplying clients' needs and tranquilizing the neighbors who resented having those on relief enjoy more than they could themselves afford. Even among those who did not themselves feel threatened, there were the middle class and upper-middle class people who knew that the income would not be properly used; the men would drink it up, and the children would be no better off. And who would do any work at all if he could get enough to live on without working? Who would do the dirty work? Any income strategy would have to have answers to these misgivings. Protection against "chiselers" had to be built in. A spate of legislative proposals was in the congressional hopper by the early 1970s. What the effects of such legislation would have on communities was high on the agenda for study by a wide variety of communities of scientists.

There were other segments of the community besides blacks and poor who were also clamoring for change in the 1960s, including nonwhite ethnic groups, college students, and women. Some called ferociously for grand revolutions; some called mildly for simple reforms. Some commanded a national forum; some, a very local one.

But there were also segments of the community that resisted change. Stability was what they sought. They tugged as hard on their end of the rope as the "change-agents" did on theirs.

8

Defense and Resistance

THE COMMUNITY AS VICTIM

Communities are vulnerable in many ways. Sometimes they are vulnerable to the depredations of an Act of God—floods, earthquakes, famines, tornadoes, fires, or plagues—which destroy people and/or property; sometimes to the depredations of acts of men—wars, depressions, revolutions, or riots—which also destroy people and/or property. A very considerable research literature on the nature of such disasters and catastrophes and on organizational techniques for dealing with them has prepared communities in the civilized world for handling them.[1]

Our attention here, however, is focused on the community as victim from a somewhat different angle, that is, from the point of view of communities or parts of communities that feel themselves threatened by disorder, invasions of one kind or another, or change and innovation, either by loss of autonomy to extracommunity systems or by inimical forces of any kind.

---

[1] Jessie Bernard, "Community Disorganization," in David L. Sills, ed., *International Encyclopedia of the Social Sciences,* vol. 3 (New York: The Macmillan Company and The Free Press, 1968), pp. 163–68.

Although a substantial research literature, especially in the area of medical sociology, is accumulating to help us see how communities react to such threats, the research has not become the concern of any single community of scientists. Some of it fits into ecological models; some, into models of conflict or power. Some fit into psychiatric models. Much of the materials presented here could be put under the heading "anti-change." With only this unifying theme to tie the research together, the materials are offered as illustrations of a variety of community defenses and/or resistance to change. Some deal with the defense of neighborhoods, protecting themselves against internal disorder on one side or invasion of unwanted intruders from the outside; some deal with the defense of the community as a whole against outsiders. Some deal with positive resistance to innovation; or to invasion by that most difficult of all opponents, different cultural values.

"URBAN UNEASE" AND DEFENSE OF BELEAGUERED NEIGHBORHOODS

First a look at neighborhoods. A study of over a thousand home-owners in Boston showed that their major concerns were not those usually specified by urbanologists as urban problems (such as, for example, housing, transportation, urban renewal, and air and water pollution), but rather such immediate things as "crime, violence, rebellious youth, racial tension, public immorality, and delinquency," which could be succinctly summarized as improper behavior in public places, or, in brief, violations of social order.[2]

Most discussions of "social order" or "the social order" are macrosociological in scope and are not immediately applicable to small neighborhood units. Still it is in these small areas where order shows itself and where its absence hurts most, personally and immediately. Justice may be as elusive today after two thousand years as it was to Pontius Pilate. But order is not equivocal, and when confronted with a choice of one or the other, many prefer order to justice.

In the Boston study, for example, it was not only crime that bothered people but also any behavior that reflected unseemly standards of conduct. The difficulties were not always, therefore,

[2] James Q. Wilson, "The Urban Unease: Community vs. City," *The Public Interest,* no. 12 (Summer 1968), p. 26.

the sorts of things that warranted calling the police; nor, in fact, were they things the police could do much about. If people are wealthy they can buy the kind of protection against unseemly behavior they want; they move into a high-rise apartment with a uniformed doorman, door buzzers, and a television monitor scrutinizing everyone who enters. Or they may engage private police or build high walls to keep intruders out. The sights and sounds of the disorderly world are kept out of their world.

Poor people do not have such resources. Penned in their ghettos or slums they are like people in an occupied country or a country under seige. They are held in thrall by "rebellious youth" and those who engage in "crime, violence, and delinquency," as specified in the Boston study. They are, in effect, a beleaguered community pitted against an enemy they cannot openly resist.

This does not mean, however, that they do not work out their own defenses. One researcher has sketched the moral order in what he calls a "defended" neighborhood.[3] A defended neighborhood relies on a "cognitive map" of the social structure of the community, a picture in the heads of the residents which is superimposed on the physical structure. This serves to help control behavior by informal means and thus preserve order within the community's boundaries. Such social maps make clear to everyone who are the individuals with whom it is safe to associate and those from whom one must keep one's distance. Such maps do not guarantee justice, but they do facilitate order.

They define groupings of varying degrees of permissible social contact; they delineate groupings with different levels of social cohesion. Residents in these defended neighborhoods are bound together not by sentimental ties nor Gemeinschaft, but rather by structural or functional ties. Thus a major function in defending the area is that of providing identifying cues. The cognitive map supplies such information, or "inside dope" on residents and groups. Residents share knowledge of the neighborhood's underlife. They keep one another au courant by means of local gossip, rumor, and all kinds of information transmitted by word of mouth that is necessary for interpreting what goes on in the area. Outsiders or strangers can be identified; insiders can be kept track of.

One of the major specialized functions of the defended neighborhood is the protection of children, not only against the

---

[3] Gerald D. Suttles, "The Role of the Defended Neighborhood in Urban Areas" (Paper read at meetings of American Sociological Association, August 1968).

ordinary hazards of traffic, violence, and attack, but also against the subtler hazards of associations which the parents disapprove. This is a factor of major significance in efforts to secure residential desegregation. In situations where the races meet as adults, it is relatively easy to institute formal rules to control their relationships. But children meet one another in primary-group situations in which formal controls are not likely to exist. The defended neighborhood tries to insure that children will have "safe associates."[4]

Mothers or other caretakers of small children are also likely to have restricted range of movement, especially if they walk rather than drive in the course of performing their several home-related tasks. They have, therefore, a vested interest in the defense of the neighborhood and an unequivocal need to know its internal structure. The elderly may also have need of protection, but, in addition, they may also supply it. Jane Jacobs has called our attention to the watchful eyes of elderly housebound individuals keeping the streets under surveillance from upper-story windows, noting any activity that seems unusual, suspicious, or out of the ordinary.[5]

Suttles notes that in new communities, whether designed by tract developers or by city planners, the physical boundaries of neighborhoods are laid down in advance; they are not political in origin and they are economic and cultural only to the extent that they attract people of similar income level and cultural background. Their identity is established in advance by the assignment of a name. Thus many of the functions performed by the cognitive map in the inner city defended neighborhoods are, in effect, already built into these new neighborhoods. The enemies against whom they must be defended are strained out. One's guard can be lowered.

Still, according to the National Commission on the Causes and Prevention of Violence, all kinds of neighborhoods—rich, poor, and suburban—will have to accelerate their defenses and close themselves into "fortresses" unless ways are found to change the circumstances that breed disorder, including violence. People in all parts of the cities, according to the Commission's

---

4 Ibid. For an analysis of the subtleties of social order in public places, see also Erving Goffman, *Relations in Public: Microstudies of the Public Order* (New York: Basic Books, Inc., Publishers, 1971).

5 Jane Jacobs, *The Death and Life of Great American Cities* (New York: Random House, Inc., 1961), pp. 35–41.

report, were in fact already arming themselves with guns. This was defense in a very literal, almost military, sense. Vigilantism was seriously considered in some areas. Order, if not law, was the cry of those beleaguered neighborhoods.

ON NE PASSE PAS!

One of the fundamental processes in the classic ecological model was invasion of one land use by another. In the ordinary course of events succession was achieved with a minimum of disarray, as we saw in Chapter 3. When it was a matter of one ethnic group invading another, the invaders had usually achieved the class level of the residents whose area was being invaded, or the invaded residents were ready to move out anyway, or the area was to be outgrown. The new residents *re*placed rather than *dis*placed the old.

But this was not always true. Sometimes neighborhoods have felt they had to defend themselves against invasion by other ethnic groups or classes before they were ready to surrender. In the case of Orientals and blacks, so-called restrictive covenants were relied on to bar them from purchasing homes in certain areas until the Supreme Court in 1948 declared that such covenants could not be enforced by the courts. Similar devices were used against other minority groups, but when they were declared legally unenforceable they tended to disappear.

Neighborhoods may have to fight other kinds of invasion. Sometimes the defense is not against ethnic or racial groups but against city planners, bureaucrats, the real estate industry, or, for that matter, any kind of industry. Such agencies have to make decisions about locating plants, schools, renewal or clearance projects, or roads and freeways that may impinge on the areas. "Protest groups, conservation committees, land owners' groups and realty associations spring into existence, thrive, and then decline as the issue which brought them into existence waxes and wanes."[6] These emergency defenses have the appearance of being sporadic, ephemeral, and transitory. This is not so, according to one student of the subject. They leave a residue and constitute a kind of subterranean basis for cohesion. They illustrate a phenomenon not usually included in models of participation. They

---

[6] J. Clarence Davies III, *Neighborhood Groups and Urban Renewal* (New York: Columbia University Press, 1966), p. 74.

might well be called *latent* participation or *potential* participation.

Not all invasions by groups or attacks by outside agencies provoke defense. Not all neighborhoods put up opposition. Why is there a difference? Why do some resist and others not? A study of Newark reported that intense opposition came not from hardcore slums or from areas with high transience rates or from those with tenements and many rooming houses, but rather from the periphery of the affected area where there was still a high rate of home ownership, stability, and one- or two-family homes. Only those neighborhoods fight to defend themselves in which families have roots and vested interests.[7]

DEFENSE OF COMMUNITIES
AGAINST INVASION BY OUTSIDERS

Defense against outsiders has always been among the functions communities have had to assume. Many early towns were walled to protect them from such invasions. In those days it was usually military assault that the community had to defend itself against. It still is in border kibbutzim in Israel. But for the most part, that kind of defense is now far too complex for any but the national community itself. Today local communities feel they have to defend themselves against quite different kinds of attack, if not military invasion, at least other kinds almost as hard to deal with—an influx of dependents who will swell relief rolls, for example. For centuries, under the Poor Law principle, local communities had been held responsible for the care of the needy; strict residential or settlement requirements had been set up to prevent the invasion of poor people from the outside. Now such protective devices have broken down. Residential requirements for assistance are no longer permitted. Many communities with relatively high welfare payments and services feel themselves unjustly put upon as they have to assume the care of newcomers.

Some communities are willing to tolerate waves of "invasion" by outsiders if there is some kind of payoff in return. Summer people are tolerated by natives of resort towns because they bring income; tourists are welcome in cities like Washington; conventions of Legionnaires, Kiwanis, Elks, Lions, and similar

[7] Harold Kaplan, *Urban Renewal Politics: Slum Clearance in Newark* (New York: Columbia University Press, 1963).

organizations more than pay for the extra community burden required for policing and cleaning up after them. Such conventions are therefore not only welcomed but invited, courted, and wooed. Agricultural communities have long been accustomed to the necessary influx of migratory workers who come to harvest crops. Despite the indispensable function these "invaders" perform, however, the host communities have not felt it necessary to provide adequate services for them. They are viewed as a necessary evil.

But when the invaders bring neither payment nor service, they are not likely to be welcome. Coxey's Army in 1894 was the prototype of later unwelcome invasions of Washington, including the March on the Pentagon three quarters of a century later. In the summer of 1967 the sanitation department of San Francisco anticipated with anxiety the influx of thousands of runaway youth in its Haight-Ashbury district. Some foreign countries forbade the entrance of so-called hippies as undesirable visitors. Some nonconforming young people in the United States were literally driven out of certain rural areas in which they tried to establish cooperative communities. Fort Lauderdale braces itself each spring for the invasion of vacationing college students. Cities everywhere dread the threat of demonstrators who, seemingly on a moment's notice, can descend upon them to participate in "plebiscitory democracy" as in Chicago in the summer of 1968, or in Washington almost any time. And rural areas have to brace themselves for hundreds of thousands of young people who may gather in their midst at "festivals" of one kind or another.

Members of a generation accustomed to moving around freely, whose families may have moved several times as they climbed the occupational ladder (one in five families moves each year, upper class more than lower class), and who are rootless but at home everywhere, have little feeling of themselves as intruders, guests, or outsiders. "The streets belong to the people" even when they are streets kept up by local taxes. Any town is their town as much as it is anyone else's. They make themselves at home. Some of the radical invaders were, in fact, talking in the 1960s of creating a "new society in the streets . . . which continues its growth with its own natural laws, structures, languages, and symbols."[8] They were "street people." Such appropriation of the streets does not always sit well with local residents. It is their taxes that pay for the extra police protection and for the cleaning

[8] Tom Hayden, quoted in *Washington Post*, December 7, 1969.

up of litter; they are the ones whose community services are strained and interrupted; it is their traffic habits that are interfered with. Local taxpayers are inclined to think they are the only people to whom the streets belong.

So far there is little defense against these invaders. But almost without doubt communities will provide, sooner or later, for their accommodation. With the increase of ease of communication and transportation, such in-gatherings may become as commonplace as older, smaller counterparts or prototypes such as camp meetings and revivals.

STABILITY AND CHANGE

Research on community change has been largely designed from the point of view of those who want to produce change, or "change-agents," and not from the point of view of those who want to resist change. Those who resist change are viewed as obstacles, and ways to win them over or to neutralize them are included in the plans. National organizations of all kinds—but especially health organizations—invoke research findings on how to get their programs (for example, maternal health clinics, or easily accessible mental-health clinics, or sex education in the schools) accepted by local communities. In fact, the burgeoning of national organizations for reform purposes of one kind or another is, as one might have deduced from the De Tocqueville paradigm, a major feature of the American scene. For each such organization, bringing its particular brand of salvation to the grass roots is its whole raison d'être.

A specialty in the profession of social work deals precisely with "community organization," which usually involves innovations of one kind or another. It stresses the importance of indigenous plans, the growth in community capacity, and cultivation of the will to change. The trend has been to view the process as one "in which the community itself is involved in determining the nature, method, and pace of change or innovation or reform."[9] The pace might be slow or fast, the objective might be reform or "social therapy," and the method might be imposed or self-determined, the implication being that the second of each of these alternatives was better than the first.[10] It was taken for granted that

---

[9] Murray G. Ross and B. F. Lappin, *Community Organization: Theory and Principles,* 2nd ed., (New York: Harper & Row, Publishers, 1967), p. 39.

[10] Ibid., pp. 14ff.

change-agents knew best how to effect change and even the changes to effect.

But there has been no corresponding body of research to instruct local communities on how to resist change. Research has taken the form of explaining why resistance occurs rather than how to resist, from the point of view of the change-agents rather than the change-resisters, and from the point of view of the *aggressors* as we are using the term here rather than the *victims.* A great deal of attention has been devoted to "obstacles" to social change. W. F. Ogburn, in the second decade of the century, had devoted a great deal of attention to such obstacles, specifically to vested interests, the power of tradition, habit, social pressure, and the tendency to forget the unpleasant, and such psychological factors as fear, anxiety, and an attitude of "let well enough alone."[11] But resistance to change as a defensive process, which is no less dynamic than change itself, has not attracted much theoretical attention.

Still there must be a considerable body of rule-of-thumb knowledge or know-how on resistance to change. Skillful lawyers learn all the loopholes of any reform legislation. (A grateful client once pronounced the first Henry Cabot Lodge to be the greatest lawyer in the country; other lawyers only told him what he could not do, while Lodge told him what he could do.) The underworld learns how to circumvent penalties. Bureaucracies absorb efforts to change them. (It has been said that every president who has tried to change the State Department has failed.)

It is possible that those who fight change are not passive "obstacles," as the Ogburn paradigm implies, but active agents. And they may go through stages analogous to those through which those engaged in reform movements go. In laboratory studies of problem solving in task-oriented groups, R. F. Bales found a characteristic sequence of phases that moved from "(a) orientation ('what is it?'), to attempts to solve problems of (b) evaluation ('how do we feel about it?'), and subsequently to attempts to solve problems of (c) control ('what shall we do about it?'). Since (a) is functionally prerequisite to (b), which in turn is functionally prerequisite to (c), departures from this order tend to produce frustration and the process tends to backtrack until the major problem has been solved."[12] As examples we might take the

[11] William Fielding Ogburn, *Social Change with Respect to Culture and Original Nature* (New York: B. W. Huebsch, 1922), Part III.

[12] R. F. Bales, *Report for the Five Years, 1946-1951,* of the Laboratory of Social Relations, Harvard University, 1951, p. 17.

reaction of communities to the changes demanded by the action groups in the 1960s that were referred to in Chapter 7. Analogously, when reformers of more conventional style introduce a change, the resisters must ask themselves what is hitting them. What is this thing called fluoridation, for example? Once they find out, they have to evaluate it and decide how they feel about it. What will it mean for them? Then, what shall they do about it?

CASE IN POINT:
FLUORIDATION AND OTHER THREATS

We noted in Chapter 7 that, on the assumption that concentrated power was essentially evil, widespread participation in community decision making was generally believed to be desirable. The theory was that when issues are clearly presented and freely argued, competition in the marketplace of ideas will produce the winner most in line with community welfare. In a democratic system the people would be right in their decisions. Vox populi, vox Dei, and all that. This point of view is tenable, although it does not preclude negative effects for some segments of the population when there are conflicting interests. For it is, regrettably, true that what suits the majority in the community may not suit everyone or, in the long run, even the community as a whole. A community with a large component of elderly nonaffluent citizens—men and women whose homes represent their one and only lifelong investment—may, for example, turn down school bond issues or school property taxes however needed new schools may actually be.

In the movement to fluoridate community water supplies, supported by the most relevant health organizations, it was found, as noted in Chapter 5, that in communities where the decision lay in the hands of the citizens, the likelihood of accepting fluoridation was much less than it was where the decision was made by official decision makers. Among communities that held referendums, sixty percent rejected fluoridation.[13] Structural facts can be invoked to explain some of this rejection: Thus Gamson and Irons found that about fifteen percent of the difference among communities could be attributed to the age and income composition of the community, those with a large elderly and low-income

[13] Harvey M. Sapolsky, "Science, Voters, and the Fluoridation Controversy," *Science* 162 (October 1968), p. 429.

population rejecting it more often.[14] Some researchers conclude that such structural factors, political and demographic, are enough to explain the resistant behavior of communities faced with the fluoridation issue.

Others make room also for social-psychological factors which they consider as important as the structural. One sociologist, for example, noted that a study of some seven hundred communities showed that opponents of fluoridation were those "accustomed to losing their war with the mainstream of society," people who had little power. He interpreted this fact as evidence of the existence among them of alienation in the sense of feelings of powerlessness. He likened the confusion of voters faced with the complexities of the fluoridation issue to the confusion of Germans of post-Weimar Germany, the very model of alienation, that is, a "sensed inability to act intelligently or with insight in a specialized and expert-oriented world."[15]

The existence of opposition not only to fluoridation but also to many other health issues has stimulated the interest of psychiatrists as well as social scientists. Granting the importance of both structural and social-psychological factors for interpreting opposition and resistance to health programs, they feel that "the problem still remains to explain the degree of irrational anxiety which these programs often evoke."[16] Why do opponents feel so strongly about them? One team of researchers noted that it was usually the same groups of people that were involved in resisting a wide variety of health innovations, not only fluoridation but mental health programs, compulsory vaccination, vivisection, immunization, and pasteurization as well. Some include also in their stockpile of enemies drugs, narcotics, alcohol, tobacco, tea, coffee, cola drinks, and cocoa. There must be, they concluded, something in common among those who consistently opposed such a variety of enemies. And, indeed, there was. They did find a fairly clear-cut psychiatric pattern among those who showed resistance to all kinds of innovations. The specific details of this

[14] William Gamson and Peter H. Irons, "Community Characteristics and Fluoridation Outcome," *Journal of Social Issues* 17 (1961), pp. 66–74; Robert L. Crain, Elihu Katz, and Donald B. Rosenthal, *The Politics of Community Conflict: The Fluoridation Decision* (Indianapolis: The Bobbs-Merrill Co., Inc., 1969).

[15] Melvin Seeman, "The Alienation Hypothesis," *Psychiatry and Social Science Review* 3 (April 1969), p. 3.

[16] Judd Marmor, Viola W. Bernard, and Perry Ottenberg, "Psychodynamics of Group Opposition to Health Programs," *American Journal of Orthopsychiatry* 30 (April 1960), p. 338.

psychiatric resistance syndrome need not detain us here. The sociologist has to take such psychiatric analysis on faith.

What is important is that there exist in the community "blocs" or subliminal sets of groups which surface from time to time and then return to general invisibility. They undoubtedly have as much reality as such other collectivities as "labor," "ethnic groups," "Jews," "Catholics," "the South," or any other entities which are the stock in trade of social analysts. Their numbers—on the basis of fragmentary evidence and insights rather than hard research—have been variously estimated to be about thirteen to fifteen percent of the American population. They include people like the followers of Senator Joseph McCarthy in the 1950s and the Radical Right in the 1960s. As a rule the issues which engage these resisters to change are not sensitive enough to mobilize great public interest. Sometimes they arouse only limited segments of the community. Ordinarily they are well within the usual community facilities for dealing with rifts.

The emphasis here has been on the kinds of conflict in the community which are only sporadic, those which are based on latent or potential kinds of organization. They are the kinds seeking not to upset the applecart, not to inaugurate change, nor even to achieve power. It is a passive kind of conflict based on resistance rather than aggression. Stability is its goal. The support may be all but subliminal, but once change is threatened it can spring up almost like Athena, fully mature. No one who has to deal with communities can afford to ignore or disregard the thousands of individuals capable at almost a moment's notice of spontaneously crystallizing into action groups.

The conflict of interest groups in communities has received serious research attention,[17] as has also race conflict, but the kind discussed here has not. It was not provided for in the classic community paradigms, nor is it adequately accounted for in current thinking and research. It would be interesting to have "cognitive maps" of such potential groups, whether one is interested in producing change or in resisting it.

CLASS CONFLICT, NEW STYLE: EMBATTLED POPULISM VERSUS NEW URBAN LIFE STYLES

Not all opposition of local communities to outsiders is against anything as definable as a corporation or "Washington" or the

---

[17] James S. Coleman, *Community Conflict* (New York: The Free Press, 1957).

Supreme Court or hippies or masses of invading young people. Sometimes it is a vaguely menacing set of values that threaten everything on which the citizens of the communities have built their lives. A complex process is involved in which horizontal and vertical relationships intersect differentially in different segments of the population: One set is receptive to a new way of living, others resent it.

When Bensman and Vidich first studied a small town in a mass society, they thought their contribution was primarily to show how small towns were losing their autonomy to extracommunity systems. In the late 1960s these researchers reinterpreted their data and added new observations. Now they saw a fundamental historical confrontation in process. They anticipated "the probability of a continuous and enduring battle between the proponents of populist culture and the bearers of the new urban life styles, for wherever the latter group reaches sufficient size it challenges the older, traditional group for leadership. In the threat to its leadership the older group sees that it not only faces the loss of community leadership and higher real estate taxes but also the defeat of its entire way of life. This way of life, though on the decline, has long historical roots. It is identified with grass-roots democracy, with Americanism, and with all the virtues of the American past. For those committed to the past and its values, this decline is hard to digest."[18]

The new urban—"urbane"—life styles that these "old-fashioned American" groups are resisting are the result of all the organizational, economic, educational, and demographic changes that are increasingly becoming characteristic of life today. These new life styles are essentially middle class, sophisticated, permissive, avant-garde, and consumption-oriented (including, for example, such elements of "gracious living" as wine, boats, elaborate hi-fi systems, and gourmet cooking). In brief, they are the stereotyped suburban life styles that are gradually encroaching on the small town. The East and West Coasts are the centers of this new culture and it is rapidly being disseminated from these centers by the mass media. Small towns, especially in the Middle West and South, are the centers of resistance. Most susceptible to the appeal of the new life styles are, understandably, the urban college-educated new middle class and teen-age youth, especially those from middle class families.[19]

---

[18] Joseph Bensman and Arthur J. Vidich, *The New American Society: The Revolution of the Middle Class* (Chicago: Quadrangle Books, Inc., 1971), p. 346.

[19] Ibid., pp. 333ff.

What we have here is not the old intellectualistic bias against the city, nor the overrepresented farm vote in state legislatures hamstringing the cities, nor yet the old rural-urban conflict of interests that was once a major key for interpreting the history of the United States, nor even the battles against giant corporations as they increased their power over the local community, but a subtler kind of invasion of small communities by strange, unfamiliar, threatening ways of thinking, living, and valuing. And there was sullen dismay on the part of the invaded.

Vidich and Bensman see no chance for the traditional populist values to succeed in their resistance; the new life styles reflect fundamental and irreversible trends in the structure of American society that cannot, in their view, be eliminated by wishing, nor by law, and they certainly cannot be reversed. The populists may resist but they cannot prevent the changes, and certainly a confrontation should be avoided for, in their opinion, a backlash would be calamitous. What we seem to have here is a different kind of class war, one in which conservatives, high and low, confront values with which they find it hard to come to terms. It is "class" war all the more complicated because the children of some of those same "urbane" families resist the new values as vehemently as the conservatives themselves do.

So much for change at home. If there had been so little recognition of the approaching crisis in community paradigms in the 1950s it is little wonder that they were unquestioningly accepted for application in the Third World as part of the great modernizing movement there. Nor was their inability to pass that test any less dismaying than it was at home.

9

"Community Development": The Third-World Test

MODERNIZATION

Modernization is a revised version of progress—not automatic progress, but guided change in a desired direction. Several communities of social scientists in the 1950s and 1960s turned their attention to supplying and researching suitable paradigms for thinking about modernization in the Third World. All models started with economic variables, but each discipline contributed a somewhat different emphasis. A variety of new concepts appeared, such as, for example, take-off stage, social mobilization, capacity or capability, need-achievement, self-others seeking, want-get ratio, traditional society, transitional society, negative political development, prismatic arrest, political decay, mobility multiplier, law of evolutionary potential, revolution of rising expectations, revolution of rising frustration, and so on.[1]

There were three levels on which modernization was required. There had to be political modernization to create viable

---

[1] Daniel Lerner, "Modernization: Social Aspects," in David L. Sills, ed., *International Encyclopedia of the Social Sciences,* vol. 10 (New York: The Macmillan Company and The Free Press, 1968), p. 389.

nations; there had to be community development to serve as units for implementing programs;[2] and there had to be individual modernization to develop the "modal personality type" needed to operate a modern society. Community development fell to the sociologists. The community was to be the basic unit of action that would combine outside assistance and organized self-determination to achieve both material goals (e.g., a new schoolhouse) and nonmaterial goals (e.g., literacy, lowered infant mortality). Community development was to deal with consciously accelerated economic, technological, and social change in a village, town, or city. The projects were to have obvious local significance within the capabilities of local people and were to be initiated by them. Above all, the program was to be noncoercive.[3]

COMMUNITY DEVELOPMENT

In his first inaugural address in 1949, President Harry S. Truman had enunciated his famous Point Four program, stating that greater production was the key to prosperity and peace, and that the key to greater production was wider and more vigorous application of modern science and technical knowledge. He therefore invited other advanced nations to pool their technical resources to "help the free peoples of the world, through their own efforts, to produce more food, more clothing, more materials for housing, and more mechanical power to lighten their burdens."

The United Nations had already arrived at the same idea. The Economic and Social Council had appropriated funds to help governments that needed technical assistance in planning their modernizing programs to train native experts both at home and abroad and to facilitate the organization of such services. Thus by 1950, under the aegis of the simplistic theory behind Point Four, modernization was off to a flying start. And in the vanguard were the scholars and researchers, led first by anthropologists and economists and joined later by sociologists and political scientists.

Armed with what seemed like a well-stocked kit of paradigms and technical resources, they seemed confident and buoyant. The

---

[2] Irwin T. Sanders, "Community Development," in David L. Sills, ed., *International Encyclopedia of the Social Sciences*, vol. 3 (New York: The Macmillan Company and The Free Press, 1968), p. 170.

[3] Ibid., p. 171.

major problems seemed to be not so much the "people aspects" of modernization as the technological aspects. American sociologists had had considerable experience in this area.

Their experience was with the extraordinarily successful agricultural extension system by which American land-grant universities had been supporting research on agricultural and rural problems, and by which county agents had been taking the results out to the farmers and their families. This pattern was, in fact, the model for community development plans in the Third World, especially in India. The diffusion of innovations had already become a major focus of research in rural sociology, judged by one commentator, in fact, as perhaps "the most important topic that rural sociologists have ever studied."[4]

Nor were rural sociologists the only community of scientists interested in community development. We have already commented, in Chapter 8, on the specialty in social work dealing with community organization, which addressed itself to ways and means of getting communities to accept innovations.[5]

There was also a body of practical experience in back of the community development idea in the Third World. Colonial governments had done some of the spade work. So had missionaries. The original aim of the Christian missionary to bring salvation to the heathen had long since been watered down to the more modest goal of bringing medical and educational services to them. The missionaries had hoped in time to turn over to their charges the management and administration of these services. In some communities, in fact, those trained by missionaries became the nucleus for Point Four development programs.

CONFLICTING PARADIGMS

The Point Four idea, then, saw productivity as the key to community development, and it posited more application of scientific and technical knowledge to achievement. It implied, in brief, scientific agriculture. It seemed to envisage for the Third World teams of county agents who would go to the farmers everywhere with the same message they had brought to farmers at home; and farmers in the Third World would be as receptive to

[4] C. A. Anderson, "Trends in Rural Sociology," in Robert K. Merton et al., eds., *Sociology Today* (New York: Basic Books, Inc., Publishers, 1959), p. 171.

[5] Murray G. Ross and B. W. Lappin, *Community Organization: Theory and Principles,* 2nd ed. (New York: Harper & Row, Publishers, 1967).

new ideas as those in Iowa had been. The scientific knowledge was needed; it was wanted; it was available. There was just the simple matter of getting it to those who needed and wanted it. Full steam ahead. The research stemming from this model was matter-of-fact, no-nonsense, and technical. It sought to answer such bread-and-butter questions as: What is the best kind of entrée into a community? Who are the best indigenous intermediaries to work with?[6] Who are the readiest to accept innovation?[7] What kinds of innovations are most likely to be accepted?[8]

But almost from the start it was the anthropological paradigm sponsored by the United Nations, which emphasized stability, that became standard. Its orientation was quite different. When anthropologists looked at a community, they saw its culture as "a cup of life." Although it may have been unintentional, they tended to project a kind of romanticism in their picture. When sociologists looked at the same people, they saw high infant mortality rates, disease and illness, malnutrition, poverty, exploitation, low life expectancy, and inefficiency in food production. They did not see a beautiful design, nor even the more matter-of-fact "material culture" of the anthropologist, but hovels, poor tools, and low-yield strains of seeds. The technicians really did know what was the best way to achieve the ostensible and stated goals of the community development program, namely, greater productivity. They knew what was possible. But the possible was not always probable, or, as the anthropological paradigm implied, desirable.

The anthropological paradigm directed attention to stability. It led to a defensive rather than an aggressive stance, to a protective rather than a stimulating approach toward simple communities. Do not lay profane hands on them; approach change very gingerly, even fearfully. Contact with modern culture could kill some, as the experience of several of the Pacific Island cultures had shown. And look what happened to the American

---

[6] The answer was school teachers (Irwin T. Sanders in a review of Herbert H. Hyman et al., *Inducing Social Change in Developing Communities,* in *American Sociological Review* 34 [April 1969], p. 261).

[7] The answer: The influential members of a community were more ready to accept innovations, and men more ready than women (Charles P. Loomis, "Change in Rural India as Related to Social Power and Sex of Adults," *Behavioral Sciences and Community Development* 1 [March 1967], pp. 1–27). The work of Loomis is representative of the best in the down-to-earth technical tradition of community development research.

[8] Chemical fertilizers, improved seed, insecticides, and plough or cultivator have been accepted in this order (Ibid.). Most had accepted smallpox vaccination; about half typhoid and cholera immunization.

Indians. A culture is an integrated and, by implication, a fragile whole. You can't just change any part of it without disrupting the whole. It has to be sheltered. Therefore, go slow! Beware of introducing anything new; it may have wholly unforeseen—and disastrous—consequences.[9]

In order to forestall such stresses of change, UNESCO commissioned a staff of specialists under the editorial direction of Margaret Mead to draw up guidelines for orienting the experts who were to go all over the world in community development crusades. The principles enunciated in the manual became revealed writ and were repeated with monotonous regularity in all reports of community development work: Go slow, do not impose plans from the outside, let the community itself decide what it wants to do; failure will surely result sooner or later if you try to impose your own ideas on the community.

The result of the paradigmatic conflict was a paradoxical, not to say schizophrenic, call for radical change, but without any disruption of the traditional social order. Change must be profound, but it must not upset the status quo. The inconsistency was met by an optimistic belief that industrialization would itself have the appropriate "spread-effects" to induce other change where needed.

One team of scholars concluded that the emphasis on the deteriorating effects of rapid social change, "unless linked directly to policy alternatives . . . , tends to preclude the formulation of volitional or decision-making implications that suggest directed change. Instead, social determinants are placed in the realm of amorphous entities removed from the control or manipulative aspects of society," and the scholars then asked "whether American social scientists . . . [were] more worried about the psychological costs of change than are the peoples they are describing."[10]

WHERE DO YOU START?
THE VILLAGE AS A UNIT OF MODERNIZATION

The community development program had taken it for granted that the community would be the unit of modernization. The communities faced by the developers were, of course, far

---

[9] J. R. Rees, in the introductory note to Margaret Mead, ed., *Cultural Patterns and Technical Change* (New York: Mentor Books, 1955), p. 8.

[10] Charles C. Moskos, Jr., and Wendell Bell, "Emerging Nations and Ideologies of American Social Scientists," *The American Sociologist* 2 (May 1967), p. 72.

from homogeneous. Some had much farther to go than others. Some were located in the bosom of nations with traditions of literate cultures centuries old; others were in the midst of tribes that did not yet have a written language. Some had had experience with money; some had not. No universal prepackaged program would fit all of these situations. Community developers often had to play it by ear.

Certainly it seemed that nothing smaller than a village was a feasible unit. In Tanzania, for example, small groups of scattered subsistence farmers had to be brought together to create any base at all for modernizing. Voluntary Ujamaa or "familyhood" villages were set up consisting of from one to two hundred families.[11] In Israel, the villages had been successful change-agents for decades before a national state was even established, the pace of change being as rapid as the technology permitted. In Mexico, too, villages had successfully served as units of change.[12]

But in Asia, Myrdal challenged the suitability of the village as a unit of modernization. In India, the village was a "stronghold of stagnation." Some colonial regimes, notably that of the Netherlands in Indonesia, had strengthened villages, and they could therefore bypass the disorganization that occurred with independence in other areas. But in most parts of South Asia, "colonialism had ordinarily led to a decay of the ancient village organization without the creation of a substitute."[13] As a result there was almost complete lack of discipline among the villagers, and the governments of "soft states" were loath to impose any. There was, therefore, "little hope in South Asia for rapid development without greater discipline. . . . In the end nothing is more dangerous for democracy than lack of discipline."[14]

Myrdal pointed out that the class structure in the village militated against the ability of the village to implement development programs. Such programs were put into the hands of those in the village most resistant to rural reconstruction, because they were already privileged and hence in no sense ready to surrender their advantages. They were in a position to lead in technological

---

[11] Anthony Astrachan, "African Village Tries to Break an Old Habit," *Washington Post,* March 9, 1969.

[12] Robert Redfield, *A Village That Chose Progress* (Chicago: University of Chicago Press, 1950).

[13] Gunnar Myrdal, *Asian Drama: An Inquiry into the Poverty of Nations* (New York: Pantheon Books, Inc., 1968), p. 856.

[14] Ibid., p. 879.

innovation only when such change helped them, but it did not spill over into fundamental institutional changes. The Indian village was, in brief, "the very stronghold of the inequalities, conflicts of interest, and resistance to change, of all the attitudes caused by and in turn buttressing stagnation."[15]

There was also the same question we asked earlier, Where actually is the locus of power? It may have been important for the villagers themselves to decide whether they wanted a new well or a better road. But in the long run the really important decisions, those that determined the direction of change itself, were actually being made far away in the capital or in the jockeying for power among great industrial complexes. It was important to get a village to use improved farming methods, but it was a question whether the community organizer or the architect of land policies in New Delhi had greater impact on getting them adopted. When recognition of the seriousness of the problem of food shortages finally led governments to reexamine their investment priorities, and not until, as a result of this review, national policy gave priority to investments in agriculture rather than heavy industry, and in new strains of seeds, fertilizers, irrigation, and pesticides rather than steel mills or airlines, did productivity actually increase. It proved not to be the villagers' decisions but government policy that made possible the resulting "green revolution."

DISAPPOINTMENT AND DISILLUSION

After twenty years of nearly spectacular research productivity, the social scientists in all the disciplines dealing with modernization felt they had not been able to achieve the breakthrough which would have made possible suitable paradigms to guide thinking and policy in the Third World. Old Western paradigms did not apply and new ones had failed. The disappointment was so profound that social scientists vied with one another in throwing stones at themselves. There was a sort of collective competition in the late 1960s among social scientists in disparaging Western paradigms as applied to the Third World. Terms of utter self-contempt were used to castigate their "ethnocentric myopia,"[16] their "Westernized ethnocentrism,"[17] and everyone

---

[15] Ibid., p. 876.

[16] Howard Stanton in Arthur J. Field, ed., *Urbanization and Work in Modernizing Societies* (Detroit: Glengary Press, 1967), p. 3.

[17] Lerner, "Modernization: Social Aspects," p. 386.

worth his salt had to prove how wrong Louis Wirth's urbanism paradigm was in the non-Western world.[18] There was a kind of orgy of intellectual self-flagellation. The sociology of development was "empirically invalid . . . , theoretically inadequate . . . , and policy-wise ineffective."[19]

"Empirically invalid . . . . " Even Western instrumental paradigms had failed. American researchers had created an impressive literature on the pitfalls and hazards to be avoided in cross-cultural research. Still, the very idea that cross-cultural research was possible implied that the techniques developed for research at home were also suitable for application elsewhere. Now researchers learned the "rather harsh fact that a number of research techniques currently in favor in urban sociology [were] not readily exportable to other cultural settings, since they have been developed to fit a constellation of traits many of which are unique to American cities."[20] This author illustrated his point with Warner's use of residence for measuring social status, since in many parts of the world residence did not have the same relationship to class as it did in the United States.

"Theoretically inadequate . . . . " Gunnar Myrdal stated that Western paradigms were seriously distorting; they conformed to the historical experience of the West but they did not apply to the Third World. He noted, for example, that models suitable for the Third World might have to include: institutionalized corruption as a taken-for-granted variable; the existence of hunger as an influence on the effects to be expected from differing policies; and the lack of social discipline as an influence on the economic infrastructure that Western economists could take for granted. He concluded that "a major vehicle for introducing serious biases into research on South Asian problems has been the uncritical application of concepts and theories that have been developed in, and have validity for, another region or group of countries, namely, the rich Western or Communist countries."[21] Daniel Lerner concurred.[22]

[18] Gideon Sjoberg, "Comparative Urban Sociology," in Merton et al., *Sociology Today,* p. 338.

[19] Andre Gunder Frank, "Sociology of Development and Underdevelopment," *Catalyst* 3 (Summer 1967), p. 20.

[20] Sjoberg, "Comparative Urban Sociology," p. 356.

[21] Myrdal, *Asian Drama,* p. 117.

[22] Lerner, "Modernization: Social Aspects," p. 390.

Among the fallacies specified by Myrdal were: Urbanization
in the West was associated with the improvement of technology
and the level of living, whereas in South Asia it was associated
with the reverse; voluntary participation was quite different in the
two parts of the world; slums were in the central city in the United
States, but they were in the surrounding areas in South Asia.

"Policy-wise ineffective . . . . " Or worse. One team of sociologists criticized Western paradigms not so much from the point
of view of technique or theory, but from the point of view that
research on the Third World was distorted by "a bias in basic
perspective . . . deleteriously affecting our scientific construc-
tions of the social realities of underdeveloped areas," a bias
supporting stability as opposed to liberating movements,
and—worse—stability in favor of American interests. They ac-
cused American social scientists of trimming their own ideals to
fit the demands of stability. In their misguided attempt not to be
"parochial" or "biased" in their viewpoint, they had turned out to
be apologists for authoritarian regimes. They concluded that
"much of the controversy concerning ethnocentrism has been
misguided. The question is not so much the relevance of general
Western concepts to studies of emerging nations, as the more
refined one of the appropriateness of particular concepts and,
more subtly, of social science values that are uniquely American."[23] Gunnar Myrdal noted that even conservative Western
students were beginning to "ask themselves whether a social
revolution is not necessary in order to set the South Asian
countries firmly on the road to progress."[24]

The persistence of overurbanization was seen by some as a
"measure of our failure to develop a comprehensive theory and
practice of modernization."[25] Such failures called for a reex-
amination of basic conceptions and assumptions on their part.
They must reconsider "the theory and practice of social change
under conditions of extreme acceleration."[26] As yet they still
lacked "the evaluated experience needed to provide rational
guidance for such unprecedented efforts to induce comprehensive
social change."[27] Despite all their research, "the processes of

[23] Moskos and Bell, "Emerging Nations and Ideologies of American Social Scientists," p. 72.

[24] Myrdal, *Asian Drama*, p. 117.

[25] Lerner, "Modernization: Social Aspects," p. 390.

[26] Ibid.

[27] Ibid., p. 388.

economic, social, and political development of the so-called underdeveloped countries . . . remain poorly understood. Theories that were attractive because of their simplicity and because they had clear-cut and helpful policy implications have been badly battered by academic critics; worse, they have been faulted by events."[28] After almost twenty years, Irwin Sanders concluded that there was "not at the present time a body of tested theory on development. Nor do we know in any systematic way why some programs succeed, by the developers' standards, while other programs fail."[29]

When Sanders concluded that the greatest gain from the years of experience with community development was simply the better understanding of village problems it afforded to higher government officials,[30] he may have been underscoring the greatest gain it was possible for this experience to net. The researchers had told the policy makers what their society was really like down there in the villages. And that, apparently, was what was needed.

Social scientists, because it is their function to report what is non-news, were describing the Third World in terms of what was usual, unexceptional, or ordinary. Newsmen tell us about a society in reverse form. By highlighting certain events as news, they tell us what is non-news. Just as we can learn what the institutional requirements for, let us say, marriage are by studying what the grounds for divorce are, so we can learn what the fundamental nature of a community is by learning what is unusual, exceptional, or extraordinary. But when the social scientists presented their data, what everyone "knew" became news. They reported that people were hungry and that agricultural innovation lagged because of inadequate support from government policy. All the ancient stresses and strains that everyone had taken for granted and accepted without question, seen through the objective eyes of the researchers, attracted attention as news. Government policy changed; more attention was paid to agriculture.

The change paid off. The so-called green revolution which constituted a "quantum jump" in agriculture was one such payoff.

---

[28] Albert O. Hirschman, "The Principle of the Hiding Hand," *The Public Interest*, no. 6 (Winter 1967), p. 10.

[29] Sanders, "Community Development," p. 173.

[30] Ibid., p. 172.

In India, for once there were beginning to be adequate food supplies.[31]

THE COSTS OF CHANGE:
THE CULTURAL LAG PARADIGM

Although events may have "faulted" a great many paradigms and paradigm candidates, they seemed rather to confirm one of the oldest paradigms in sociology, but one currently out of fashion, namely, W. F. Ogburn's paradigm of the cultural lag. Although, like the anthropological paradigm, it recognized that any culture is, indeed, an integrated whole, it did not draw the same corollary, namely, that the relations among the component structures remained fixed. It recognized that they changed. And, precisely because all were parts of a whole, change in one part called for change in other parts.

Ogburn was concerned primarily with the material or technological aspects of culture and what he called the adaptive culture, especially "customs, beliefs, philosophies, laws, [and] governments,"[32] which adjust people to the material conditions of life. He did not deny that the adaptive culture might precede or go along *pari passu* with technological change, "but such a situation presumes a very high degree of planning, prediction, and control," so that the usual situation was one in which material culture changed first and adaptive culture lagged behind. Ogburn listed a number of causes of cultural lag, including the difficulty of, and hence the scarcity of, inventions in the adaptive culture; the heterogeneity of society which created conflict of interests with respect to change; and group valuations, expressed in morals, mores, and customs, which became embedded in the habits of many people and thus resisted change.

The lesson of the cultural lag paradigm for community development was not, like that of the anthropological paradigm, Go slow. Nor was it, as suggested by some, to place a moratorium on technological advance. The lesson was, combining the anthropological cautiousness and the Point Four emphasis on technology, that since stresses and strains could be expected from techno-

---

[31] Wolf Ladejinsky, "Ironies of India's Green Revolution," *Foreign Affairs* 48 (July 1970), p. 758.

[32] William Fielding Ogburn, *Social Change with Respect to Culture and Original Nature* (New York: B. W. Huebsch, Inc., 1922), p. 202.

logical changes, anticipate them, plan inventions in the adaptive culture to prepare for them. The best course for development lay not in less but in more speed—speed, that is, in keeping institutional structures or adaptive culture up to date, in minimizing the inevitable dislocations resulting from differing rates of change in different aspects of culture.

The green revolution was almost a textbook case of the kind of lag Ogburn was analyzing. The technological change that produced it—improved techniques, better seed, use of fertilizer—was producing the expectable disruptions in the adaptive culture in the form of conflict over the best way to share in the increased production. Only rich farmers could take advantage of the new technologies, mechanization of agriculture reduced the status of tenants to that of hired labor, tenancy reform became less feasible, the disparity between rich and poor farmers became greater, and threats of peasant uprisings became ominous. "The village poor were not averse to forcible occupation of land, harvesting standing crops, and violent attempts to secure better wages."[33] Forcible occupation of land, murder, casualties: It was well understood that all this was but "a foretaste of an enormous 'law-and-order' problem." And the prime minister herself warned that the revolution might not remain green unless there was also a revolution in the adaptive culture—Ogburn's term, not hers—based on social justice.[34] It sounded very much like a paraphrase of Gunnar Myrdal.

Another example of the cultural lag theory, this one in the field of health and medical technology, was almost a textbook illustration of another paradigm, the Malthusian. During the 1950s there had seemed to be time to follow the go-slow policy. There appeared to be no special urgency. So let the village set its own pace. Let it decide what it wanted to do. We might think the best thing would be Program X; but if it wanted Program Y, which seemed totally irrelevant, who were we to say no? We'd go along. By the 1960s, however, things began to look different. The whole community development approach itself began to seem rather feeble when the national and international forces within which it had to operate posed such almost insuperable obstacles. Agricultural improvement in the village had been hard to achieve when the national policy was one of steel mills rather than fertilizers, or,

---

[33] Ladejinsky, "Ironies of India's Green Revolution," pp. 766–67.

[34] Ibid., p. 767.

more ominously, if the increase in population outstripped the increases in production. Even the green revolution was no guarantee of plenty. "Continued uncontrolled population expansion could . . . still cause . . . hopes to be dashed."[35] By the late 1960s the go-slow policy confronted serious challenge. Modernization had been "too fast" in some areas of culture, too slow in others. Things were out of kilter.

The health and medical technicians who brought sanitation and modern health sciences to the villages of the Third World had succeeded very well.[36] But attempts to bring corresponding changes in the adaptive culture—lower birth rates—had not. An emergency was suddenly—actually not at all suddenly—enveloping many parts of the Third World. Time was of the essence. We could not wait. We had to limit the birth rate. The anthropological paradigm seemed a luxury the Third World could no longer afford. Difficult questions began to be raised, like "How long can we wait? How slow can we go? How much can we depend on community development?"

How long can authorities desiring rapid social change wait for positive results from a slow educational process? Or in working out national economic and social plans, how much weight can they give to the priorities of villagers throughout the land? To what extent can those sponsoring community development rely on local leaders to initiate projects in terms of the "felt needs" of their fellow citizens, or must this initiative come from outside professional workers who stimulate and help local people bring into being some form of local action?[37]

In the Third World no more than at home were community paradigms passing the tests imposed by the "novelties of fact" being generated today. Where, then, are we left? What are we to do? Continue to tinker? Give up the whole idea of suitable paradigms? Or seek the revolutionary breakthrough so many members of the community of scientists interested in the community are calling for? These are questions easier asked than answered.

[35] A. H. Boerma, Foreword to *The State of Food and Agriculture* (New York: Food and Agriculture Organization of the United Nations, 1968), p. 1.

[36] See footnote 8.

[37] Sanders, "Community Development," p. 171.

Part Four

Revolution Anyone?

The Future of the Concept of the Community and Community Paradigms

TWO QUESTIONS

Granted that "novelties of fact" both at home and in the Third World have weighed the classic community paradigms down with a heavy load of anomalies, two questions currently being asked are addressed here: (1) Is the very concept of the community necessary for an understanding of how our society operates and, if it is, (2) is normal-science research guided by the classic paradigms adequate for the purpose, or are we in need of a scientific revolution in this area to supply us with more appropriate paradigms for the postcity world of today? The discussion here has to do with community in the settlement sense in which locale is an intrinsic component. Our answer to the first question is affirmative; our answer to the other one is negative to the first part and affirmative to the second. But before proceeding, a parenthetical aside may be in order for the case of community conceived without the locale component or even, for that matter, without a high level of interaction.

"COMMUNITY" SANS LOCALE

R. E. Park had noted that for many people profession rather than locale was the basic bond. More recently, W. J. Goode, on the basis of eight criteria—none of which are specified by students of spatial communities as intrinsic—has argued that the professions could fruitfully be viewed as communities.[1] Thomas S. Kuhn's use of the concept of a "community of scientists," which we have found so useful in the present book, is an example of the application of such a nonspatial concept of community. We are told that on the jets carrying technocrats hither and yon all over the world, people identify with their professional affiliations rather than with their geographic communities. An individual is with IBM, not from Bethesda; with AID, not from Washington; with the International Monetary Fund, not from New York; and so on. The point is interesting, but hardly crucial.

One more parenthetical comment is appropriate. The concept of "consciousness" seems to be in the process of revival. It was once prominent in the thinking of labor organizers who sought to create "class consciousness" in workers and, in effect, to create a kind of class-based community that would transcend locale and, in the case of Marxists, in fact, one that would transcend nationality. More recently women have spoken of "consciousness-raising" which is a process of achieving the "consciousness of kind" that Franklin H. Giddings was writing about half a century ago. The idea is to create "sisterhood," which, more than the professions, conforms to the eight criteria of community that Goode specified.

Whatever may be the fate of such related concepts—their persistence hints at a felt need for a better-supplied conceptual armory for understanding how modern societies operate—the question here has to do with the settlement concept of community in which locale is intrinsic.

IS THE CONCEPT
OF THE COMMUNITY VIABLE?

Is such a concept worth keeping? Is it any longer necessary? Is it even usable? And, even if it is, is it important enough to retain? Is it essential for understanding societies today? Although

---

[1] W. J. Goode, "Community Within a Community: The Professions," *American Sociological Review* 22 (April 1957), pp. 194–200.

an affirmative reply to these questions is given here, it is essential to state the case for a negative reply also, the case, that is, for abandoning the concept of the community.

It is granted that for subhuman, preliterate, agricultural, and, to a large extent, preindustrial societies, the concept of local community is indispensable. Indeed, in the case of preliterates, the concepts of community and society are identical; we speak of preliterate societies or preliterate communities almost interchangeably. The boundaries of one are the boundaries of the other. In the past community depended on spatial propinquity. It was not easy for social relationships to have intimacy and emotional depth or for social cohesion and continuity to persist in the absence of nearness. And since the beginnings of agriculture, except in such anomalous cases as gypsies and other wanderers, spatial propinquity was related to a fixed settlement. Locale was thus fundamental.

But those who think the concept should be jettisoned argue that it is now anachronistic since improvements in communication, especially the mass media, and most especially television, as well as in transportation, have profoundly changed the significance of space for human relationships.[2] Modern communication and transportation technology mark the end of the community just as agricultural technology marked its advent at the beginning of human history. Once individual mobility has reached a certain level, once speed and feasibility of communication have reached a certain level, and once economic and political integration have reached a certain level, we do not need the concept of the community at all to understand how a society operates. Retention of the concept may, in fact, actually prevent us from seeing the really relevant phenomena on today's scene. The city, for example, has ceased to be an urban community; approaching it as such is distorting rather than helpful.

THE MASS MEDIA
AND THE EROSION OF COMMUNITY

In Chapter 4 we spoke of the contra-class effect of the "massification" of society. There has been a contra-community effect also. The housewife watching television while she irons her

---

[2] For the best statement of the case against the concept of the community, especially of the urban community, see the Fall 1968 issue of *Daedalus,* "The Conscience of the City."

family's clothes feels closer to the female talk-show star than to her neighbor across the hall. New York City is visually closer than the neighborhood on the other side of the tracks. The hometown of the soap opera family is more familiar to her than her own. The mass media tend to dissolve community barriers for the "masses" as rapid air transportation does for the "classes."

True, those who wish to reach members of mass society do still have to take community factors into account; they know that what one community will accept, another will reject; they still have to pay obeisance to community standards (and a vast research apparatus keeps them informed on these matters). Still, sellers can beam their messages to an audience that is almost independent of the local community. The part of mass society that lives in Tuscaloosa, Alabama, is about the same as the part that lives in Bangor, Maine. It is in this sense that the mass media may be said to dissolve community boundaries. One good poll, it is argued, can tell us more about the way our society operates than a dozen community studies.

THE DISAPPEARANCE OF SPACE

Increased speed in transportation has had an analogous contra-community effect. It has become a cliché, for example, that it takes longer to get to the airport than it does to get to a city hundreds of miles away. Just as a man in New York might once have said, "I'll meet you for lunch at the Waldorf," he may now say, "I'll meet you for lunch in Washington." A member of a scientific community can meet his confreres half a continent away almost as easily as he can meet with local colleagues on the other side of town. It is not that territoriality is no longer a basic variable for some administrative purposes, but that space relationships take on a different aspect when transportation puts Chicago and New York closer together for some decisions than Harlem and Wall Street, or London and Washington closer together than Georgetown and Anacostia.

Since so many of the most vital social systems thus now transcend local communities, the urban settlement can no longer be viewed as an appropriate unit of observation, let alone as a community. It has to be viewed simply as a nodal point of a region, country, or international system. What happens in a certain part of a settlement like New York, for example, may be more related to what is happening in Mississippi than to what is happening down- or uptown. What happens in a certain part of

Chicago may be more related to what is happening in Appalachia or the Ozarks than to what is happening on the North—or South or West—Side. The use of land on the Savannah River may be more influenced by what is happening in the Pentagon than by what is happening locally.

The distribution of people in dispersed social systems is not only spatial but "mental." Some people are in a planetary community; some are in a national community; still others are in a community bounded by their limited interests. The bodies of people might be in one spatial area, but not their social worlds. The concept of locale has little meaning in this context. The concept of "communality" was once proposed to refer to these locale-independent relationships.[3] Now the implications for the community of the independence from locale as shown by these new kinds of relationships are becoming overwhelming.

The allegedly anachronistic nature of the local concept of the community was being noted all the way from the smallest to the largest territorial units, from neighborhood to parish to city to nation. For some, even the neighborhood was already out. Saul Alinsky, for example, who had himself pioneered neighborhood action groups, was questioning the use of the neighborhood concept: "I do not think the idea of geographical areas, especially of neighborhoods, is any longer applicable. . . . People no longer really live their lives in neighborhoods. . . . The life of the people is elsewhere. We are going to have to find out where it really is and how to organize it."[4] He noted that the compelling interests of people were no longer "in what we habitually call the community," and, in fact, he did not believe that "we know what the community is now." Even the Catholic Church, which has succeeded for millennia in administering a world-wide organization on the basis of the local parish, is now finding it inadequate. Thus a Louisiana monsignor is quoted as admitting that "the Catholic parish system is an anachronism. Its basic concept is territorial, and nothing but sewer districts operate that way today. How can you gather and relate people of common interests when you are dividing them up according to geographic accident?"[5] The management of impersonal engineering housekeeping and sanitary

[3] Bessie McClanahan, "The Communality: The Urban Substitute for the Traditional Community," *Sociology and Social Research* 30 (March-April 1946), p. 267.

[4] Quoted by D. J. R. Bruckner, "Alinsky Rethinks Idea of Community," *Washington Post*, February 20, 1969.

[5] Unsigned, "The Struggle to Find Meaning," *Newsweek*, October 4, 1971, pp. 88–89.

services was, in brief, necessarily based on locale. But what did that have to do with community?

The city as a whole was also being conceptualized out of existence as a community. In the postindustrial age most people would have only very minor ties to any particular place; their lives would be lived in the global village and communities would remain only for those who could not make it in the modern world. In fact, Melvin M. Webber says that "we may not be far from the time when the vernacular [locale-based] meaning of 'community' will be archaic and disappear from common usage. It has already lost much of its traditional meaning for a great many of those on the leading edge of the society."[6] He argues not only that the concept of community is anachronistic but also that, since it could not interpret what is happening today, its retention is positively distorting:

> We are passing through a revolution that is unhitching the social processes of urbanization from the locationally fixed city and region. . . . Deficiencies of our language and . . . the anachronistic thought-ways we have carried over from the passing era [now create confusion]. We still have no adequate descriptive terms for the emerging social order. . . . We seem still to assume that territoriality is a necessary attribute of social systems. . . . The error has been a serious one. . . . In the novel society now emerging . . . the influence and significance of geographic distance and geographic place are declining rapidly.[7]

Even the nation as a community was being expunged by some. The important structural units to understand now transcended nations too, for modern societies were increasingly run by technocrats who identified with their fellow technocrats wherever they were rather than with fellow nationals. Some saw the emergence of an international society in the Western world as the fifteenth century had seen the emergence of the nation-state. It was not only jet-set technocrats who crossed national boundaries as casually as their forebears crossed state lines in the past. A generation of young people has grown up, who swarm from one country, one continent, or one hemisphere to another, and who are about equally at home in one place as another.

[6] Melvin M. Webber, "The Post-City Age," *Daedalus,* Fall 1968, p. 1099.

[7] Ibid., pp. 1092–94.

Although the importance attached to the nonspatial aspects of society in the future might seem to be exaggerated by dwelling on the jet set and peripatetic young people, there can be no denying the fact that international contacts are, indeed, the wave of the future for more and more people. Louis Kriesberg has analyzed international nongovernmental organizations, and he reports that they have increased tenfold in this century, from fewer than two hundred to almost two thousand. They vary widely in the degree of community or consensus they have achieved—the degree being greatest among those concerned with technology, science, medicine, and sports and lowest among those concerned with humanistic and artistic matters—but he believes they may be "an index of the extent to which a world society already exists."[8]

The conception of this postcity, in fact, postcommunity, society that comes through, then, is of a great locale-independent sea of contacts with little vestigial locale-anchored pockets of communities here and there; a great impersonal world where groups, classes, coalitions, and alliances form and re-form, but remain always in flux, unanchored to any settled locale. It is a conception of a society in which it makes little difference to people where they live. If the housekeeping were in good order and the amenities observed, one place would be as good as another. Locale as such would have little significance.

Those who argue against the relevance of locale put up a very persuasive case. And it may well be that they do indeed presage a scientific revolution. I am also aware of the fact that my own resistance to the abandonment of locale in the conceptualization of the community may be a classic example of the inertia of paradigms. Still, a good case can also be made for the retention of the settlement conceptualization, at least for the present.

THE PERSISTENCE OF LOCALE

Not many people seem to be ready yet for complete abandonment of locale. And so long as locale means anything for many people, the concept of the local community has validity. Thus, despite the vehemence with which some observers were conceptualizing the local community out of existence, whether at the neighborhood, city, or national level, there were others who were still finding it indispensable.

[8] Louis Kriesberg, "How a Plowing Contest May Ease World Tensions," *Transaction*, December 1967, p. 36.

Gerald Suttles, for example, argues that the neighborhood remains "an independent feature of social organization which must be examined in its own right."[9] Physical boundaries are still meaningful to residents and, "in this sense, territorial boundaries between neighborhoods are a proper element of social structure."[10] Morris Janowitz concurred. Commenting on the decline of interest in urban community studies in the 1960s he noted that the intrinsic vitality of the subject kept it alive nevertheless; interest in the local community, in fact, was now reviving it and he concluded that "community study remains a basic vehicle for holistic and comprehensive understanding of the metropolitan condition."[11] So far from having obliterated the community, modern life was calling for more of it; students who went out to study the city found residents almost pathetically eager to make some sort of local identification, to attach some sort of significance to locale. Scott Greer was also still finding locale a key concept in studying the urban community.[12] Even today researchers in large cities are finding "some cells with a unity similar to that of the medieval town."[13] So long as locale continued to mean so much to so many people, the concept of local community retained validity.

While some social scientists were decrying the concept of community as anachronistic, Terry N. Clark was calling for a revival of interest in community research. He noted that, although the American Sociological Association had dropped programs on the subject at its annual meetings in 1957, "the growth in interest and research in the community area in recent years suggests that more permanent attention by the ASA might be in order," and he suggests the organization of a Section on the subject.[14] (There had, understandably, always been a Committee for Community Research in the International Sociological Association.) In 1971 a

[9] Gerald Suttles, "Territoriality and the Urban Community" (Paper read at the 1968 meetings of the American Sociological Association, Abstract D3969 in the 1968 Supplement to *Sociological Abstracts.*)

[10] Ibid.

[11] Morris Janowitz, in the preface to Gerald Suttles, *The Social Order of the Slum* (Chicago: University of Chicago Press, 1968), p. vii.

[12] Scott Greer, *The Emerging City* (New York: The Free Press, 1962), p. 64.

[13] Janet Abu-Lughod, "The City Is Dead—Long Live the City: Some Thoughts on Urbanity," in Sylvia Fava, ed., *Urbanism in World Perspective* (New York: Thomas Y. Crowell Company, 1968), p. 155.

[14] Terry N. Clark, Memorandum on Several Community Research Activities, April 12, 1971.

plan for the reorganization of the executive branch of the federal government called for the establishment of a Department of Community Development.

It is true that as administrative or management units, localities can be dealt with without reference to the concept of community. Such phenomena as crime or race relations, for example, may be abstract, formal, and impersonal. One studies them by way of tables, maps, charts, and long-term trends. As such they may be viewed as little different essentially from ocean currents or meteorological phenomena. As a matter of fact, this conception of communities has been attributed to military flyers who see not cities of human beings down there on the ground but simply targets for their mission, physical rather than human entities. But down there on the ground there were men, women, and children into whose eyes one could look, whose pain one could see, whose rage or whose apathy one could almost touch.

At the local community level there is confrontation, visual if not tactile, emotional if not intellectual. People still live next door to others, they eat, sleep, love, hate, avoid, or seek one another in a given locale. Whether or not they have much to do with their neighbors, they use the same grocery store or supermarket, attend the same movie houses, and patronize the same beauty parlors or barber shops. Owners or renters, they depend on the same community services such as, humble as they may be, garbage collection, street cleaning, and police protection. However emancipated from spatial barriers and however independent of locale the élite may be, it is still on the community scene that for most human beings interaction takes place. These phenomena cannot be just read out of the discipline.

Unless everything we have learned so far about human relationships is dated—and the possibility of this contingency cannot be dismissed—communities will persist. Nor is the concept of local community irrelevant in the Gemeinschaft sense. Our attention is being increasingly called to the almost compulsive "quest for community" among thousands of seekers in rural and urban communes of many kinds all across the country, and to them the concept of local community is far from anachronistic. There is evidence here of great lacunae in our knowledge and a need to fill them in. What do all those substitutes for intimacy mean, all those sensitivity training groups, T-groups, encounter groups, and communities designed to supply—for a fee—the much longed-for closeness, physical as well as psychological? Do they mean that life in the postcity era is washing out?

Still, the fact that one does not reject the concept of community even in this day and age does not necessarily mean that one also accepts the classic paradigms. Even though, for the present, community continues to make a difference in the lives of most people, its significance both as a structural and as a social-psychological factor is by no means clearly interpreted by the old paradigms. A scientific revolution may still be needed.

Before passing on to the second question posed earlier—the problem of community paradigms—a parenthetical aside is needed on the never articulated but generally recognized status system among communities of scientists, one of those extrinsic factors affecting the growth of science that Kuhn discusses. A science—any science—is a mosaic of paradigms adhered to, cultivated, and cherished by a set of communities of scientists. There may be little in common between or among these communities. Each has its own pantheon, its own cherished symbols and beliefs. And each has its own rank in the status hierarchy. The people who study the postcity age are themselves on the leading edge of our society, and that is the part of it they are interested in studying. They inhabit the global village, the world of the top echelons of industry, government, and academia, the world of the highest status, and this high status reflects back on those who study it. At the other extreme is the relatively low prestige level of research on the nitty-gritty of the small local community units. We have here a curiously familiar replication of the old city-slicker, rural-hayseed picture. On the one hand are the super-mobile, wide-ranging upper echelons of industry, government, and academia, who are at home everywhere, moving about from one part of the world to another in the ordinary course of their lives. And on the other hand are the nonmobile people in settlements set aside for children and their caretakers and for "those adults who have not gained access to modern society."[15] It is among these unimportant people that community remains significant. "In the Harlems and South Sides of the nation are some of the last viable remnants of preindustrial societies, where village styles are most nearly intact. Here the turf is the city block, and teenage gangs wage war in its defense. Here in the slum blocks of the central cities may be the only pure place-based social neighborhoods we have left."[16] It sounds curiously like an old regime contemplating the lower orders. Only now it is a new regime looking down its nose at the old one.

[15] Webber, "The Post-City Age," p. 1099.

[16] Ibid., p. 1102.

REVOLUTION ANYONE?

The call for new community paradigms is coming from many corners. Thus Morris Janowitz, for example, although he believes that "the direct interaction of man and his spatial and economic environment conditions all forms of urban life," still recognizes that "the constructs of the social scientists have . . . become out of date."[17] And Janet Abu-Lughod, who also believes that locale remains important, nevertheless concludes that "to comprehend the nature of . . . urbanism and urbanity . . . measures more sophisticated than those hitherto employed will be needed."[18] Alfred Dean has noted that "the complexity of modern communities defies traditional conceptualizations and . . . taxes empirical techniques and strategies."[19] And, although Roland L. Warren deplores the trend among some students to discard the concept of the community as a useless will-o'-the-wisp, he nevertheless is calling for a "relatively simple model of the community which can permit meaningful analyses and testable research hypotheses."[20] The lack of such needed models, constructs, or paradigms, Edmund N. Bacon warns, is the cause of our failure in dealing with cities. Most of the concepts we are applying were inherited from the past and are "not only no longer relevant, but positively inhibitory to clear thinking."[21] And E. Digby Baltzell, apparently giving up on paradigms which assume either locale or kinship or patriarchal relations as community bonds, asks "how can a society institutionalize new social and legal relationships which will best promote a mature and responsible neighborliness appropriate to an urban, bureaucratized, and rational (rather than local and patriarchal) social order?"[22] A scientific revolution is clearly being called for.

[17] Morris Janowitz, *The Community Press* (Chicago: University of Chicago Press, 1967), p. xviii.

[18] Abu-Lughod, "The City Is Dead—Long Live the City," p. 157.

[19] Alfred Dean, in a review of *Community Dynamics and Mental Health* by Donald C. Klein in *Social Forces*, September 1969, p. 142.

[20] Roland L. Warren, *The Community in America* (Chicago: Rand McNally & Co., 1963), pp. ix, 2, 6, 9.

[21] Edmund N. Bacon, "Urban Process," *Daedalus*, Fall 1968, p. 1165.

[22] E. Digby Baltzell, ed., *The Search for Community in Modern America* (New York: Harper & Row, 1968), p. 11.

HOW ABSTRACT? HOW GENERAL?

The classic community paradigms have been criticized not only on the basis that the kinds of communities they dealt with have become passé, anachronistic, and on their way out, but also on the basis that they are not universal enough, that they are ethnocentric or parochial. They are thus deficient in both time and place. They are limited by the setting in which they were designed, the United States at a certain historic moment. Under the conditions prevailing at that historic moment, they tell us how settlements grew up, differentiated and structured themselves internally, and allocated space; how the components—class and ethnic—interacted among themselves; and how they affected the social relationships and hence the personalities of their residents. It all seemed very natural. And so indeed it was. But as we later learned, it was not the only natural way, nor was it equally natural under all conditions.

Two hazards have characterized the sociology of the community. At one extreme has been the temptation to play up the concrete, descriptive materials, to emphasize "'fact-finding' to the neglect of broader theoretical issues";[23] and, at the other extreme, to emphasize the abstract, theoretical aspects, seeing the community as simply an illustration or exemplification of principles of social systems in general. In support of this latter point of view it is argued that, in order to be universal, a model has to be abstract and general. And it is true that if one wants timeless, universal paradigms, which are invulnerable to "novelties of fact," they do have to be of a high level of generality—so general, in fact, as to be quite irrelevant to concrete, specific communities as we know them.

If one is looking for such timeless, universal paradigms, as stable as those in the physical sciences, the cause is indeed lost. Every community paradigm has to race the "novelties of fact" that modern life generates. But if one is willing to settle for less than such timeless, universal constructs, the cause is more promising. At least it is not hopeless. True, as Gideon Sjoberg says, "to isolate similar patterns among different cultures, urban sociologists must operate on a rather abstract level of analysis,"[24] but not impossibly so.

---

[23] Gideon Sjoberg, "Comparative Urban Sociology," in Robert K. Merton et al., eds., *Sociology Today* (New York: Basic Books, Inc., Publishers, 1959), p. 356.

[24] Ibid.

IF . . . THEN

Every physical science paradigm may be stated in the "if . . . then" form. If, for example, an object falls in a vacuum at sea level, then $v^2 = 2gh$; that is, "any body falling freely under the action of gravitation has uniform acceleration." To be sure, few objects ever fall in a vacuum at sea level. Still, knowing how they would makes it possible for the gunner to compute how fast his missile will "fall" by supplying the unique parameters of his position, far from sea level and far from a vacuum. And so with community paradigms. They may also take the "if . . . then" form. In this sense all the classic paradigms may be said to be still valid for the circumstances they were designed to interpret. (Paradigms are not right or wrong, correct or incorrect, but only more or less useful.) The difficulty is that the data, literally the "givens" that supply the "ifs," change very fast.

Although I am loathe to give up the insights of the current critics of our locale-based conceptions of social structure, I am equally loathe to abandon the concept of locale. The "if . . . then" statement of community paradigms makes possible the retention of both. "If space is obliterated for more and more people, and if . . . , and if . . . , then we can expect . . . ." Or, "if locale remains a basic factor in the relationships of groups and individuals, then . . . ." The statement of paradigms in such a form directs us to sharpen our "ifs." It also offers us options in the selection of models. It makes possible the competition among paradigms essential for the growth of science.

It does not, however, provide the scientific revolution for which activists, planners, and sociologists are calling. We still need such a revolution to help us see the "ifs." While we are waiting for the revolution that will tell us what the new "ifs" are, we may have to rely on simply tinkering with the old paradigms.

It is conceivable, however, that all the components of a scientific revolution are already at hand, as they were in the second decade of the century when Park and Burgess crystallized them in the new ecological paradigm. Someone may soon step forward with a paradigm or set of paradigms that will make so much sense out of the seeming anomalies that sociologists will accept it, and it will then become the basis for a new spurt in normal-science research.

Achieving a successful paradigm would not necessarily mean that we could also achieve control over the functioning of communities, badly needed as such control may be. But at least it would help us understand them better; it would help in the formulation of issues. And that is perhaps all that sociology can be expected to do. Policy makers would still have to carry the ball from there.

Selected Readings

[Books available in paperbound editions are indicated by an asterisk.]

I. ARTICLES

The usual process of discipline development is by way of articles in the professional journals. In the case of the sociology of community, analysis of the articles in the *American Journal of Sociology* and the *American Sociological Review* gives a synoptic overview of what the course has been in this century.

An analysis of the items indexed in the first seventy volumes of the *American Journal of Sociology,* from 1895 to 1965, shows three "waves" of interest, peaking in 1909–1913, 1928–1933, and 1953–1958. There is also an irregular peak in 1938–1943, which is somewhat surprising since in 1936 a new periodical, *Rural Sociology,* was established which drained off a source of articles on the rural community.

The classification of the indexed articles permits two kinds of comparisons, namely, between the frequency of articles on (1) the rural and the urban community and (2) ecology and stratification. Except for the period 1914–1934, the number of articles on urban communities surpassed the number on rural communities especially, of course, after 1936, when *Rural Sociology* was established. The peak for articles on the rural community came in the 1929–1933 period; the peak for articles on the urban community, in 1954–1959.

The articles reveal a far greater preoccupation with stratification than with ecology. Only in the period 1924–1928—the heyday of the Chicago ecological paradigm—did articles on ecology surpass those on stratification. The high point for the stratification articles occurred in 1949–1953; the high point for the ecology articles, in 1959–1963. Overall, stratification in the urban community was the major preoccupation of those writing the articles in the first seventy volumes of the *American Journal of Sociology*.

A similar analysis of the *American Sociological Review,* summarized in the accompanying table, shows that overall, with the exception due to an efflorescence of interest in the urban community in the late 1950s, there has been a steady decline in the average number of articles dealing with community. There has been a precipitous decline in articles dealing with ecology, and articles on rural communities, villages, and neighborhoods have all but disappeared. In general, the *American Sociological Review* has shown less interest in the sociology of community than has the *American Journal of Sociology.* Like the *American Journal of Sociology,* the *American Sociological Review* has shown greatest concern for the urban community; but unlike the *Journal,* the *Review* has been more interested in ecology (often in its technical aspects) than in social structure (social stratification and social class).

Not all of the articles published are received by the respective communities of scientists as equally significant for the sociology of community. Even so, the number finally becomes too large for convenient accessibility through the journals. It becomes essential to winnow them and present them in some more compact and convenient form. Compilations then begin, the editors selecting according to their own editorial concerns, offering something for everyone though not necessarily everything for any one.

II. COMPILATIONS: READERS, ANTHOLOGIES, AND SOURCEBOOKS

The burgeoning of compilations may be taken as an index of the degree to which a discipline is "getting out of hand." Members

TABLE A. NUMBER OF ARTICLES AND ANNUAL AVERAGE NUMBER INDEXED UNDER SPECIFIED CATEGORIES IN *AMERICAN SOCIOLOGICAL REVIEW*, 1936-1970

Category	1936-1955 No.	Av.	1956-1960 No.	Av.	1961-1965 No.	Av.	1966-1970 No.	Av.	1936-1970 No.	Av.
Community	36	1.8	3	.6	7	1.4	4	.8	50	1.4
Urban	38	1.9	26	5.2	2	.4	2	.4	68	1.9
Rural	20	1.0	2	.4	2	.4	—	—	24	.7
Village	7	.35	—	—	—	—	—	—	7	.2
Neighborhood	4	.2	—	—	2	.4	1	.2	7	.2
Ecology	51	2.55	8	1.6	4	.8	1	.2	64	1.8
Structure	15	.75	12	2.4	13	2.6	3	.6	43	1.2
Community power	—	—	9	1.8	9	1.8	6	1.2	24	.7
Total	171	8.55	60	12.0	39	7.8	17	3.4	287	8.2

of the community of scientists are giving up attempts to achieve anything more in the way of integration than the imposition of a classification on the flood of normal-science research that gushes forth from the computers. In the field especially of urban community study increasing numbers of such volumes have been appearing in recent years.

One of the earliest and greatest classics was that compiled by Pitirim A. Sorokin, Carle C. Zimmerman, and Charles J. Galpin, *A Systematic Source Book in Rural Sociology*, 3 vols. (Russell & Russell Publishers, 1930–1932; reprinted in 1965). Another was by R. E. Park, E. W. Burgess, and R. D. McKenzie, *The City**** (hardbound: University of Chicago Press, 1925, reissued in 1967 under the editorship of Morris Janowitz; softbound: Phoenix Books, University of Chicago Press, 1968). The first reflected the cosmopolitanism and enormous erudition of the senior author who could bring to bear on the subject the literature of many languages, and the three volumes are still of considerable interest; the second included papers only by the three authors, but was, in a way, a landmark. The early papers on community by R. E. Park (1916–1939) have been edited by E. C. Hughes in an anthology on *Human Communities: The City and Human Ecology* (The Free Press, 1952), making more widely available these important and seminal articles. Carl J. Friedrich has edited a volume on *Community* (Liberal Arts Press, 1959), which includes a variety of approaches.

The recent compilations have tended to be weighted heavily in the direction of urban communities and have a distinctly demographic and/or ecological bent. Among the most important are those by Paul K. Hatt and Albert J. Reiss, Jr., *Reader in Urban Sociology* (The Free Press, 1951), revised and updated as *Cities and Society* (The Free Press, 1957); William M. Dobriner, *The Suburban Community* (G. P. Putnam's Sons, 1959); Marvin B. Sussman's *Community Structure and Analysis* (Thomas Y. Crowell Company, 1958); O. D. Duncan et al., *Metropolis and Region* (Johns Hopkins Press, 1960); George A. Theodorson, *Studies in Human Ecology* (Harper & Row, Publishers, 1961); Philip M. Hauser and Leo F. Schnore, *The Study of Urbanization* (John Wiley & Sons, Inc., 1965); and Sylvia Fleis Fava, *Urbanism in World Perspective: A Reader**** (Thomas Y. Crowell Company, 1968). James F. Short, Jr., and Morris Janowitz have assembled some of the more seminal articles dealing with the Chicago paradigm in *The Social Fabric of the Metropolis* (University of Chicago Press, 1970). Articles dealing with all levels of urban organization, including many of the classics, have been collected by Robert Gutman and David Popenoe in "an integrated reader in urban sociology," under the title, *Neighborhood, City, and Metropolis* (Random House, Inc., 1970). The rural community was the subject of a compilation by James H. Copp, *Our Changing Rural Society: Perspectives and Trends* (Iowa State University Press, 1964).

To counteract the heavily urban and ecological emphasis of so many of the readers and compilations, there is the book edited by David W. Minar and Scott Greer, *The Concept of Community: Readings with Interpretations** (Aldine Publishing Company, 1969). It deals with the nonlocale aspects of community. Community is nonterritorial, independent of place. The editors grant that locale was important in the past, but today it is significant only or primarily in declining small towns and in primitive villages and tribes.

An important sourcebook is *The Search for Community Power** (Prentice-Hall, Inc., 1968), edited by Frederick M. Wirt and Willis D. Hawley. They have assembled all the important studies to date dealing with the community power structure, including the élitist and the pluralist, and the Hunter and the Dahl approaches. They criticize the community power structure research as showing too little concern for large cities, for its ignoring of poverty, race, and ethnicity, and for not recognizing adequately the possible existence of several power structures in a community. They also criticize the "so what?" position of many of those who study community power structure.

Related to power, especially in connection with urban problems, are three other compilations. Alan Shank, editor of *Political Power and the Urban Crisis** (Holbrook Press, 1969), defines the urban crisis in terms of the black ghetto; the readings he has selected are very current, most dating since 1965. David Popenoe has edited *The Urban Industrial Frontier: Essays on Social Trends and Institutional Goals in Modern Communities* (Rutgers University Press, 1969), which deals with schools, organized religion, local government, social welfare, mass culture and arts, and work and employment. Especially useful is the essay by Norton Long which criticizes the work of C. W. Mills and Floyd Hunter, much of which he labels as social-science fiction. Terry N. Clark's *Community Structure and Decision-Making: Comparative Analysis* (Chandler Publishing Company, 1968) assembles a variety of politically oriented studies with a more theoretical slant.

In quite the opposite direction is the sourcebook edited by

Anselm L. Strauss, *The American City: A Sourcebook of Urban Imagery* (Aldine Publishing Company, 1968) in which he criticizes the narrow problem orientation and scope of much urban community research. He would like to have us study the odd, the seemingly trivial, such things, for example, as symbols of time and space, urban icons, and related aspects of urban life not accommodated by most approaches.

The war on poverty of the 1960s elicited great interest in the subject of participation and several compilations have resulted. Hans B. C. Spiegel has edited two volumes on *Citizen Participation in Urban Development* (Institute for Applied Behavioral Science, NEA, 1968, 1969), one on *Concepts and Issues* and one on *Cases and Programs*. Robert R. Alford and Harry M. Scoble have assembled several case studies in their *Bureaucracy and Participation: Political Cultures in Four Wisconsin Cities* (Rand McNally & Co., 1969), criticizing both the political scientist's and the sociologist's approach to the power structure, both of which, in their opinion, give inadequate recognition to the limitations imposed on both leaders and voters by political structures and culture.

Interest in the history of communities, especially urban communities, has produced two excellent compilations. One is *Nineteenth-Century Cities: Essays in the New Urban History** (Yale University Press, 1969), edited by Stephan Thernstrom and Richard Sennett, in which such topics as social class, status, and stratification; élites; social, occupational, and ethnic mobility; slums; and violence are discussed, serving as an excellent perspective on twentieth-century studies of these phenomena. The other is *American Urban History: An Interpretive Reader with Commentaries** (Oxford University Press, 1969), a collection of 44 papers edited by Alexander B. Callow, Jr.

Development or modernization has also called forth its compilations, again primarily as related to urban communities. Philip M. Hauser's *Urbanization in Latin America* (UNESCO, Columbia University Press, 1961) is more sociological than some of the others, especially Ray Turner's *India's Urban Future* (University of California Press, 1962), which is primarily economic, or Hilda Kuper's *Urbanization and Migration in West Africa* (University of California Press, 1965). Sylvia Fava, commenting on these three volumes, notes that the "data challenge many of our assumptions regarding the ecological patterns of cities, city-hinterland relationships, and the inevitability of an 'urban way of life' for urban dwellers" (*Social Problems* 14 [Summer 1966], p. 95).

A series of studies on modernization in the Philippines—*Modernization: Its Impact in the Philippines* (Manila University Press, 1967, 1968)—by Walden F. Bellow et al. is fairly specialized, but of interest to those who wish to delve into one special area. Also of specialized concern is Horace Miner's compilation, *The City in Modern Africa* (Praeger Publishers, Inc., 1968), based on 21 papers given at a Conference on Methods and Objectives of Urban Research in Africa. Paul Meadows and Ephraim H. Mizruchi have assembled a book with cross-cultural comparisons as a major concern under the title *Urbanism, Urbanization, and Change: Comparative Perspectives* (Addison-Wesley Publishing Co., Inc., 1969). Ira M. Lapidus has edited *Middle Eastern Cities: A Symposium on Ancient, Islamic, and Contemporary Middle Eastern Urbanism* (University of California Press, 1970). Gerald Breese, editor of *The City in Newly Developing Countries: Readings on Urbanism and Urbanization* (Prentice-Hall, Inc., 1969), bypasses the problem of the applicability of western models to the Third World but offers a wealth of empirical and interpretive materials.

III. TREATISES

Treatises and texts call for a higher level of integration and synthesis than compilations since the data must be processed by a single mind or set of minds. One of the earliest was Adna Ferrin Weber's *The Growth of Cities in the Nineteenth Century* (The Macmillan Company, 1899; republished in 1963 by Greenwood Press, Inc.), and one of the most impressive was Sorokin and Zimmerman's *Principles of Rural-Urban Sociology* (Holt, Rinehart & Winston, Inc., 1929).

As in the case of compilations, so also in the case of treatises, the emphasis tends heavily in the direction of urban communities. C. Arnold Anderson rebukes rural sociologists for their aversion toward codification and synthesis ("Trends in Rural Sociology," in Robert K. Merton et al., *Sociology Today** [Harper & Row, Publishers, 1962], p. 366), and the relative paucity of books performing these functions is indeed notable. An important exception is *The Agrarian Transition in America: Dualism and Change* (The Bobbs-Merrill Co., Inc., 1968) in which the authors, Wayne C. Rohrer and Louis H. Douglas, show how tenacious the no-longer-valid agrarian myth remains and how dysfunctional it is for those trying to solve urban problems. Gideon Sjoberg's treatise on *The Preindustrial City: Past and Present* (The Free Press, 1960) attempts to broaden the perspective of community study by including cities in both "historical societies and in surviving literate nonindustrial orders." Technology and power are his "crucial" variables. An interesting oriental counterpart is Takeo Yazaki's *Social Change and the Citizen in Japan from the Earliest Times Through the Industrial Revolution,* translated by David L. Swain (Japan Publications Trading Co., 1968). C. C. Harris' *Cities of the Soviet Union* (Rand McNally & Co., 1970) is another perspective-broadening volume, filling a lacuna of long standing with data not otherwise easily available.

Almost in a class by itself is Jane Jacobs' *The Death and Life of Great American Cities* (hardbound: Random House, Inc., 1961; softbound: Modern Library, Inc., 1969). She became the outstanding advocate of diversity in city planning. In order to make her point, she wrote about why some parts of cities were safe, and others not; why some slums regenerate themselves and others do not; "in short . . . about how cities work in real life." Her ideas had enormous impact on thinking about cities.

Evidence for the persistence of the ecological approach may be garnered from several books in the more academic tradition. Leo F. Schnore's *The Urban Scene: Human Ecology and Demography* (The Free Press, 1965) deals with social morphology with a strongly ecological orientation. Even more strongly ecological in emphasis are the two following books. One is Ralph Thomlinson's *Urban Structure: The Social and Spatial Character of Cities* (Random House, Inc., 1968), which offers nine theories to explain the spatial patterning of cities, and William Michelson's *Man and His Urban Environment: A Sociological Approach* (Addison-Wesley Publishing Co., Inc., 1970).

In *Cities of the Prairie* (Basic Books, Inc., Publishers, 1970), Daniel J. Elazar, incorporating analyses of the impact of the frontier, migration, sectionalism, and federalism, arrives at a modified ecological conceptualization, the "linear conurbated metropolis."

An excellent counterfoil to these ecological books is Scott Greer's *The Emerging City* (The Free Press, 1962). He sees the city as "product and producer of mass society" and even foresees the possibility that the city as we know it may come to an end, supplanted by the metropolis which is quite a different phenomenon and not, as Sylvia Fava has noted, simply the city "writ large."

An interesting attempt to consolidate several approaches to

the urban community is James M. Beshers' *Urban Social Structure* (The Free Press, 1962). It seeks to integrate the ecological, the functional, and the sociopsychological approaches, including historical data where available, and to use marriage and family patterns as a focus for integrating ecological distribution, social structure, and individual behavior. As between class and ethnic groups, he tends to see a continuance of the second, so that class will not be the sole factor in community structure.

Leonard Reissman, in *The Urban Process* (The Free Press, 1964), believes Western paradigms are suitable for the Third World; but C. A. O. Van Nieuwenhuijze, in his *Development: A Challenge to Whom?* (Humanities Press, Inc., 1970), warns against ethnocentrism and the application of Western models to the Third World.

IV. COMMUNITY STUDIES

In contrast to the paucity of generalizing treatises on the sociology of community is the abundance of studies describing concrete, specific communities. These have taken a myriad of forms, from loving, nostalgic accounts by local historians of their hometowns based on community records and old-timers' memories to militantly muckraking and reformist surveys to sophisticated analyses of individual cities and suburbs.

One of the earliest of the great classics was Numa D. Fustel de Coulanges' *The Ancient City* of 1864 (Doubleday & Company, Inc., 1956), which was a study of the city in Greece and Rome. Of quite a different slant was Charles Booth's monumental study of poverty in London, *Life and Labour of the People in London: Final Volume* (Macmillan & Co., Ltd., 1902). The great *Pittsburgh Survey* by the Russell Sage Foundation (1914) was another landmark.

Elin L. Anderson's *We Americans* (Harvard University Press, 1937; reprinted in 1967 by Russell and Russell Publishers) was an interesting account of the ethnic structure of a New England town. C. Arnold Anderson is of the opinion that J. M. Williams' *Our Rural Heritage* (Alfred A. Knopf, Inc., 1925), a study of a New York community, has not been surpassed by any later studies ("Trends in Rural Sociology," in Merton et al., *Sociology Today,* p. 168). *Crestwood Heights: A North American Suburb* (University of Toronto Press, 1956) by John R. Seeley, R. Alexander Sim, and Elizabeth W. Loosley is an outstanding study of a Canadian upper-middle class suburb.

Among the most recent studies of specific communities might be mentioned Elmora Messer Matthews' *Neighbor and Kin: Life in a Tennessee Ridge Community* (Vanderbilt University Press, 1966), which is of special interest because she reports no stratification in at least one of the communities. At the other end of the class ladder is Dennis P. Sobin's study of an upper class suburb, *Dynamics of Community Change: The Case of Long Island's Declining Gold Coast* (Ira J. Friedman, Inc., 1968). Theodore Caplow, Sheldon Stryker, and Saul E. Wallace have given us *The Urban Ambience: A Study of San Juan, Puerto Rico* (Bedminster Press, Inc., 1964). And among the almost endless flow of community studies in other countries might be mentioned: *Two Pakistani Villages: A Study in Social Stratification* (Punjab University Press, 1969) by Muhammad Rafique Raza, and *Moshava, Kibbutz, and Moshav: Jewish Rural Settlement and Development in Palestine* (Cornell University Press, 1969) by D. Weintraub, M. Lissak, and Y. Azmon.

The sociological use to which community studies can be put is illustrated by the insightful interpretation of the findings of the great community studies from Middletown to suburbia by Maurice R. Stein in *The Eclipse of Community: An Interpretation of American Studies** (Princeton University Press, 1960; softbound: 1971). He sees them as documentations of the processes of urbanization (Chicago), bureaucratization (Yankee City), and industrialization (Middletown). His conclusion that community was in eclipse was one of the earliest statements of this increasingly heard claim.

V. SPECIALIZED STUDIES

In addition to studies that attempt to give an all-around description or analysis of individual communities are studies that focus on special aspects of community processes. Thus, for example, studies of communities in disaster do not tell us so much about communities as they do about collective behavior. Still they are useful by providing data on what happens when community structures break down. Allen H. Barton's *Communities in Disaster: A Sociological Analysis of Collective Stress Situations* (Doubleday & Company, Inc., 1969) is an excellent example. A different kind of "survival" is dealt with in *Jewish Identity of the Suburban Frontiers: A Study of Group Survival in the Open Society* (Basic Books, Inc., Publishers, 1967) by Marshall

Sklare and Joseph Greenblum. Numerous studies of action groups in the war on poverty in the 1960s were made in communities all over the country to determine how much change, if any, had been effectuated. One example was *A Relevant War Against Poverty: A Study of Community Action Programs and Observable Social Change* (Metropolitan Applied Research Center, 1968) by the Dynamics Research Institute of the City University of New York. The enormous research referred to in the body of the present book on the fluoridation issue falls into this category also.

Experimental research in the development tradition may also be viewed as specialized community studies. Prodipto Roy, Frederick B. Waisanen, and Everett M. Rogers' *The Impact of Communication on Rural Development: An Investigation in Costa Rica and India* (UNESCO, 1969) and Lalit K. Sen's *Opinion Leadership in India: A Study of Interpersonal Communication in Eight Villages* (Hyderbad: National Institute of Community Development, 1969) may be taken as representative of this genre. Like so many others, it might be added parenthetically, the results, so far as learning how to produce desired change is concerned, are disappointing.

One specialized study that is almost unique is Maren Lochwood Carden's *Oneida: Utopian Community to Modern Corporation* (Johns Hopkins Press, 1969). It carries the history of the Oneida community down to the time it ceased to be, in effect, the shadow of John Humphreys Noyes and became incorporated. The author interviewed the oldest survivors and is thus able to give a down-to-earth authenticity to the materials. This is a story of a different kind of "transition."

Among specialized studies may be listed those that deal with enclave communities. Broadly defined, the term refers to any settlement that maintains a separate racial, cultural, ethnic, or class identity within the bosom of a widely different environment. It may refer to an area of old mansions inhabited by "old families" surrounded by a seething slum that has engulfed it, a pocket of "poor white trash" surviving in developing suburban areas, a military base in a foreign country, or, especially in multiracial societies under colonial regimes, compounds of one kind or another or restricted areas in which the rulers lived apart. Of particular interest are diasporan communities, or enclaves in which the residents consider themselves as belonging to a distant homeland rather than to the host country. An excellent example is Sheldon Stryker's "Social Structure and Prejudice," *Social Problems* 6 (Spring 1959), pp. 340–54, which shows resemblances among the Jewish ghetto in Germany in the eighteenth and nineteenth centuries, the Christian Armenian community in Turkey in the nineteenth and twentieth centuries, and the Parsi community in India in the seventeenth to the nineteenth centuries. In all three, the critical but denigrated functions—primarily trading, commerce, and banking—were assumed by or assigned to these diasporan communities. In the Third World today the Chinese and Indians have constituted diasporan communities in Southeast Asia and in East Africa. Agehananda Bharati, in "The Unwanted Elite of East Africa," *Transaction* 3 (July-August 1966), pp. 38–41, and Lea E. Williams, in "The Overseas Chinese and Peking," *Transaction* 4 (January-February 1967), pp. 9ff., have described such diasporan enclaves.

Of quite a different kind are the highly specialized technical studies dealing with the engineering, financial, and technical aspects of the community as illustrated by J. P. Crecine and Louis H. Masotti's *Financing the Metropolis,* vol. 4 (Sage Publications, Inc., 1970).

VI. METHODS OF COMMUNITY STUDY

A quarter of a century ago, August B. Hollingshead could summarize the trends in community research in an article ("Community Research: Development and Present Condition," *American Sociological Review* 13 [April 1948], pp. 126–46). Since then there has been a burgeoning of methods and techniques.

The first great research approaches to community study in the nineteenth century were those of the early anthropologists and the reformers. One was primarily descriptive and suitable for small preliterate and rural communities, the other primarily quantitative, in the form of surveys suitable, especially and increasingly, for more complex urban communities.

The survey has remained a major methodological tool for community research (Hanan C. Selvin, "Methods of Survey Analysis," in David L. Sills, ed., *International Encyclopedia of the Social Sciences,* vol. 15 [The Macmillan Company and The Free Press, 1968], pp. 411–19); some of the greatest names in the history of sociology are associated with this method. The early counting approach has become increasingly analytic and a large part of community research has turned to the improvement of measurement techniques.

Thomas S. Kuhn's conception of paradigms includes instrumentation, and in the body of this text we used the Simon-Binet tests of intelligence as an example. Community study has depended to a large extent on instruments and indexes of one kind or another. Indeed, the ecological paradigm rested on measures and indexes of such sociological phenomena as delinquency, mental illness, family breakdown, vice, and racial segregation, among others. Much of the normal-science research in the study of community is still concentrated on improving techniques of measurement designed to do better the kinds of things which have already been done: better indexes of segregation, better understanding of why people move, and more attention to the time element—"diachronic" as well as "synchronic" measures—rather than fundamental challenges to the ecological paradigm as a whole.

A great deal of urban community study has become demographic. Already in the 1920s the study of urban communities was beginning to profit from improved census data and the imaginative innovations that sociologists, especially those in the Chicago tradition, were asking for and getting, such as, for example, data by census tracts and later by metropolitan districts. They were asking for and getting data on mobility, housing, income, education, and families. With improved census data it became possible to make more detailed and accurate studies of the structure and functioning of urban communities. In 1961 Beverly Duncan, O. D. Duncan, and Ray P. Cuzzort published *Statistical Geography: Problems in Analyzing Areal Data* (The Free Press). In the same year Jack P. Gibbs edited a compilation on *Urban Research Methods** (Van Nostrand-Reinhold Books).

In recent years games and simulation have served as both research and teaching devices. The work of William A. Gamson is noteworthy in this connection, especially his *SIMSOC: Simulated Society** (The Macmillan Company, 1969), which shows student-players the nature and operation of power, class, authority, voluntary associations, leadership, and other phenomena of community life. Power, stratification, and class are also dealt with in R. Gary Shirts' *Star Power* (La Jolla: Similie II, 1969). Another, for training planners, was *Urban Systems Simulation* (Washington Center for Metropolitan Studies, 1968). A valuable statement of the simulation approach in sociology may be found in Cathy S. Greenblatt's article, "Simulation, Games, and the Sociologist," *The American Sociologist* 6 (May 1971), pp. 161–64.

VII. HOW-TO-DO-IT MANUALS AS SOURCES FOR COMMUNITY SOCIOLOGY

Ever since community organization became a social-work specialty there has been a growing literature, primarily based on experience and data-gathering research rather than on sociological paradigms or data, on how to organize communities for general welfare and human services. A recent example of such a how-to-do-it book is Irving A. Spergel's *Community Problem Solving: The Delinquency Example* (University of Chicago Press, 1969). Spergel distinguishes four types of community organizers, namely, the enabler, the advocate, the organizer, and the developer. The general emphasis tends to be on stability rather than on change. At the opposite pole is the kind of community organization represented by Saul Alinsky who also published a recipe book, *Rules for Radicals* (Random House, Inc., 1971), but with an emphasis on change rather than on stability. Alinsky was as manipulative as the social worker, but more cynical. His analysis of "the poor" is less romantic but also less patronizing. Alinsky was trained in the labor movement, but was also trained in sociology, and his analyses, although far from the sociological model, supply data useful for understanding how power operates.

Somewhere between these two extremes in Michael Walzer's *Political Action: A Practical Guide to Movement Politics** (Quadrangle Books, Inc., 1971). It falls in the area of the sociology of participation. The author participated in the peace and civil rights movements and tries here to systematize what he learned about power from those experiences. He has relearned the old adage, attributed to Lincoln Steffens, that "the professional always wins over the amateur" in community reform. He argues for the semiprofessionalization of citizen politics, that is, for paying citizens for the time they invest in political action. Otherwise citizen politics becomes the prerogative of only those who have the leisure to engage in it and the patience to sit through interminable meetings. Such citizen action has little chance against "established political parties and labor unions which are essentially associations of adult males rooted in their communities." Walzer is reformist rather than revolutionary in orientation, but the reforms he seeks go beyond conventional reformism.

VIII. OTHER SOURCES

In addition to treatises, community studies, and research

reports, which do all the intellectual work for the reader, there are other sources from which a competent sociologist should be able to winnow out a great deal of nonsociological chaff to find the kernel of sociological wheat they contain. Among these sources of data about communities are the numerous publications of governmental units, especially at the national level. By their very nature they must pay a great deal of attention to community factors. They have to reflect the wide diversity of communities. Federal boards, commissions, and committees often hold hearings in different parts of the country. Regional and community comparisons have to be built into the research.

Among these sources of data are the annual reports of such government agencies as the U.S. Housing and Home Finance Agency (1947–). (In 1963 this agency also published *Metropolis in Transition* by Roscoe Coleman Martin.) Also important are the great commission reports made from time to time for presidents or congresses to serve as the basis for legislation. They are usually fact-finding in nature. The data are gleaned for purposes of reform rather than science-building. But, approached with a suitable paradigm, they can be made to yield useful insights. And increasingly they include important contributions by trained social-science researchers.

An early example was the U.S. Industrial Commission of 1900–1901. A great classic example was the report of the U.S. Immigration Commission (1911), which gathered huge quantities of data on urban immigrant colonies and presented massive, detailed data, almost block by block, on ethnic groups, their concentration and distribution. Other famous commission reports which have provided relevant data on urban communities, though beamed at other targets, are the so-called Wickersham Report of the National Commission on Law Observance and Enforcement, dealing with crime and delinquency (1930); the so-called Hoover Report of the U.S. Commission on the Organization of the Executive Branch (1949) on government reorganization, which covered the waterfront from Indians to transportation; and the several reports of the Committee on Economic Security, on which the Social Security Act of 1935 was based.[1]

More recently, the U.S. Commission on Civil Rights (1959–), the Commission on the Impact of Defense and Disarmament

[1] One sociologist expressed great satisfaction at the passage of this Act, noting what a rich source of data its statistical records would make available. Only when a ripple of amusement ran through the audience did the speaker add that, of course, it was a great humanitarian breakthrough also.

(1965), the so-called Kerner Report of the National Advisory Commission on Civil Disorders (1968), the Eisenhower Report of the U.S. Commission on the Causes and Prevention of Violence (1969), and the Report of the Commission on Obscenity and Pornography (1970) have assembled a great deal of research data by social scientists, as well as hearings, which, although they may have to be winnowed, do offer a wide variety of specific sociological data on how communities, especially urban communities, compare and contrast with one another in race relations, proneness to riots, violence, sexual standards, and related phenomena. The National Commission on Urban Problems has published an important report specifically on the urban community, *Building the American City* (1968).

Agricultural Experiment Stations attached to land-grant universities also publish important studies on rural communities, as do also many large urban centers on their communities.

IX. BIBLIOGRAPHIES

Most articles, texts, treatises, and research reports contain bibliographies. In addition, from time to time, independent bibliographies appear. Jack D. Mezirow listed 1589 items up to 1963 in the field of community development alone in *The Literature of Community Development* (AID and Peace Corps, 1963). Robert Lorenz, Paul Meadows, and W. Bloomberg have put together *A World of Cities: A Cross-Cultural Urban Bibliography* (Syracuse University Press, 1964). *Urbanization in West Africa: A Review of Current Literature** (Northwestern University Press, 1965) by R. P. Simms contains 306 items. A bibliography, *New Communities,* published by the Housing and Home Finance Agency in 1965 included 292 items since 1950. And Sylvia Fava, in the Summer 1966 issue of *Social Problems* has an extremely useful essay review of recent books in the urban field (pp. 93–104).

Index

A

Abu-Lughod, Janet, 186, 189
Adrian, Charles R., 81
Agriculture
  and community, 4
  and physiocratic paradigm, 19
Alford, Robert R., 198
Alinsky, Saul, 183, 206
Allen, James S., 132
Anderson, C. Arnold, 165, 199, 201
Anderson, Elin L., 201
Anomalies
  in class structure model, 64–70
  in ecological model, 42–50
  in Gesellschaft and Gemeinschaft,
    91–93
  in paradigm of capitalism, 20
Apathy, 82–83
Arnold, Thurman, 20
Astrachan, Anthony, 168
Azmon, Y., 202

B

Bacon, Edward N., 5, 189
Bales, R. F., 157
Baltzell, E. Digby, 77, 189
Baron, Harold M., 134

Barton, Allen H., 202
Bealer, Robert C., 100
Bell, Wendell, 167, 171
Bellow, Walden F., 199
Benedict, Ruth, 93
Bensman, Joseph, 64, 108, 161, 162
Berger, Bennett M., 56, 117, 128
Bernard, Jessie, 10, 12, 19, 52, 124, 141,
  149
Bernard, L. L., 141
Bernard, Viola, 159
Besher, James M., 201
Bettelheim, Bruno, 105
Bharati, Agedananda, 204
Black, Bertram M., 140
Black community, 123–139
  class in, 58–62
  collectivist paradigm of, 128–129
  ecology of, 39–40
  and Gemeinschaft-Gesellschaft,
    114–120
  new criteria of, 126
  power struggles in, 137–139
  social mobility in, 127–128
  urbanism and, 112–114
Black power, 133–139
  achievement of, 135

violence and, 135–136
Black powerlessness, 134–135
Blacks
  class mobility among, 124
  in classic community paradigms,
    124–129
  community power, 125
  ecological, 124
  Gemeinschaft-Gesellschaft, 125
  dysfunctionality for, of individual
    social mobility paradigm, 127–128
  rejection by, of classic community
    paradigms, 125–126
Blalock, H. H., 124, 133
Blau, Peter, 63
Bloom, Harold, 79
Bloomberg, W., 208
Boerma, A. H., 175
Booth, Charles, 49, 99, 113, 115, 140,
  201
Boulding, Kenneth E., 5, 30, 49
Breese, Gerald, 199
Bruckner, J. R., 183
Buck, Roy, 96
Buckley, Walter, 27
Bunzel, John H., 129
Burgess, E. W., 34, 37, 191, 196

C
Callow, Alexander B., Jr., 198
Capitalism, paradigm of, 16–22, 92
  beliefs and assumptions in, 17
  characterizing concepts of, 16–18
  competition exalted in, 18
  conflict deplored in, 18–19
  corollaries of, 18–19
  and ecological paradigm of com-
    munity, 16
  fate of, 20–22
  as Gesellschaft, 16, 21, 92
Caplow, Theodore, 202
Carden, Maren Lockwood, 203
Carmichael, Stokeley, 134
Cayton, Horace R., 61, 128, 134, 138
Chadwick, Sir Edwin, 113
Change
  costs of, 173–175
  resistance to, 157–160
  stability and, 156
Change agents, 156–157
Cities, animus against, 107–109
Clark, Terry, 79, 186, 197
Class
  in black community, criteria of,
    58–59
  at community and at societal levels,
    52–53

  criteria of, 53
  in ecological model, 51
  and ethnic groups, 55–58
  in functional paradigm, 51–52
  mobility, 56–57
  new, in black community, 126
  in paradigm of capitalism, 51–52
  paradigms, poor in, 139–141
  schismatic nature of, 59–60
  structure of communities, 53–55
  in Yankee City, 54–55, 56
Class conflict, new style, 160–162
Coleman, James S., 160
Committee on Economic Security, 207
Common ties, as characteristic of community, 3
Communities
  communitarian, 100–102
  competition among, 191
  diasporan, 203–204
  enclave, 203–204
Community
  black, 58–62, 123–139
  breakdown, 106
  class structure of, 51–70
  common ties in, 3, 4
  concept of, 179–181
  conservation of, 11
  continuity of in time, 4
  as co-unity, 4
  defense of, 149–154
  definition of, 3–5
  against disorder, 150–152
  ecological model of, 33–50
  emotional depth in, 4
  erosion of, 181–182
  future of, 179–190
  as Gemeinschaft, 4
  Gemeinschaft-Gesellschaft, 91–120
  in "if . . . then" form, 8, 191–192
  against invasion, 153–155
  invasion of, 154–156
  locale in, 3
  and mental health, 102–103
  moral commitment in, 4
  against outsiders, 154–156
  paradigms of, crisis in, 3–14
  perishability of, 13
  personal intimacy in, 4
  power, paradigm of, 8
  power structure, 71–89
  responsibility of, for needy, 154
  sans locale, 180
  of scientists, 5–6
  settlement concept of, 3, 4
  social cohesion in, 4
  social interaction in, 3, 4

sociology of, hazards of, 190
study, paradigmatic context of, 15
technology and, 4, 180–183
and "the community," 3–4
as victim, 149
viability of, 180–181
Community class structure, paradigm of, 51–70
anomalies in, 64–70
nature of, 52–55
Community development, 163–175
conflicting paradigms in, 165–166
technology in, 164–165
Community integration
collective representations, 63–64
conflict with outside enemy, 63
factors in, 62–64
fate of, 68–70
upward mobility, 63
voluntary associations, 62
Community paradigms
class structure, 51–70
ecological, 33–50
future of, 179–192
Gemeinschaft-Gesellschaft, 91–120
power structure, 71–89
Western, failure of, in Third World, 169–172
Community power structure, paradigms of
élitist, 75–76, 82
pluralist, 76–78, 82
Competition
in ecological model, 38
exalted in paradigm of capitalism, 18
replaced by conflict as decision-making process, 47–50
stalled, 45–47
Comte, Auguste, 52
Conflict
deplored in paradigm of capitalism, 18–19
paradigmatic, 165–167
as replacement of competition as decision-making process, 47–50
and resistance to change, 157–160
Copp, James H., 197
Crain, Robert L., 159
Crankshaw, Edward, 26
Crecine, J. P., 204
Cuzzort, Ray P., 205

D

Dahl, Robert A., 76–78, 83, 85, 87, 119, 197
Darwin, Charles, 18
Davies, J. Clarence, 153

Davis, Kingsley, 24, 27, 52
Dean, Alfred, 5, 189
Dean, Lois, 87
Decisional method, 76–77, 78
Defended neighborhoods, 150–152
Defense of community, 149–154
against disorder, 150–152
against invasion, 153–155
against outsiders, 154–156
De Tocqueville, Alexis, 82–83, 144, 156
Diamond, Stanley, 105
Direct action, 84–85
Dobriner, William M., 196
Douglas, Louis H., 199
Drake, St. Clair, 61, 128, 134, 138
DuBois, W. E. B., 59, 60, 61, 129, 134, 144
Duncan, Beverly, 205
Duncan, O. Dudley, 46, 63, 97, 124, 196, 205
Durkheim, Emile, 18, 63, 91
Dynamics Research Institute, 203

E

Eaton, Joseph W., 103
Ecological paradigm of community, 8, 33–50
allocation of land in, 34–35
community structure in, 37–38
conflict rather than competition as decision-making mechanism, 47–50
congeries versus structure, 43–45
crisis in, 41–50
dysfunctional results of, 49–50
ecological processes in, 38–39
intervention, 42–43
natural areas in, 35–37
normal science in, 39–40
as scientific revolution, 34
stalled processes, 45–47
Eells, Kenneth, 61
Elazar, Daniel J., 109, 115, 200
Erikson, Kai, 25
Ethnic groups, 55–58
and "melting pot," 55–58
and upward mobility, 56–58
versus class structure, 55

F

Fanon, Frantz, 130, 131, 135, 136, 137
Fava, Sylvia Fleis, 41, 43, 48, 186, 196, 198, 200, 208
Field, Arthur J., 95, 169
Firey, Walter, 40
Fiske, John, 18
Fluoridation, resistance to, 83, 158–159

Foster, George M., 94
Frank, Andre Gunder, 170
Frazier, E. Franklin, 39, 59, 60, 113, 124
Friedrich, Carl J., 196
Function
  latent, 25–26
  nature of, 23–24
Fustel de Coulanges, Numa Denis, 201

G
Galbraith, J. K., 20
Galpin, Charles J., 95, 96, 196
Gamson, William A., 159, 205
Gans, Herbert, 42, 48, 55, 95, 111, 112, 117, 118, 140
Gemeinschaft, 4, 5, 16, 91–107
  and the folk, 93–96
  influence of, 106–107
  mystique, 92–93
  patterns of settlement and, 95–96
  and rural life, 94–98
Gesellschaft, 8
  as antithesis of community, 21
  as paradigm of capitalism, 16, 21, 91, 92
  and rural life, 94
Gibbs, Jack P., 205
Giddings, F. H., 35
Glazer, Nathan, 55, 56
Goffman, Erving, 152
Goode, W. J., 180
Gouldner, Alvin W., 22
"Green revolution," 169, 174
Greenblatt, Cathy S., 205
Greenblum, Joseph, 203
Greer, Scott, 111, 186, 197, 200
Gutman, Robert, 197

H
Hare, Nathan, 128, 129
Harris, C. C., 200
Harris, Chauncey D., 37
Hatt, Paul K., 97, 196
Hauser, Philip, 94, 110, 111, 196, 198
Hawley, Amos, 36, 38, 47, 52, 71, 72, 73, 86
Hawley, Willis D., 197
Hayden, Tom, 155
Herberg, Will, 57
Hickey, Gerald Cannon, 93
Hillery, George A., 3
Himes, Joseph S., 123
Hirschman, Albert O., 172
Hoffsomer, H. C., 96
Hollingshead, August B., 204
Hoyt, Homer, 37, 44
Hughes, E. C., 196

Hunter, Floyd, 75–76, 83, 85, 197
Hyman, Herbert A., 166

I
Ideology, and paradigmatic predilections, 26–27
Integrating factors in community, 62–64
  fate of, 68–70
Invasion
  defense against, 153–156
  as ecological process, 38
Irons, Peter H., 159

J
Jacobs, Jane, 48, 152, 200
Jacoby, Erich H., 93
Janowitz, Morris, 73, 186, 189, 196
Johnson, Charles S., 124, 134
Johnson, Erwin H., 95

K
Kain, John F., 45, 47
Kanter, Rosabeth Moss, 102
Kaplan, Harold, 154
Katz, Elihu, 159
Kaufman, Harold F., 96
Keniston, Kenneth, 5
Kerner Report, 133
Kibbutz, 103–106
King, Martin Luther, 136, 137
Kinsey, Alfred C., 98, 100
Klein, Donald C., 15
Kleiner, Robert J., 128
Kornblum, William, 79
Kornhauser, William, 65, 66
Kriesberg, Louis, 49, 185
Kuhn, Thomas S., v, 5, 6, 9, 10, 11, 12, 13, 41, 188, 205
Kuper, Hilda, 198

L
Ladejinsky, Wolf, 173, 174
Lapidus, Ira M., 199
Lappin, B. W., 165
Larson, Olaf F., 97
Lebeaux, Charles N., 95, 139
Lerner, Daniel, 163, 169, 170, 171
Leventman, Seymour, 138
Lewis, Claudia, 100
Liebow, Elliot, 115
Lindblom, Charles E., 17
Lipset, Seymour Martin, 96
Lissak, M., 202
Locale, 3, 4, 180
  persistence of, 185–188
Long, Norton, 80, 81, 197
Loomis, Charles P., 21, 91, 166

Loosley, Elizabeth W., 201
Lorenz, Robert, 208
Low, J. O., 65, 67
Lowenthal, Leo, 67
Lunt, Paul S., 54
Lynd, Helen M., 73, 75
Lynd, Robert S., 73, 75

M
McClanahan, Bessie, 183
McKenzie, R. D., 37, 196
McLuhan, Marshall, 119
Marmor, Judd, 159
Martin, Roscoe Coleman, 207
Marx, Karl, 20, 72
Masotti, Louis H., 204
Mass media, and erosion of community, 181–182
Mass society
  and blurring of ranked status, 65–66
  and community class structure, 64–68
  contra-class effect of, 66–68
Matthews, Elmoore Messer, 202
Mead, Margaret, 167
Meadows, Paul, 199, 208
Meeker, Marchia, 61
"Melting pot," 55–58, 131–133
Mental health and community, 102–103
Merton, Robert K., 22, 23, 26, 165, 199
Mezirow, Jack D., 208
Michelson, William, 200
Middletown, 73–74
Miller, D. C., 65
Miller, Herman P., 127
Mills, C. Wright, 74–75, 197
Minar, David S., 197
Miner, Horace, 199
Mizruchi, Ephraim H., 199
Mobility, residential, and class, 56–57
Modernization
  disappointment and disillusion with, among social scientists, 169–170
  emphasis on technology in, 164
  and Point Four program, 164–165
  of race relations, 123–139
  three levels of, in Third World, 163–164
  village as unit of, 167–169
  of welfare system, 139–147
Moore, Wilbert E., 25
Moskos, Charles, Jr., 167
Moynihan, Daniel Patrick, v, 5, 55, 56, 146
Myrdal, Gunnar, 22, 136, 168, 169, 170, 171

N
National Advisory Commission on Civil Disorders (Kerner Report), 133, 208
National Commission on Law Observance and Enforcement (Wickersham Report), 207
Natural Resources Committee, 108
"Negritude," 131
Neighborhoods, 150
  beleaguered, 150–152
Newman, Dorothy K., 127
Nisbet, Robert A., 4, 5
Normal science, 10–11
Nossiter, Bernard D., 137, 138

O
Off-beat communities, 106
Ogburn, W. F., 157, 173
Olson, Mancur, Jr., 28
Order, 150–151
Ottenberg, Perry, 159
Owen, Robert, 99

P
Paine, Thomas O., 50
Paradigm
  anthropological, in community development, 166–167
  of capitalism, 16–22
  characterizing concepts of, 16–18
  of community class structure, 51–70
  of community power structure, 71–89
  corollaries of, 18–20
  cultural lag, 173–175
  De Tocqueville, 156
  ecological, 33–50
  functional, as framework for community study, 22–26
  of Gesellschaft and Gemeinschaft, 91–120
  of urbanism, 109–111
  of *Volkgeist,* 130
Paradigms
  anomalies and, 10–13
  anomalies in, 10–11
  changes in, 11–13
  conflicting, in community development, 165–167
  "current history" and, 12–13
  debacle of, 119
  definition of, 6
  inertia of, 8–10
  key role of, 6–7
  outside influences and, 12–13
  overarching, 15–30

resistance to, 12
sciences as mosaics of, 188
and scientific revolutions, 10–11
technology and, 12
"tinkering" with rather than revolution, 13
Western, failure of, in Third World, 169–172
Park, R. E., 33, 34, 37, 108, 109, 119, 180, 191, 196
Parker, Seymour, 128
Parsons, Talcott, 22, 88
Participation, 82–83, 84, 156
effect of, on decisions on complex issues, 83
as strategy in war on poverty, 144–146
Persky, Joseph J., 45, 47
Peters, Victor, 102
Political resources, 76–77, 84
Poor, in class paradigms, 139–141
Popenoe, David, 197
Populism, 160–161
Poverty, war on, 142–147
income maintenance strategy in, 146–147
job strategy in, 142–143
"maximum feasible participation" in, 144–146
service strategy in, 143–144
Power
black, 133–138
and class, 72, 74
of direct action, 84–85
as dominance, 72
functional approach to, 72–73
impersonal, 71–73
locus of, 84–89, 146
in Middletown, 73–74
personalization of, 73–74
resource, white guilt as, 136
struggles in black communities, 137–138
in Yankee City, 87–88
Power élite, 73–75
Power stasis, 82
Power structure, 75–82
absence of, 82
differences in results of research on, as related to discipline, 78
differences in results of research on, as related to ideology, 79
differences in results of research on, as related to method, 78–79
differences in results of research on, as related to nature of community, 79

élitist model of, 75–76, 82
hollow, 80–81
normal-science research on, 78–79
phantom, 79–80
pluralist model of, 76–78, 82
Powerlessness, black, 134–135

Q
Quinn, James A., 36, 47

R
Rainwater, Lee, 115
Raza, Muhammad Rafique, 202
Redfield, Robert, 168
Rees, J. R., 167
Regional City, 75
Reiss, Albert J., 96, 97
Reissman, Leonard, 201
Reputational method, 76, 78
Resistance to change, 157–160
Revolution, scientific, called for, 189
Richardson, Benjamin Ward, 113
Riesman, David, 100
Rogers, Everett M., 203
Rohrer, Wayne C., 199
Ross, E. A., 98
Ross, Murray G., 156, 165
Roy, Prodipto, 203
Rural community, 92–100
Rural-urban differences, 97–98
Rural-urban migration
and "folk depletion," 99
selectivity of, 98–100
Rurality, criteria of, 96–98

S
Sanders, Irwin T., 22, 164, 166, 172, 173, 175
Sapolsky, Harvey M., 83, 158
Schnore, Leo F., 94, 196, 200
Schuler, E. A., 96
Scientific revolution, called for, 189
Scientific revolutions, 10–11
Scoble, Harry M., 198
Seeley, John R., 5, 25, 201
Seeman, Melvin, 159
Selvin, Hanan C., 204
Sen, Lalit K., 203
Sennett, Richard, 198
Settlement concept of community, 3
Settlement patterns and Gemeinschaft 95–96
Shank, Alan, 197
Shils, Edward, 65
Shirts, R. Gary, 205
Short, James F., 196
Sills, David L., 97, 163, 164, 204

Sim, R. Alexander, 201
Simmel, Georg, 109, 114
Simms, R. P., 208
Sjoberg, Gideon, 170, 190, 199
Sklare, Marshall, 203
Social class paradigm of community, 8, 51–70
Social interaction, as characteristic of community, 3
Social mobility, belief in, as factor in community integration, 63
Sorel, Georges, 84
Sorokin, Pitirim A., 97, 196, 199
Soul
  as black version of *Volkgeist,* 130
  mystique of, 129–131
  and "negritude," 131
Space, disappearance of, and community, 182–185
Spencer, Herbert, 18
Spengler, Joseph J., 19
Spergel, Irving S., 206
Spiegel, Hans B. C., 198
Srole, Leo, 56, 57, 58
Stability
  and change, 156–158
  emphasis on, in anthropological paradigm, 166–167
Stanton, Howard, 169
Stein, Maurice R., 74, 202
Stendler, Celia Bunes, 52
Strauss, Anselm L., 198
Stryker, Sheldon, 202, 203
Suburbanism, as a way of life, 115–119
Suburbs, 115–118
  old and new, 116–118
Succession, as ecological process, 38
Sumner, W. G., 23
Sussman, Marvin B., 22, 196
Suttles, Gerald D., 112, 114, 115, 151, 152, 186

T
Tauber, Alma, 127
Tauber, Karl, 127
Technology
  and community, 4, 5, 181–183
  emphasis on, in Point Four program for community development, 164–165
"The community"
  as distinguished from "community," 3–4
  locale as basic component of, 3–4
Theodorson, George A., 196
Thernstrom, Stephan, 198
Thomlinson, Ralph, 200

Tobias, Susan, 79
Tönnies, Ferdinand, 21, 91, 92, 95, 107
Turner, Ray, 198

U
Ullman, Edward L., 37
U.S. Commission on Causes and Prevention of Violence (Eisenhower Report), 152, 208
U.S. Commission on Civil Rights, 207
U.S. Commission on Obscenity and Pornography, 208
U.S. Commission on the Organization of the Executive Branch (Hoover Report), 207
U.S. Housing and Home Finance Agency, 207
U.S. Industrial Commission, 207
Urban unease, 150–151
Urbanism
  black version of, 112–114
  coping with, 111–112
  paradigm of, 109–111
  as a way of life, 109–111

V
Van Nieuwenhuijze, C. A. O., 201
Veblen, T. B., 20, 51, 52
Vidich, Arthur J., 64, 108, 161, 162
Violence, 134–136

W
Waisenen, Frederick B., 203
Wallace, Saul E., 202
Walton, John, 78, 79
Walzer, Michael, 206
Warner, W. Lloyd, 51–58, 61–70, 74, 87, 88, 117, 137
Warren, Roland L., 5, 22, 88, 189
Washington Post, 38
Webber, Melvin M., 5, 81, 188
Weber, Adna Ferrin, 48, 98, 99, 199
Weil, Robert J., 103
Weintraub, D., 202
Welfare, 139–147
  modernizing of, 139–147
White, Lucia, 107, 108
White, Morton, 107, 108
Whyte, William H., Jr., 117
Wilcox, Herbert C., 52
Wilensky, Harold, 66, 95, 139
William, Lea., 204
Williams, M. M., 201
Willits, Fern K., 100
Wilson, James Q., 56, 137, 150
Wirt, Frederick M., 197

Wirth, Louis, 109, 110, 114
Wolfinger, Raymond E., 78

Y
Yankee City, 54, 74
    criteria for selection of, for study, 54

Yazaki, Takeo, 200
Young, Roland, 65

Z
Zimmerman, Carle C., 97, 196, 199
Zorbaugh, Harvey W., 36

1 2 3 4 5 6 7 8 9 10 11 12 13 14 15 16 17 18 19 20 21 22 23 24 25   80 79 78 77 76 75 74 73 72